Good Housekeeping

Family Guide to
Over-the-Counter
Medicines

Good Housekeeping

Family Guide to Over-the-Counter Medicines

Consultant Pharmacist:
Pamela Mason BSc, MSc, PhD, MRPharmS

Consultant General Practitioner:
Dr Marion Newman MBBS, BSc, MRCGP

EBURY PRESS LONDON

The information and advice contained in this book are not intended to replace the services of a trained health professional, whom you should consult for individual medical problems. The products listed are not intended as endorsements.

Some product formulations may have changed since this book was written. Always check the contents of each product before you buy. **If you are in any doubt, check with your pharmacist or GP** before buying or using.

First published in 1999

1 3 5 7 9 10 8 6 4 2

Text © Ebury Press Limited 1999

First published in the United Kingdom in 1999 by Ebury Press
Random House, 20 Vauxhall Bridge Road, London SW1V 2SA.

Random House Australia (Pty) Limited
20 Alfred Street, Milsons Point, Sydney, New South Wales 2061, Australia

Random House New Zealand Limited
18 Poland Road, Glenfield, Auckland 10, New Zealand

Random House South Africa (Pty) Limited
Endulini, 5a Jubilee Road, Parktown 2193, South Africa

Random House UK Ltd Reg. No. 954009

A catalogue record for this book is available from the British Library.
ISBN 0 09 186851 3

Consultant Pharmacist: Pamela Mason BSc, MSc, PhD, MRPharmS
Consultant General Practitioner: Dr Marion Newman MBBS, BSc, MRCGP
Writer and researcher: Clare Hill
Design: Paul Saunders
Editors: Catherine Bradley and Molly Perham
Proofreader: Peter Gibbs

Printed and bound by Mackays of Chatham plc, Chatham, Kent

ACKNOWLEDGEMENTS

Many people have helped with the writing and production of this book and deserve to be singled out for praise.

I would like to thank Catherine Bradley of Ebury Press and designer Paul Saunders, who both made the book happen and believed it would get finished!

My particular thanks and gratitude go to both Pamela Mason and Marion Newman for their great expertise, professionalism and helpful comments and advice during the writing of this book. I am particularly indebted to them for their cheerful willingness to 'go the extra mile'.

Lastly, I would like to thank my husband Jonathan – a lovely man with saintly patience.

CONTENTS

Foreword

Welcome to the *Good Housekeeping Family Guide to Over-the-Counter Medicines*. I hope you will find it a useful guide to common minor ailments and the medicines that you can use to treat them. The past 50 years, and especially the last 20 years, have witnessed an enormous revolution in medicine and the ways in which illnesses are treated. When I first qualified as a pharmacist, the National Health Service was already nearly 30 years old, but fewer than half of the medicines we have today were then available.

These enormous strides in medicine, together with the availability of NHS prescriptions, although welcome, have tended to increase people's reliance on their general practitioners. Yet managing your own illness, especially when it is a minor one, can be just as effective as a visit to your GP – and often more convenient. Moreover, if you pay for your prescriptions, buying your own medicines over the counter can often be cheaper. However, never let cost deter you from visiting your GP or taking your pharmacist's advice.

Always treat medicines – whether you obtain them on a doctor's prescription or over the counter – with great respect. Never make the mistake of assuming that medicines that you can buy yourself are like other items of household shopping. A growing number of strong and effective medicines – some of which, until recently, were available only on prescription – can now be bought over the counter, but this does increase the chance for mishap and the need for careful use.

Taken inappropriately with disregard to the instructions on the package or used to treat a condition for which you should visit your doctor, over-the-counter medicines can actually do more harm than good. However, if they are used appropriately, over-the-counter medicines can play a useful role in alleviating symptoms associated with common family ailments such as coughs, colds, sore throats, indigestion, skin complaints and hay fever.

Using over-the-counter medicines safely means always reading the instructions on the package very carefully. Check what the medicine is for and how to take it. Never take more of the medicine than it says on the bottle or packet. If you are planning to give the medicine to a child, check the age range and the dose very carefully and consult your pharmacist or doctor if you have any doubt. Many medicines, for example, are not suitable for children. It is also important to find out exactly what the medicine contains. You may need to avoid certain ingredients, perhaps because of an existing medical condition you have (for example, asthma or a heart condition), other medicines you are taking or because you are allergic to a certain substance. Be especially careful if you are pregnant or breast feeding. Many over-the-counter medicines are not suitable in these circumstances.

Better still, ask your pharmacist for advice. You do not need an appointment to see a pharmacist and there is usually at least one pharmacy on every high street, so they are very convenient to visit. Your pharmacist is an expert on medicines and is there to help you to choose a medicine which is appropriate for you. In addition, your pharmacist will advise when you should see your doctor – advice which should always be acted upon. To help your pharmacist help you, always tell him or her if you are taking any other medicines, herbal or homoeopathic remedies or vitamin supplements, and if you have any existing medical conditions. Also remember to say if you have already tried any over-the-counter remedy for your ailment.

This book will help to reinforce the advice given by your pharmacist or doctor. It is certainly not a substitute for professional advice. However, we all know how easy it is to forget things we have been told, particularly in times of stress when we, or perhaps someone else in the family, does not feel well. This book is intended to remove some of the concerns you might have when you arrive home with your medicine. It gives straightforward information on the symptoms and treatment of a range of common ailments. It tells you about over 1000 over-the-counter remedies, complementary medicines and vitamin supplements, giving you authoritative information on how to use the remedy, what and when to use it and – very importantly – when not to use it.

The more you know about any medicine you use, the more likely you are to use it safely and appropriately – which is to your ultimate benefit. I hope that this book will help you to manage minor ailments and use over-the-counter medicines effectively. Keep it handy.

Pamela Mason BSc, MSc, PhD, MRPharms

How to Use this Book

This book aims to describe common ailments by their symptoms, followed by a comprehensive listing of the most widely available over-the-counter remedies. It also includes commonly available vitamin and mineral supplements which you may want to consider to improve or maintain good health.

Chapter 1 provides an overview of choosing and using over-the-counter remedies, outlining the legal position for remedies – whether orthodox or complementary – and stressing the importance of using remedies safely.

Chapter 2 describes a wide range of common ailments that you or your family may experience. Symptoms are described and general guidelines are given for treatment. This is followed by the 'Remedies' section, which indicates where you should go in Chapter 3 for details of relevant remedies.

Chapter 3 is divided into 13 sections, each containing a comprehensive listing of the vast range of over-the-counter remedies commonly available. Entries with a 🐎 symbol denote remedies specifically designed for children and complementary products are also clearly identified with a ✿. An introductory section describes typical ingredients contained in the remedies and their safe usage. Also included is a **Warning Note**, which you should **always** read before considering which remedy to select. This contains information about safe usage and also details of who should not use a particular remedy. This information, however, is only a guideline and should not be used as a substitute for receiving expert advice from your pharmacist or GP.

Each listing gives the name of the product, a brief description of its active ingredients and what it treats, followed by dosage or usage instructions. However, in the intensely competitive world of the over-the-counter industry, products and their formulations are changing all the time, so always check the contents and usage details on the product packaging before you buy it. If you are in any way confused or require further information **ask your pharmacist or GP**.

Chapter 4 describes commonly available vitamin, mineral and food supplements, together with an outline of the effect the main ingredients have. However, you should **always** check with your pharmacist or GP if you wish to use any of the supplements to treat an ailment, rather than just using them as a preventative against ill health. Self-dosage of vitamin, mineral and other supplements to treat ailments is **not recommended** unless on medical advice.

CHAPTER 1

Choosing and Using Over-the-Counter Remedies

This chapter provides information on how to select over-the-counter remedies and use them safely. It explains the legal obligations that pharmaceutical companies have to ensure that their products are safe for the widest number of people. It also explains how important it is for you to use them wisely.

Some people dislike going to the doctor and rely on over-the-counter medicines as a substitute for receiving proper medical attention. This book is not for them. The purpose of this chapter is to emphasise the importance of taking an active and responsible part in your health – and that includes knowing when it is more suitable to seek expert help from your pharmacist or your GP.

There is a remedy for almost any type of ailment – and in many cases there are hundreds of remedies for a single ailment. With such a vast array of products available, it can be difficult choosing the right remedy for you. Packaging and the quantities contained within it change, for example paracetamol and aspirin are only available in smaller quantities (of 16 tablets or capsules) from non-pharmacy outlets, such as supermarket or general stores. Larger packs (a maximum of 32 tablets or capsules) may be obtained from pharmacies. This is a recent legal development in Britain designed to prevent misuse. This chapter emphasises the role of pharmacists in making information available to you and encourages you to consult them when making your choice of remedy.

This chapter also provides advice on using herbal and homoeopathic remedies, which are becoming ever more popular. As with all remedies, these have to be used wisely and carefully, and should not be used as a substitute for receiving proper medical diagnosis and treatment.

Caring for your health – and the health of your family – is an important responsibility. This book will help you choose suitable over-the-counter remedies and this chapter will explain how you can do it.

What are over-the-counter remedies?

Over-the-counter medicines are those which you can buy without a doctor's prescription from various high street outlets, including your local pharmacy, supermarket or corner shop. Over-the-counter medicines are used to treat minor symptoms of common complaints which do not require the attention of a doctor. Such complaints, given time, will generally rectify themselves without any treatment at all by relying on the body's own in-built ability to heal itself and fight off infection.

Nevertheless, over-the-counter remedies play a useful role in helping to alleviate some of the symptoms experienced while this natural healing process is going on. For example, if you have flu it will last approximately 7–10 days, whether you treat it with an over-the-counter remedy or not. This is the time it takes for the body's defence system to fight the infection and rectify the chemical balance within the body. However, taking cold and flu remedies during this time will help alleviate the unpleasant symptoms – not the cause – of headache, muscle ache, fever and nasal congestion that may be experienced. Should the flu and/or some or all of its symptoms linger, you may require prescription drug intervention in the form of antibiotics to kill the germ 'invader' if the body is struggling to fight it.

Over-the-counter remedies and the law

The pharmaceutical business is extremely big business. Many millions of pounds are spent on buying remedies and further millions of pounds are spent in trying to ensure that they are safe for the widest number of people.

In order to be called a medicine in the United Kingdom, a product has to be licensed under the Medicines Act 1968. A licence can only be given if the product has been successful in controlled studies and after it has proved its safety, efficacy and quality of ingredients. Licensing controls the contents of a product, the way in which a product is advertised, where it can be sold, the doses it is sold in, the form in which it can be administered (for example, as tablets, liquids, patches, etc.) and how it should be used by the consumer.

The Medicines Control Agency (MCA) is the official body that deals with the licensing of new products. There are three categories of medicines in the United Kingdom: prescription-only medicines (which feature POM on their packaging) to treat serious conditions, for example high blood pressure, asthma or depression; pharmacy-only medicines (which feature P on their packaging), such as certain cough mixtures that contain powerful ingredients; and General Sales List medicines (which feature GSL on their packaging). The General Sales List includes all medicines that do not need to be sold in pharmacies. Such remedies can be bought from grocery stores, garage forecourts and supermarkets, as well as pharmacies. Their ingredients are considered to be safe in the dosages made available and so there is no restriction on their sale or supply.

Testing over-the-counter remedies

The amount of any medicine required depends upon the patient's age, weight, diet, genetic make-up and the existing state of his or her health. Pregnancy, breast-feeding and existing medical conditions, such as asthma, allergies, heart and blood conditions, are all factors that affect whether a remedy is suitable. Taking prescription medicines also affects which over-the-counter treatments should be used. For this reason, over-the-counter medicines have to be tested and found suitable for a wide range of the general population – and they must clearly advise when anyone with an existing medical condition should not use an over-the-counter remedy. Pharmaceutical manufacturers must provide detailed medical information on the product – either on the label and/or included on an information sheet within the packaging. This information will include a list of ailments for which the product is suitable, a list of contraindications that states who should not use the remedy (because of age, existing medical condition, pregnancy or breast-feeding, or because of taking certain prescription drugs and so on). This list is quite long – but you should always read it thoroughly to check whether the remedy is suitable for you and your individual needs. The information on the label and inside sheet will also list potential side-effects that may be experienced by some individuals, such as a rash, drowsiness, constipation, and other physical reactions.

Complementary over-the-counter remedies are becoming increasingly popular in the United Kingdom, and some are now widely available in high-street pharmacies. Homoeopathic and herbal remedies sold over-the-counter in Britain are considered safe, although in many cases there is no clinical proof of their effectiveness. However, strict labelling laws apply to them also. Legally, no mention can be made of treating symptoms if the remedy is not licensed. For this reason you may find that there is precious little information on the labels to tell you about what they are suitable for treating. For example, the herb St John's wort is considered a suitable treatment for mild, transient depression and is often prescribed in Germany for this use. However, if you buy St John's wort in your local health food shop, no mention may legally be made about this, and the only details you will be able to read about the product are those regarding ingredients and dosages.

Any medicines with POM (Prescription-Only Medicines) on the packaging can only be obtained via a prescription from a doctor or dentist. In recent years, many preparations which were once available only on prescription have now come 'off the List' and can be bought over-the-counter. Likewise, some other medicines that were once generally available have been added to the List and now require a prescription.

Types of remedies

There are several methods of taking over-the-counter and prescription drugs – orally, through the rectum or vagina, locally/topically or by inhalation. In addition, for ear and eye conditions drops may be inserted directly into the ear or onto the eye. Only a medical practitioner can prescribe medications that are administered by injection (that is, by inserting a needle into the body to deliver a medication).

Oral medication

Oral medicines are those which have to be swallowed. These come in the form of tablets, liquids, powders for dilution and capsules. Oral medications are quick and convenient. The active ingredients within the medication are absorbed by the gut and then carried around the blood stream. However, the extent of absorption can vary from patient to patient, some absorbing them quickly, others more slowly.

Vaginal and rectal medication

These medicines usually come in the form of pessaries (for vaginal insertion) and suppositories (for rectal insertion). Sometimes the pessaries or suppositories are sold with an insertion tube, making them easier to position. Suppositories can be useful for those who have difficulty swallowing medicines or who are being repeatedly sick.

Topical and local medication

Topical or local medications usually act locally on the skin to ease skin complaints. Sometimes, however, their active ingredients are absorbed through the skin and into the blood stream to treat other areas of the body. Nicotine patches, for example, work in this way. Most topical and local medications are in the form of ointments, creams, lotions, gels and sprays. These products are applied directly to the skin and release their active ingredients directly to the affected area. Skin conditions such as eczema, dermatitis, cold sores, cuts and bruises and fungal infections can all be treated in this way. Sometimes certain conditions, such as athlete's foot, are treated by dusting powder over the affected area. This helps dry out the area and to cure the infection.

Inhalation

Certain conditions are most successfully treated by inhaling the medicine either through the mouth or nose so that it enters the respiratory system directly and has a rapid impact. Asthma, hayfever and some cold and flu remedies are administered in this way.

How to take over-the-counter medicines

When taking over-the-counter medicines, you should ensure that you know what you are taking and why you are taking it. Check exactly what you are treating. Is it skin-related (such as a rash, spot, cut, irritation), a fever, or an ache or pain? Sometimes, the condition may be a combination of several symptoms, as in the case of a cold or flu where you may experience a variety of symptoms including a raised temperature, cough, sore throat, sneeze, headache or muscular pain.

Most conditions suited to self-treatment are easy to recognise. They are relatively minor and unlikely to spread or cause complications. Ask your pharmacist's advice on which remedy will most successfully treat your symptoms, or combination of symptoms, giving him or her details of your general health and any other treatments you are taking. However, if the condition does not respond to self-treatment, you should not hesitate to seek further advice and information. If you feel the condition is minor rather than severe, talk first to your pharmacist. You should definitely see your doctor if advised to do so by the pharmacist or if you are at all concerned about your symptoms – especially if you consider them to be worsening or to be severe.

You should also always see your doctor if the ailment you are treating with over-the-counter remedies does not appear to respond to treatment, or if you experience unpleasant side-effects.

There are various ways of taking over-the-counter preparations. Some remedies have the same effect but may be taken in different ways, to suit the preference of the individual user. For example, those who find swallowing tablets difficult may prefer a liquid remedy. The effect is the same.

Following dosage instructions

When self-treating for common ailments, it is essential always to read the instructions that appear on the medicine, or – in the case of medicines contained within packaging – to read the packing box and the patient information details contained in the leaflet inside. Always take the over-the-counter remedies as instructed on the preparation. If it says: 'Do not exceed 4 doses in 24 hours' this should be adhered to. Also note the details given in the 'Contraindications' section. This will advise you of a range of circumstances in which the medicine is not suitable. For example, some medicines may not be suitable for diabetics, asthmatics or those taking certain prescription drugs.

The contra-indications section will also alert you to side-effects that may be experienced in a minority of people. If you experience any of the side-effects listed, seek your pharmacist's advice for an alternative remedy. For example, many cough remedies include an antihistamine ingredient which may make you feel drowsy. If your cough is minor and you need to remain alert – for example, if you need to work, drive or operate any machinery – your pharmacist can recommend an alternative remedy for you that is suited to your symptoms but that does not contain antihistamine or a 'non-drowsy' variety.

The number of times you should take or use a drug, and the amount you should take (dosage) are always advised on the product, whether it is a prescription remedy, an over-the-counter remedy or a complementary remedy. In addition to ensuring that you take the correct dosage, you should also be aware that it is extremely easy to exceed this dosage if you mix remedies. For example, taking a cold and flu remedy together with an analgesic, such as aspirin, ibuprofen or paracetamol, is not advisable. See the Warning Box on page 20.

Remember, if you are in any doubt about your medication, consult your pharmacist for advice.

The role of the pharmacist

Pharmacists are highly trained professionals who dispense and make up prescription and over-the-counter remedies. The most familiar pharmacist is the one found in any high street pharmacy, but they also work in hospitals, the pharmaceutical industry and in research.

The pharmacist's knowledge about drugs and drug treatments is wide and he or she is there to pass on this knowledge to the consumer, so always feel free to ask any questions of the pharmacist about any remedy – prescription or over-the-counter. This will, in many cases, save a time-consuming trip to the doctor's surgery.

Pharmacists are specialists in how drugs work, how they interact with each other and what their potential side-effects may be. They will be able to advise you about the suitability or otherwise of any preparation, given information about your own individual needs and state of health. They can provide supplementary information for you if the packaging or labelling of the over-the-counter remedy does not give you enough detail, and they can in many circumstances advise on which is the better-value product, such as a generic version of a high-profile branded product.

Pharmacists are registered by the Royal Pharmaceutical Society and have to follow a Code of Ethics. This states that, on request, the pharmacist must provide advice on medication, and that he or she should not rely on the customer's own diagnosis of what is wrong but should ask for additional information to assess the accuracy of the customer's self-diagnosis. To this end the pharmacist may ask for details on all or some of your personal details, including information about:

• your age

• your symptoms

- how long you have had the ailment

- whether you are pregnant or breast-feeding

- if you have any existing or past medical conditions

- what other medication you are taking – whether prescription, over-the-counter or complementary

- any allergies you may have

- what vitamin, mineral or other supplements you are taking

In return, you should try to be as accurate and helpful in your responses to the pharmacist's questions as possible so he or she can give you the best advice. If you feel uneasy about providing intimate details of your health in the middle of a busy pharmacy request to see the pharmacist in a more private setting. Many have a private area or room specifically for this purpose. Based on your responses, the pharmacist will direct you towards the most suitable remedies.

As well as helping you to choose the correct remedy, your pharmacist can advise you if you are unsure what is causing your problem or what to do about it. He or she will also tell you whether, based on your answers to the questions outlined above, you should see your doctor for an accurate diagnosis and/or appropriate treatment.

When to see your doctor

Most minor ailments will resolve themselves, with or without treatment. However, if an ailment persists and if over-the-counter remedies fail to ease the symptoms, you should always make an appointment with your GP for investigation and treatment. If the condition gets worse, despite using the remedy, or you become at all worried about your symptoms, you should seek medical attention without delay. **This is important for everyone, but especially so for babies, children and the elderly.**

Always stop using a remedy if it seems to make your ailment worse, for example if you develop a rash, breathing difficulties, or other unwanted side-effects. If the side-effects are disturbing or get worse, you should seek medical advice and/or treatment as soon as possible. Always see your doctor if you have any of the following symptoms: heart palpitations, blurred vision, chest pain, excessive pain or bleeding, suspected broken bones, or injuries to the eyes.

Always seek medical treatment for a child if his or her temperature reaches above 39°C (103°F) and remains that high for longer than 2 days, or earlier if you are alarmed by any of the symptoms. You should also contact a doctor if there is drowsiness, vomiting, a rash or severe diarrhoea.

Complementary remedies

In recent years there has been a rapid growth of interest in taking complementary remedies and sales of these products have increased accordingly. It is estimated that as many as 4 out of 5 people in Britain have used a complementary therapy or remedy at some time and, according to the Consumer's Association, 75 per cent of those who have claim that it has helped to ease their condition or cure it.

The remedies featured in this book are those that are most widely available and which can easily be found in any high street pharmacy, health food shop or large supermarket. Own-brand products are also available from major supermarkets and pharmacies, but these are not covered in the book.

A common misconception is that a 'natural' remedy is a 'safe' remedy. **This is not necessarily true.** As with all the remedies featured in this book, you should treat the preparations with respect, use them as directed on the labels, and not mix remedies unless advised that it is safe to do so. Always seek medical advice if your ailment does not respond to complementary treatment.

None of the remedies featured in this book, be they orthodox or complementary, should be used by pregnant or breast-feeding women, those with existing medical conditions or those taking any form of prescription medication without first checking that it is safe to do so with their pharmacist or GP.

MIXING REMEDIES

It is just as possible to overdose on over-the-counter medicines as it is for prescribed medicines. Many over-the-counter preparations contain a mix of ingredients which, if combined with another remedy, can cause overdose. For example, many cold and flu remedies contain paracetamol, as do preparations for headaches and coughs. **Do not combine the remedies.** Paracetamol can cause nausea and vomiting if taken to excess. In severe cases it can cause liver failure and death.

Herbal remedies

Modern herbal remedies are largely based on a variety of folk-lore remedies which, in many cases, have been used for centuries. They are made from the leaves, bark, roots, flowers, seeds or oils of plants and can be used or taken in a number of ways, for example as tablets, drops, syrups or teas. Others may be applied as creams or ointments.

During the late 19th and early 20th centuries, traditional herbal remedies were generally supplanted by the orthodox forms of medicine that we know today. The use of herbal treatments fell into a rapid decline but, as the 20th century draws to a close, interest in this traditional medicine is growing significantly.

The pharmaceutical industry is also now taking more interest in herbal remedies. As options for laboratory-based drug developments reduces, they are increasingly looking to the plant world to identify active substances that can be used in orthodox medicine. When used as directed on the packaging, the remedies can be safely taken. As with all drugs or remedies, however, they can be harmful if misused and they may cause unwanted side-effects. For this reason it is essential that you always read the dosage labels carefully and do not exceed them. You should always seek medical advice if your ailment does not respond to the remedy.

Homoeopathic remedies

Homoeopathy is a system of complementary medicine which takes the view that a substance that causes an illness or ailment may also be used to cure that illness or ailment. This is known as treating 'like with like'. This is in direct opposition to the orthodox medical view that each illness or ailment can only be cured by an antidote. For example, antibiotics are used to fight disease by killing off the invading infection. By contrast, homoeopathic remedies introduce a minute substance of the cause of the illness into the body in order to fight the infection. This is often referred to as the law of similars, in which it is thought that the body does not allow two similar diseases to exist in the body at the same time. By introducing a minute amount of the illness via a homoeopathic remedy, the infection or illness can be made to go.

Homoeopathic remedies are made from animal, vegetable, mineral and human sources. These substances are diluted in water or alcohol until no trace of the original substance is discernible in the liquid. This extreme dilution is thought to produce the curative effect without harmful side-effects. In Western scientific terms this is impossible, yet homoeopathy is indisputably becoming more popular as an alternative form of treatment to orthodox medicine. Homoeopathic remedies are now widely available in most high street pharmacies and health food shops.

The Homoeopathic Registration Scheme controls the sale of all homoeopathic remedies to ensure safety and quality of the item. Products that have been tested for safety are marked 'HR' on the label. Only prescription homoeopathic remedies are licensed (see page 15).

How to take complementary remedies

It is a common misconception that complementary remedies are safe and harmless to take because they are made from natural ingredients. They are not safe and harmless: if they were, they would have no curative effect – indeed no effect at all.

All complementary remedies should be viewed with the same respect as orthodox medicines. Do not exceed the stated dose. Do not mix different complementary treatments without taking advice. Do not mix complementary and orthodox over-the-counter medicines, unless your GP or pharmacist tells you it is safe to do so. Always follow the instructions on the label and packaging – and stop using the remedy immediately if you experience any unwanted side-effects. If there is no improvement in your condition, seek your pharmacist's advice on other available remedies – either orthodox or complementary.

Taking homoeopathic remedies

Self-treatment with homoeopathic remedies is only advised for minor ailments. Homoeopathic treatments can often be used in conjunction with orthodox remedies, but you must first check that it is safe to do so by asking your pharmacist, homoeopath or GP.

As with orthodox remedies, homoeopathic remedies must be taken responsibly. Remember that taking more of a remedy than the recommended dosage will not make the remedy more effective. Always follow the dosage instructions shown on the label. The remedies should be taken at least 20-30 minutes after eating, smoking or drinking to ensure that your tongue is clean. You should avoid handling the remedy by tipping the tablets into the lid of the bottle and then dropping them under your tongue and allowing them to dissolve.

Throughout the book you will see dosages for homoeopathic remedies as either 6x, 6c or 30c. These figures denote the potency of the remedy. Although other potencies are available, these are not usually readily obtainable.

When the remedies are being made, they are diluted and then rapidly shaken (succession) until they reach the potency required. 6x is diluted in a 1 to 9 ratio, with a shaking process repeated 6 times. This progresses to 6c diluted in a 1 in 99 ratio and shaken 6 times. The highest dilution is 30c which is diluted in a 1 to 99 ratio and shaken 30 times. Following the homoeopathic principle of the smallest dilution being the most effective, 30c is more potent than 6x.

Continue to take the remedy for as long as is advised and in the dosages

---

HOMOEOPATHIC DOSAGES

The homoeopathic dosages described in Chapter 3 describe only the amount contained within each tablet or single dose. The label will tell you how many of the tablets or what amount of the liquid you should take. This very much depends on why you are taking it so **always read the label** thoroughly first.

given on the packaging. If your symptoms do not respond to treatment, seek the advice of a fully trained homoeopath and discuss the situation with your GP. Self-treatment with homoeopathic remedies is limited. Most homoeopaths prefer to 'prescribe' only after considering the mental and emotional wellbeing of the patient, as well as referring to past medical history, physical appearance and mental attitude. This holistic approach to diagnosis may mean that your choice of over-the-counter remedy is not the same as the remedy a homoeopath might recommend.

Vitamin, Mineral and Food Supplements

Although medical experts are divided about the long-term value of taking vitamin, mineral and food supplements, they are very popular – in 1997 over £367 million was spent on buying them. In theory, eating a balanced diet should provide you with all the vitamins and minerals you require. However, those who smoke or drink heavily, those under extreme stress or those recovering from illness can benefit from supplements – although in certain circumstances a healthier lifestyle would bring greater benefit.

Vitamins and minerals, fish oils and other products, such as ginseng and evening primrose oil, are classified as food supplements rather than medicines. Provided that they fulfil the requirements of the food laws, there is no restriction on their sale. However, if a vitamin, mineral or supplement is used to treat or prevent a specific condition, it will have to have a licence and will only be available through a pharmacy. An example of such a supplement is Pregaday, a treament for pregnant women containing iron and folic acid.

For more information about vitamin and mineral supplements, see Chapter 4 (page 285).

Home first aid

Keeping over-the-counter remedies in the home enables you to treat minor illnesses and accidents as and when they occur. On page 25 is a list of useful items to have to hand to cope with such events. However, before stocking up your home first aid cabinet you should think about what your needs and your family's needs are. For example, if you have young children, you should ensure that you have a range of children's-strength products such as a children's version of liquid paracetamol, and a wide range of sticking plasters for the inevitable bumps and scrapes children suffer.

Your needs may also vary according to the seasons. For example, during the winter months an over-the-counter cough remedy or combined cold and flu remedy is a useful standby and in the summer months you may want to ensure you have a hayfever remedy or a remedy for bites and stings to hand.

When stocking your cabinet, you should always keep the medicines in their original containers, preferably also with their outer packaging and any inner leaflets that give guidance on the product's safe usage. This will ensure that you know what they are for and how to use them properly.

Siting your cabinet

Your medicine chest should **always** be lockable. This will enable you to also keep any prescription medications alongside your over-the-counter remedies in a safe, secure place. Where you keep your first aid cabinet is also important. It should be kept high up and safely out of the reach of children in a dry place – not in the bathroom where heat, humidity and steam can infiltrate the cabinet and cause a rapid deterioration of the contents. It should also be sited in a communal area so all members of the family who need access to first aid can use it – for many reasons the kitchen is an obvious place.

Although vitamins, minerals and other supplements are not usually kept in the medicine cabinet, they should also be kept safely out of reach of children – many are attractively coloured and look like sweets and may tempt children.

Maintaining your first aid cabinet

You should check the contents of your cabinet on a regular basis to ensure you do not run out of a particular remedy. Although we have made general suggestions as to what you might need to keep in your chest, ask your pharmacist's advice if you have specific needs.

Regularly clearing out the first aid cabinet will enable you to make a note of any products which are no longer required or which have outlived their 'Use By' date. These should not be used as many of them will have become ineffective or degraded. You should also throw away any ointments or lotions which have discoloured, become cloudy or have changed texture, for example if the ingredients have become separated, runny or thickened. Preparations in tubes should be thrown away if they are leaking, cracked or if their contents have hardened.

If you are not sure what a remedy is for – throw it away. If you are not sure what a prescription remedy is, check with your GP or pharmacist. If it is no longer required for treatment – throw it away.

Emergency telephone numbers

It is a good idea to keep a list of emergency telephone numbers taped to the outside or inside of the cabinet for easy reference. These could include your GP's telephone number, together with surgery times, your local hospital's accident and emergency number and the numbers of your health visitor, district nurse or dentist.

Safe disposal

When throwing away any medications – be they over-the-counter remedies or prescription medications – you should do so safely. Do not flush them down the lavatory or throw them in the rubbish bin. You risk harming the environment and wildlife as well as humans. Instead, take them to your GP's surgery, your local pharmacy or to a hospital pharmacy department for safe disposal.

HOME FIRST AID CABINET

Many of the remedies listed in this book are suitable for keeping at home to deal with emergencies. You may also wish to include herbal or homoeopathic remedies. A possible home first aid cabinet is suggested below, but you should tailor-make yours to suit your own or your family's requirements.

- Bandages, plasters, surgical tape and safety pins for dressing cuts and wounds, sprains, etc

- An antiseptic for cleaning cuts and wounds, gargling for sore throats and treating mouth ulcers, etc

- A general painkiller (also children's version of liquid paracetamol or ibuprofen, if appropriate)

- Thermometer

- Burn cream

- A bites and stings preparation

- An oral rehydration solution to replace lost salts caused by repeated diarrhoea

- A mild laxative

- An indigestion remedy

- Travel sickness tablets, if appropriate

- A cold and flu remedy (also a children's version, if appropriate)

- A joint and muscle easing spray or cream for sports injuries

- A hayfever remedy, if appropriate

- Arnica cream for bruises and joint and muscle problems

- A cream containing calendula for cuts, grazes and minor skin irritations

CHAPTER 2

Common Family Ailments and Conditions

Throughout life we will experience a range of common ailments. They are usually temporary, not liable to spread elsewhere in the body and easy to identify. Unless complications develop, these conditions do not warrant treatment from a doctor and their symptoms can be eased by taking over-the-counter remedies. Of all the ailments, coughs and colds and flu and digestive conditions, such as indigestion and constipation or diarrhoea, are some of the most common and these all respond well to self-medication and treatment.

This chapter describes a wide range of common ailments, outlining their key symptoms and then providing general advice and guidelines for treatment. At the end of each entry is a 'Remedies' section, which indicates where you should go in Chapter 3 for details of relevant over-the-counter remedies.

If you have any concerns about diagnosing a condition, **always ask your pharmacist or GP for advice**. This is important for you, but is even more important if you are diagnosing a child's condition.

If you have an existing medical condition, are pregnant or breast-feeding or taking prescription medication you should be very careful about self-diagnosis. If you have any concerns at all, it is safer and wiser to seek medical advice.

ABSCESSES (SKIN)

An abscess occurs when the skin has become punctured and infected, usually by one of the staphylococci bacteria. Sometimes they develop when a hair follicle, skin pore or sebaceous cyst becomes infected. To fight the infection, the body seals off the area, forming a pus-filled swelling on the site. Abscesses are painful, particularly when pressure is applied, and can occur on any part of the body. Large sites of infection can cause a fever and sweating.

TREATING SKIN ABSCESSES

Most abscesses burst and drain of their own accord. Once burst, the area should be kept clean to prevent further infection. Bathe in salt water and allow to dry out. If the abscess is persistent, your doctor may drain it. Antibiotics will be required if you are feverish or if there is a large area of redness around the area, suggesting spreading infection.

☙ REMEDIES see page 185

ABSCESSES (TOOTH)

Tooth abscesses occur when bacteria are able to enter the central cavity of the tooth. The cavity houses pulp, the nerves and blood vessels of the tooth. If the tooth's dentine and enamel are destroyed by dental caries, the inside of the tooth becomes vulnerable. The bacteria enter the tooth, infecting the pulp and spreading into the surrounding gum tissue, forming an abscess. Abscesses can also form when bacteria collect in the areas between the teeth and gums. Sore, red and swollen areas appear on the gums and there may be facial swelling. This makes chewing extremely painful.

TREATING TOOTH ABSCESSES

Abscesses should always be treated by a dentist, as the infection can spread to the surrounding tissues and bones. Dentists will usually prescribe an antibiotic if the infection has spread. Although the dentist will try to save the tooth, an extraction or root canal treatment may be necessary. Painkillers will usually help ease the pain until you can see a dentist.

☙ REMEDIES Mouthwashes; **General Pain Relief**, see page 78

ACNE and SPOTS *(See also Blackheads, page 34)*

Acne is the appearance of spots on the face and upper body. They most commonly appear during adolescence and the early twenties, although they can affect all age groups. Usually spots are nothing more than a temporary and minor inconvenience but, for some, the outbreaks can be more serious, more frequent and may in some cases be disfiguring.

Excess production of sebum, the skin's natural oil, gives rise to the spots. Normally, the sebum flows out of the follicle along the hair but if the flow is blocked by a plug of skin debris or hardened sebum, a comedone (blackhead or whitehead) forms. Behind the debris, bacteria multiply on the site, causing infection and inflammation. Acne and spots can be caused or aggravated by certain drugs and cosmetics. It can also be genetic and there is a link with hormone production within the body.

TREATING ACNE AND SPOTS

Keeping the skin clean and regularly exfoliating the skin will help stop sebum from blocking the pores. Mild exposure to sunlight also helps clear up the skin – but exposure should be strictly controlled and provide no risk of sunburn. Eating a healthy diet with plenty of fruit and vegetables and taking daily vitamin supplements of vitamins A, C and E should also help (see pages 285 and 286). Avoid picking at the skin, as this can cause scarring.

Over-the-counter lotions and creams, mostly containing benzoyl peroxide, are available which clean the skin and dry out the spots. There may be skin flaking as the surrounding unaffected skin will be sloughed off along with the spot.

Severe acne requires medical treatment with stronger creams and lotions and antibiotics or possibly hormone-regulating drugs.

✿ REMEDIES see page 187

ANAEMIA

Anaemia is the presence of a lower concentration of haemoglobin in the blood than is normal for a person's age and sex. This impedes the supply of oxygen to the cells, causing tiredness, shortness of breath, and sometimes headaches or dizzy spells.

There are various types and causes of anaemia, most of which require medical investigation and treatment. The most common form is iron deficiency anaemia. Heavy menstrual flow often causes a lack of sufficient iron in the body. A diet that does not contain enough vitamins and minerals can also lead to anaemia. Pregnant women, children, the elderly and those who eat a diet low in iron-rich foods are typical sufferers.

TREATING ANAEMIA

If you suspect you have anaemia, you should see your doctor for an accurate diagnosis. The best source of iron, and the food from which it is best absorbed, is red meat. Other sources include wholemeal bread, leafy green vegetables and breakfast cereals fortified with iron. Taking a multi-vitamin and mineral supplement with adequate quantities of iron will help make up any iron deficiency in the diet. If these measures do not improve the anaemia, you should go back to your doctor for more specific treatment. Anaemia can be a symptom of serious illnesses.

✿ REMEDIES see page 257

ANXIETY

Anxiety is a normal emotional response to a wide range of worrying or stress-inducing situations. However, for some, anxiety can occur for no known reason or may be experienced to an extent that is not warranted by the cause. Anxiety causes a sense of dread, fear and mental upset that can manifest itself in a wide range of physical symptoms including palpitations, breathlessness, aches and pains, sleeping problems, headaches and shakiness in the limbs.

TREATING ANXIETY

As anxiety can be a normal reaction to a normal but stress-inducing event, treatment is not usually necessary – you will return to normal once the anxiety-inducing event has passed. However, for those who regularly face stressful events, coping techniques such as stress management, breathing exercises and visualisation exercises can help. The support of friends and family can help tremendously. Herbal remedies can help calm you down and assist with sleep disturbances.

Anxiety brought about by more serious emotional disturbances – for example, divorce, bereavement, separation, financial worries, serious illness, phobias and panic disorders – may require help from your GP. You may be prescribed anti-anxiety drugs or referred for counselling.

Sometimes symptoms from an over-active thyroid gland may resemble anxiety, and a blood test to exclude this possibility may be useful.

⊕ **REMEDIES** (COMPLEMENTARY) see page 270

ARTHRITIS

Arthritis is a blanket term used to cover a wide range of joint disorders, including osteoarthritis, rheumatoid arthritis and gout (see page 49). The term arthritis describes inflammation of the joints, but other soft tissues and muscles in the body may also be affected.

Arthritis causes joint pain, stiffness and loss of movement. Some find that moving the affected joint eases it, while others find this too painful to do. Osteoarthritis may be hereditary but a poor lifestyle, previous joint injury and being overweight are all aggravating factors.

Osteoarthritis is the most common form of arthritis, tending to affect those over 50 years of age. It is generally more common in women. Deep, aching pain is experienced in the joints, usually those at the ends of the fingers and base of the thumbs, the base of the large toe and the neck, spine, hips and knee.

Rest, rather than movement, tends to ease the pain. As osteoarthritis progresses the joints become sore and tender, and when moved there may be a grinding noise or sensation. There is increasingly stiffness and pain in the hips at night, and the knees may give way. Sometimes, because of an over-production of joint fluid, the joint (often the knee) becomes hot, red, swollen and painful.

Rheumatoid arthritis is much more serious than osteoarthritis and much less common. It usually develops in those aged 20 to 50 years and it affects three times as many women as men.

With rheumatoid arthritis, the body's immune system turns against itself and attacks the lining of the joints. This causes the joints to become inflamed. At first, rheumatoid arthritis affects the hands and feet but it can progress to all the other joints, making them swollen, painful and difficult to move. Although rheumatoid arthritis is thought of as just a joint disease, it affects the body as a whole, causing other symptoms such as feeling tired, losing the appetite and generally feeling unwell. Severe rheumatoid arthritis can affect other organs in the body such as the heart and lungs.

TREATING ARTHRITIS
All forms of arthritis can be eased by taking painkillers. Treatment is aimed at relieving pain and inflammation and promoting – or preserving – mobility. Rheumatoid arthritis, particularly at its more advanced stages, requires prescription drug and medical treatment. Sometimes splinting affected joints can help ease the pain.

✚ REMEDIES Non-steroidal anti-inflammatory preparations; **General Pain Relief**, see page 78

ASTHMA

Asthma is a common condition where the tubes in the lungs are over-responsive to a wide range of stimuli that results in constriction of the muscles of the bronchial airway and inflammation of the lining. During an attack, sufferers experience difficulty in breathing, wheezing, sensations of tightness in the chest (often wakening them in the night) and suffocation. In very severe attacks there may be a rapid pulse, sweating, an inability to speak without gasping for air, mental confusion and severe anxiety. Some sufferers tend not to wheeze but to have paroxysms of coughing that may lead to a misdiagnosis of bronchitis.

Asthma can be aggravated by a sensitivity to irritants such as pollen, dust mites, feathers and animal dander. Air pollution, food allergies, extremes in air temperature, exercise and some drugs may also bring on an attack. Asthma tends to also affect those who have a family history of allergy, including eczema (page 46), hayfever (page 50) or hives (page 51). Children who have asthma usually improve in adolescence.

TREATING ASTHMA
Asthma is a serious condition and requires medical diagnosis and treatment. A severe attack requires urgent medical attention. However, during an attack it may be possible to keep calm using breathing exercises. Complementary therapies may also help calm the sufferer during an attack. Allergen avoidance, for example using synthetic bedding, may be helpful.

✚ REMEDIES (COMPLEMENTARY) Homoeopathy, see page 101

ATHLETE'S FOOT

Athlete's foot is a contagious fungal infection that affects the webs of the feet between the toes. It can also spread to the soles of the feet. The condition can be either dry and scaly or wet and blistery. It can be painful, particularly when the skin cracks between the toes. Sometimes the fungus that causes the infection can spread to the toenails. Damage to the skin predisposes to skin infections, and the foot may become red, swollen and tender.

Warm, moist conditions can encourage the fungus, which is passed on from someone else with the infection when small bits of shed skin drop from their bare feet. For this reason, swimming pools are a prime site for contracting the condition, although sharing towels, bath-mats and shoes or socks of those with the infection is another form of transmission.

TREATING ATHLETE'S FOOT

For dry athlete's foot there are various cream preparations containing antifungal ingredients. For wet athlete's foot, dry powders can be used. Keep the feet dry and avoid passing the infection on to others. Wear cotton or wool socks to help the feet stay aired and dry, and change socks daily. At home, wear sandals. Severe cases of athlete's foot, or cases which do not respond to over-the-counter remedies, will need medical treatment. Your doctor may take samples to confirm the diagnosis and prescribe a stronger anti-fungal preparation. If the condition continues, you may be referred to a dermatologist.

✚ **REMEDIES** see page 191

BACK PAIN (See also Sciatica, page 64)

Most people will have experienced a bout of back pain at some time in life. The severity of a bout can range from a minor ache or twinge that disappears of its own accord, to extreme and acute agony brought on by a movement, either obvious or unidentifiable.

There are numerous causes for back pain, the most common being misusing the back by overstraining or incorrect lifting techniques and poor posture – sitting at a computer screen without getting up and stretching regularly is just one of the very many postural causes of back pain.

Other causes of back problems include minor structural abnormalities, arthritis, prolapsed lumbar or cervical discs, osteoporosis and other medical problems. Low back pain is also common at the time of the menopause.

TREATING BACK PAIN

Resting the back, combined with taking painkillers, will help ease immediate pain. Usually a bad bout of back pain will resolve itself within a week or so. If the pain is severe or repeated, you should see your GP, who may arrange appropriate investigations, prescribe stronger painkillers or refer you to a consultant and/or physiotherapist. You may alternatively wish to consult a registered osteopath or chiropractor. Chronic back pain requires re-educating the body to move correctly.

Yoga and Alexander technique can help achieve this. Strengthening the back muscles through mild exercise will also help. Ask your GP or physiotherapist for advice.

✚ **REMEDIES** see page 228

BAD BREATH

Bad breath can simply be the result of eating strong, pungent and spicy foods, particularly garlic, onions and curries, or it can be caused by food particles being trapped between the teeth and not dislodged when brushing. Tooth decay may also cause bad breath, as can tonsillitis, gum disease, chronic catarrh, sinus infections, smoking and constipation. Sometimes, bad breath is a symptom of a more serious underlying problem.

TREATING BAD BREATH

Brushing and flossing the teeth properly after each meal and seeing the dentist and hygienist regularly will help. Avoiding strong foods or using mouthwashes can help mask the smell. All other conditions causing bad breath will either resolve once the infection has passed or will remain. These should be investigated by your GP to rule out a more serious condition.

✚ **REMEDIES** see page 248

BITES and STINGS

Bites and stings, whether caused by animal bites, insect stings or certain plants, pierce the skin and cause redness, local swelling and sometimes infection. Some insects and plants transmit poisonous substances when they pierce the skin. An allergic reaction may occur.

TREATING BITES AND STINGS

If an animal bite pierces the skin, you should go to your doctor, who will check if your tetanus jabs are up to date and may prescribe antibiotics to fight any infection. Alternatively, go to the Accident and Emergency Department of your local hospital. Rabies is a potential problem if you are bitten when abroad, so seek medical attention at the local hospital immediately.

For insect stings, remove the sting with tweezers if it is visible. Spray or dab on an over-the-counter sting calming product. An antihistamine will reduce the swelling. Traditionally people dab a solution of bicarbonate of soda on to a bee sting to neutralise it. To neutralise wasp stings, dab on lemon juice or vinegar.

If you develop a fever, nausea, dizziness or vomiting, have difficulty breathing, or experience swelling of the lips and mouth, seek urgent medical attention. People who develop a severe allergic reaction to insect bites may need to carry an adrenaline syringe.

✚ **REMEDIES** see page 195

BLACKHEADS

Blackheads are small, black dots that appear on the skin, usually on the oilier parts of the face and body. They appear where the pores of the skin have become blocked with sebum, the naturally oily substance which is produced by the skin. The blockages are caused by dead skin cells, bacteria and grease building up in the pore and forming a plug.

Sometimes the blackheads become infected, particularly if dirty hands are used to squeeze them out. Blackheads are one of the types of spot in acne (see page 28).

TREATING BLACKHEADS

Keeping the skin clean and exfoliating regularly will help keep the pores clean and prevent a build-up of oil and skin debris.

A beauty therapist can remove the blackheads during a facial. There are now adhesive strip products that help clear the blocked pores: the strip is stuck on the affected area and then peeled off, removing the blackheads with the strip. If you attempt to squeeze them, always make sure you have scrupulously clean hands and that you dab the area with a mild antiseptic or facewash.

✚ **REMEDIES** Antiseptics, see page 93, and Acne and Spots, see page 28

BOILS and CARBUNCLES

Boils are painful, pus-filled skin abscesses (see Skin Abscesses, page 28) that are red and swollen and very tender to the touch. They tend to appear on the neck or buttocks, but they can appear elsewhere on the body and are caused by a scratch or break in the skin that becomes infected, so conditions such as eczema, scabies, nits or ringworm increase the likelihood of skin infections and sometimes sebaceous cysts become infected.

Carbuncles are a group of inter-connected boils. These are extremely painful and require medical attention. Both are more likely to occur if you are run down, for example with diabetes, as the body has a harder time fighting off the infection. They also tend to spread within the family or an institution.

TREATING BOILS AND CARBUNCLES

If the boil comes to a head of its own accord, wipe away the infected pus, dab on some antiseptic and cover with a clean dressing. Let the healing take place, keeping the area clean and dry. If the boil does not respond to treatment, you may need to have it lanced by your doctor. This will remove the infected pus. You may be given antibiotics as a precautionary measure.

Carbuncles always require medical attention. They will be treated in the same way as boils but you may need to be treated by a dermatologist at a hospital.

✚ **REMEDIES** see page 185

BRONCHITIS

Bronchitis is due to an infection and inflammation of the mucus membranes (bronchi) that line the bronchial tubes in the lungs. It is often a complication of a viral infection, such as flu. Symptoms include coughing, which produces large quantities of green-yellow phlegm, fever and chest pains. Coughing may be accompanied by a wheezing or 'rattling' noise and there may be pain in the breastbone when coughing.

An acute attack of bronchitis usually takes one or two weeks to disappear. However, over the years after repeated episodes bronchitis can become chronic and is usually the result of narrowing and damage of the airways. Smoking is the prime cause of chronic bronchitis, as it stimulates the production of phlegm and damages the bronchi's muscle walls and also the walls of the smaller airways of the lungs (bronchioles). This makes the sufferer more susceptible to infection and other irritants.

TREATING BRONCHITIS

Acute bronchitis can be treated with over-the-counter remedies. If it accompanies flu, a flu remedy that also treats coughing may be taken.

Chronic bronchitis, depending on its severity, may require bronchodialator drugs to expand the constricted airways. Antibiotic drugs may be prescribed to treat bacterial lung infection. Your GP may need to monitor your progress and provide further tests and treatment, depending on the severity of the attacks. You should have the flu jab annually and the anti-pneumonia jab every ten years.

For both acute and chronic bronchitis, avoiding irritants will help considerably, particularly by stopping smoking.

✚ **REMEDIES** see page 102

BRUISES

Bleeding beneath unbroken skin causes a bruise to form. This can happen due to a knock or prolonged pressure on the area. Blue-black in colour at first, bruises gradually fade to yellow and then disappear. The impact causes damage to the blood vessels, causing the blood to leak out underneath the skin. Sometimes the bruised area swells.

TREATING BRUISES

Bruises usually disappear of their own accord. If they are particularly large and painful, putting a cold water compress over the area will help calm it down. Frozen peas or rice bags can be used instead.

Always see your doctor if the bruising is around the eye, causing a black eye. This is especially important if you have any disturbances to your vision.

Bruising is common in the elderly as the skin is thin and the blood vessels poorly supported. Children tend to get bruises as a result of enthusiastic play. Spontaneous bruising without a history of injury may indicate a medical disorder and should be investigated. In addition, if you notice a child who is regularly bruised, consider making further investigations and, if required, report your findings to the police or Childline (Tel: 0800 1111).

✚ REMEDIES see page 199

BUNIONS

Bunions are usually caused by wearing ill-fitting shoes and affect three times more women than men. The joint at the base of the big toe bulges outwards and a thick, fluid-filled sac develops over the inflamed area. This is called a bursa (see Bursitis, page 37). Bunions can be very painful and cause pressure and crowding of the toes, which makes wearing shoes of any kind difficult.

TREATING BUNIONS

Small bunions may benefit from a toe pad to straighten the toe and padding in the shoes, particularly in the area around the big toe. If the bunion becomes swollen and infected your doctor may prescribe antibiotics and painkillers. Large bunions require surgery to straighten the toe.

✚ REMEDIES see page 227

BURNS and SCALDS

Heat, extreme cold and certain chemicals can cause burns to the skin. Sunburn, (see page 69) fire and other heat sources, such as irons or ovens, are common causes of burns. Burns caused by steam or hot fluids are known as scalds.

TREATING BURNS AND SCALDS

You should only self-treat minor burns or scalds. If a minor burn or scald becomes swollen and infected, you should see your GP for treatment.

To treat a minor burn or scald, put the affected part underneath a tap of running cold water. This will take the heat out of the area and prevent any further damage. Keep the affected area there until the acute pain subsides and then dry carefully. Apply burn creams or sprays and cover with a non-stick dressing to protect the area. Painkillers will help ease the pain. Do not puncture any blisters that may develop as the raw, tender flesh underneath may become infected.

Large burns with large blisters should be dressed by your doctor or a hospital's Accident and Emergency Department.

Major burns or scalds require emergency treatment. Place the affected area under cold water and call an ambulance or ask someone to take you to the nearest hospital's Accident and Emergency Department.

✚ REMEDIES see page 200

BURSITIS

Bursitis is an inflammation to the bursa, a fluid-filled sac that forms over an area subjected to excessive pressure. It can occur on the knees, elbows and shoulders but most commonly on the toe of the big foot (see Bunions, page 36). Bursitis can be associated with rheumatoid arthritis (see page 63) and gout (see page 49).

TREATING BURSITIS

Rest the affected part for a few days to allow the fluid in the bursa to subside. If the area is particularly painful, hold a bag of frozen peas or rice over the area. Aspirin or ibuprofen may help.

If the swelling persists, you should see your doctor. You may be prescribed antibiotics if the swelling has become infected. Your GP may drain the bursa or refer you to hospital for this to be done.

✚ **REMEDIES** see page 227

CALLUSES

When the skin is subjected to heavy use from friction or pressure, the horny layer of the skin becomes thicker and forms calluses. Those who do heavy manual work, a lot of gardening, or who wear ill-fitting shoes may develop calluses on their hands or feet.

TREATING CALLUSES

The calluses will fade if they are no longer put under pressure or intensive use. Gently removing the hardened skin with a soapy pumice stone will help new, softer skin to form. Always moisturise after scraping the skin off. If badly fitted shoes are the cause, stop wearing the shoes. Thick calluses on the feet may require a visit to the chiropodist.

✚ **REMEDIES** see page 203

CATARRH

Catarrh occurs when the nose lining is inflamed and causes a nasal discharge. This can be thin and watery, but more often is thick and yellow or green in colour. Catarrh is very often a symptom of other respiratory disorders such as colds and flu. It can also be caused by irritant substances, such as dust or smoke, or allergies to substances such as pollen. Severe catarrh can block the nose and sometimes causes headaches due to sinus congestion. The over-production of mucus, which trickles down the throat, may cause an irritating cough and the inflammation can cause nasal obstruction, sneezing or a watery nasal discharge. In this situation, a viral upper respiratory tract infection or cold can cause acute sinusitis with fever, facial pain and green nasal discharge.

Smokers often suffer from smokers' cough, because of over-production of mucus in the lungs.

TREATING CATARRH

Catarrh due to a cold or flu will usually disappear of its own accord. Steam inhalations can reduce the effects. Nasal decongestants and cold remedy preparations may help alleviate symptoms. Painkillers may ease the pain of sinusitis. Giving up smoking can help alleviate chronic catarrh.

✚ **REMEDIES** see page 119

CHICKENPOX

This very common and highly infectious viral illness is characterised by tell-tale red raised spots with a water blister on top. Before the spots appear, the child may feel generally unwell and have a slight fever. Once the spots appear, they form blisters that crust over. They can appear all over the body, including inside the mouth. They are very itchy and it will be difficult for a child to resist scratching them. However, try to prevent them doing this because it may leave scars or cause infection. After a few days the crusts fall off. From the day before the spots appear to when the spots crust over, your child will be infectious to others.

TREATING CHICKENPOX

Child versions of paracetamol will help reduce fever – do not give a child under the age of 12 any product that contains aspirin. Calamine lotion or antihistamines will calm the itchy skin.

Call your GP if your child's scratching has made the spots infected, if their temperature exceeds 104°F (40°C), or if the child still has a cough or is coughing up phlegm after the spots have gone. Antibiotics may be given to fight any secondary bacterial infection.

Pregnant women who have been in contact with chicken pox should see their doctor for advice. All adults develop the disease should see their doctor for specific treatment.

✚ **REMEDIES** see page 274

CHILBLAINS

Excessive constriction of the small blood vessels under the skin brought about by exposure to cold causes itchy purple-red swellings to appear on the toes or fingers.

TREATING CHILBLAINS

Chilblains usually heal without treatment but dusting the affected area with talcum powder will help relieve itching. Prevent chilblains by keeping yourself warm in cold weather with a hat, scarf, gloves, thick socks and a warm coat.

✚ **REMEDIES** see page 257

COLD SORES

Small sores that develop around the lips, mouth and nose are caused by the herpes simplex I virus. They are highly contagious and passed from one person to another via physical contact, often from kissing, or by using an infected person's towels on the face. Once acquired, the virus remains in the body for life, flaring up from time to time, usually when the sufferer is run down or experiencing a lot of stress.

TREATING COLD SORES

Keep the area clean by bathing the sore in a salt water solution and try to avoid touching the sores with your hands. Be scrupulous in your hygiene to avoid giving the virus to others. An attack can be averted by applying a cream containing aciclovir the minute the tingly sensation is experienced at the site of the about-to-develop sore. Occasionally cold sores become secondarily infected and may need antibiotics.

✚ **REMEDIES** see page 250

COLDS

Colds are contagious and are spread through tiny droplets in the air caused by an infected person's sneeze. Cold symptoms include a runny nose, sneezing, sore throat, coughs and headache, and sometimes a slight temperature.

Colds are caused by a viral infection. When you catch a cold your body produces antibodies to the virus, helping to ensure you will not be vulnerable to that virus again. However, as there are so many different viruses this does not mean that you will never have a cold again. In fact, the average adult is likely to have three colds a year, although, depending on the type of virus and the overall state of your health, the severity of the colds will vary.

Complications of colds include acute bronchitis (see page 35), sinusitis (see page 65) and ear infections (see page 145).

TREATING COLDS

Get plenty of rest and stay at home to avoid passing the virus on to others. Keep warm and drink plenty of fluids such as water, herbal teas and fresh citrus fruit juices. Get some fresh air if you feel up to it, as it may help clear the blocked sinus passages. Eat healthily, increasing your intake of fruit and vegetables. If you don't feel like eating, try taking small, light meals such as soups and juiced fruits and raw vegetables. Hot honey and lemon drinks will help ease a sore throat. Take a multi-vitamin and mineral supplement to help replace lost nutrition.

Colds usually go within a week to ten days. Try to build up your strength, however, as you may still be weak and therefore vulnerable to another cold virus. People with a history of chest problems or sinus infections may require antibiotics.

✚ **REMEDIES** see page 122

COLIC

Infantile colic is a childhood ailment that causes severe abdominal pain. Spasms of pain are felt in waves, causing the baby to cry in pain. Although colic is common and harmless, it is very distressing to both the child and the parent. The cause of colic is unknown and it tends to disappear once the infant is over three months old.

If episodes of colic are accompanied by constipation, diarrhoea and fever, and if the baby is failing to gain sufficient weight, you should see your GP as there may be a more serious underlying problem that requires treatment.

TREATING COLIC

Cuddling and soothing your baby may help ease the infant's distress during spasms of colic. Stroking the baby's back or placing a warm pad on the baby's abdomen may help soothe an attack. Rocking the baby rhythmically or taking it for a ride in the car are both worth trying.

Milk is sometimes implicated in colic – either the infant formula or foods eaten by the mother. However, don't try changing your baby's milk without medical advice.

✚ **REMEDIES** see page 274

CONJUNCTIVITIS

When the conjunctiva membrane lining the eyelids and covering the front of the eyeball becomes inflamed the condition is known as conjunctivitis. The eyes become red and itchy, and may be sticky, particularly in the morning. They are often painful and may feel as if there is some gritty substance under the eyelids. Sometimes there is a blurring of vision and if there is an infection, there may be a discharge of pus.

Allergies such as hayfever and other irritants in the eye may cause conjunctivitis, as can bacterial invaders.

TREATING CONJUNCTIVITIS

Bathe the affected eye with warm water and remove any hardened pus by holding a wet cotton-wool pad over the area until the pus is moist. Avoid rubbing the eye.

Allergic conjunctivitis can be treated with antihistamine eye drops. A bacterial infection may require antibiotics.

✚ **REMEDIES** see page 246

CONSTIPATION

Having difficulty passing stools or passing them less frequently than is normal for you is known as constipation. Usually constipation is temporary and bowel movements will return to normal after a few days. A diet lacking in fibre, insufficient exercise, some medicines, stress and a change in routine can all upset bowel habits.

If constipation continues for more than ten days, or if bowel movements are painful and accompanied by blood, you should see your GP so that any underlying illness can be eliminated.

TREATING CONSTIPATION
Taking more exercise and increasing the amount of fibre in your diet will improve constipation. Eat more wholemeal bread, fresh fruit and vegetables and drink orange or prune juice (increasing the amount of fluids generally will help). Laxatives can be used with caution, although prolonged use is not advised.

🔋 REMEDIES see page 149

CORNS

Corns are small, circular and cone-shaped areas of thickened skin on the feet which sometimes also have a small central core. They usually develop as a result of friction or pressure caused by ill-fitting shoes.

There are two types of corns: hard corns, which develop on the upper surface of the toes or on the outside of the little toe; and soft corns, which are usually white and develop between the fourth and fifth toes.

Pain is experienced when the centre of the corn is subjected to pressure, usually from shoes. Sometimes a corn can become infected. If this occurs you should see your doctor.

TREATING CORNS
Minor corns can be pared down with an emery board or pumice stone. More troublesome corns can be treated by applying paints containing salicylic acid or by putting impregnated pads over the area to soften and remove the corn.

▶ **Caution** Diabetics must not self-treat corns or any other foot problems.

🔋 REMEDIES see page 203

COUGH (See also Bronchitis, page 35, Sinusitis, page 65, Colds and Flu, page 122)

A cough is a reflex action designed to clear the throat, windpipe and lung airways of excess mucus, catarrh or irritants such as dust, smoke or foreign bodies. The cough may be either productive, causing mucus or catarrh, or dry and non-productive.

The majority of coughs are due to viral infections that produce irritation and cause increased mucus production in the lungs and back of the nose, frequently a symptom of colds, flu, bronchitis and sinusitis. However, coughing can sometimes be a symptom of asthma and other serious diseases such as heart failure. If you feel generally unwell, have a persistent cough, breathlessness, chest pain, or are producing masses of green sputum, you should see your doctor.

TREATING COUGHS

There is a vast array of over-the-counter cough remedies available so it may be difficult to make a choice. There is, however, an important distinction to make: if the cough is dry and unproductive, select cough remedies that include a suppressant; if the cough is chesty or congestive, use an expectorant to clear the phlegm.

▶ **Caution** Never treat a chesty cough with a suppressant, unless it is in a specially combined formula, as the congestion will remain in the lungs and may cause a chest infection. Many cold and flu remedies include cough suppressants (see Cold and Flu, page 122). Coughs connected with Sinusitis (see page 65) and Bronchitis (see page 35) also have specific over-the-counter remedies.

✚ **REMEDIES** see page 102

CRADLE CAP

Young babies often develop cradle cap, a thick scaly dandruff that forms over the scalp and eyebrows. It is not a serious condition and does not cause any pain or irritation. Avoid putting irritant clothing such as wool on the baby's head.

TREATING CRADLE CAP

Shampoo the baby's head with cradle cap preparations or use a cream overnight to loosen the scales and wash it off in the morning. Do not use an adult shampoo as this may irritate the delicate skin. Take care to keep lather out of the baby's eyes. If the condition does not clear, ask your doctor for advice.

✚ **REMEDIES** see page 276

CRAMP

Cramp is an involuntary contraction or spasm of the muscles. Typically it lasts for only a few seconds or minutes, but it can be extremely painful. It usually occurs in the legs, feet or hands and often develops after repetitive movements reduce blood flow to the area. Cramps can also occur during sports or when limbs are cold and have not been warmed up adequately.

TREATING CRAMP

Minor cramp can be treated by gently massaging the affected area. Warming the area up will help. Calf cramps can be eased by gently pressing the foot on the floor and moving the toes upwards. Most cramps will abate but they can be extremely painful at the time.

✚ **REMEDIES** see page 227

CUTS

Most cuts are not serious. However, it is important to guard against serious infection, especially if the cut was caused by a dirty implement or by an animal scratch or bite. If the cut is major or is causing excessive bleeding, it will require medical attention. If the cut is deep it may require stitches.

To stop bleeding, raise the affected part and apply firm continuous pressure using a clean folded tea towel or handkerchief for 15 to 20 minutes. A cut that continues to bleed despite first-aid treatment should be seen by a doctor at the Accident and Emergency Department of your nearest hospital.

TREATING CUTS

Treat minor cuts by cleansing the wound and wiping away any dirt with a pad soaked in a dilute solution of antiseptic. You can also use antiseptic wipes designed for the purpose. Cover the cut with a clean dressing.

If the cut was caused by an animal, or if you had been gardening and have not recently had a tetanus injection, you should see the doctor for treatment.

❋ REMEDIES see page 205

CYSTITIS

Pain when passing urine is the most common symptom of cystitis. It is caused by bacteria infecting the bladder and is more common in women because the tube leading to the outside of the body, through which the urine passes, is much shorter in women than in men and also nearer the anus, where the bacteria, which live in the gut, leave the body. This makes it easier for bacteria to enter the tube and pass up to the bladder.

Passing urine is painful and causes a burning sensation. The urine may be cloudy and there is usually a strong odour. Some women find urinating so painful that they put off going to the toilet for as long as possible, which aggravates the condition further.

Sexual intercourse can trigger attacks of cystitis, and it is more common in women who use the diaphragm for contraception. You can reduce the frequency of attacks by emptying the bladder before and immediately after intercourse.

Sometimes the infection can pass from the bladder to the kidneys.

TREATING CYSTITIS

Flush out the urinary system by drinking lots of water. Take care to wipe yourself from front to back after going to the toilet, to avoid infection. Drink cranberrry juice, because it contains a substance that prevents bacteria from multiplying in the urinary tract. Over-the-counter remedies can quickly and effectively help relieve symptoms, but if symptoms persist or you are unwell, consult your doctor.

❋ REMEDIES see page 177

DANDRUFF

A form of seborrhoeic dermatitis, dandruff causes flaky bits of skin to be shed from the scalp. Although this is a normal process, dandruff becomes a problem when it is excessive. Also, with dandruff the shed skin clumps together, making shedding more obvious.

Dandruff can occur if you are allergic to the contents of certain shampoo preparations, so it is worth switching products to see if there is an improvement. Using too many hair styling products such as conditioners, mousses, gels and sprays, or over-washing the hair, can also cause dandruff.

TREATING DANDRUFF

When washing your hair, make sure you rinse thoroughly. Be gentle when drying it, avoiding the high setting on the hairdryer. Use a coal tar based medicated shampoo – all pharmacies stock a wide range of preparations. For more persistent dandruff, more specialist over-the-counter preparations are required.

Sometimes seborrhoeic dermatitis causes dandruff. This is an adult form of cradle cap (see page 42) and mild cases will respond to over-the-counter remedies. If there is no improvement, you should see your doctor for advice.

✚ **REMEDIES** see page 207

DEPRESSION

Depression has many causes and its effect on the emotions ranges from a temporary feeling of being 'fed up' to more serious, depressive states of thinking that life is not worthwhile. Moods are affected by many factors, so it is understandable to be unhappy when unpleasant life events occur. However, depending on how well you cope and how supportive your friends and family are, you should survive a short period of depression without harm.

What distinguishes depression from unhappiness is a persistent low mood, difficulty sleeping, loss of appetite and weight loss, poor concentration, loss of interest in appearance, work, hobbies and friends, and negative thoughts with self-blame, guilt and hopelessness.

TREATING DEPRESSION

During periods of mild depression it is particularly important to eat well and to get enough sleep. Taking regular exercise can boost the hormones that raise mood, lifting the depression for several hours. Talk about your feelings to a supportive partner or friend.

Prolonged or severe depression should always receive medical attention. Your doctor may be able to help the symptoms of depression, such as insomnia, and may prescribe a course of anti-depressant drugs to help you over the worst times. Counselling can also be arranged so that you can talk through your feelings and deal with your problems.

✚ **REMEDIES** see page 264

DERMATITIS

The usual cause of dermatitis is an allergy to a substance with which the skin comes into contact, but it can also be caused by sensitivity to sunlight. Stress can also trigger a bout of dermatitis.

Symptoms include dry, scaly skin that can often be red and itchy (see Eczema, pages 46-47). It affects small or large areas of the body, appearing in one site or several. The most common areas are on the hands, face, scalp (see Dandruff, page 44), chest and back as well as the legs and arms.

TREATING DERMATITIS

Mild dermatitis can be eased by moisturising the skin with an emollient lotion or cream. Avoid using perfumed soaps, creams and cosmetics if these tend to make your dermatitis worse. Wearing rough cloth next to the skin can also aggravate dermatitis. Wear cotton-lined rubber gloves when washing up or cleaning with detergents.

For dermatitis that is painful, disfiguring or persistent, you should see your GP for an accurate diagnosis and appropriate treatment.

✚ **REMEDIES** see page 211

DIARRHOEA

Diarrhoea may be decribed as the frequent passing of loose or watery stools. Causes can be varied and include eating or drinking aggravating food, such as large quantities of fruit or vegetables, food-borne infections, food allergies, emotional problems such as anxiety and fear, and sometimes as a side-effect of taking medication, for example antibiotics. Sometimes the diarrhoea is accompanied by pain in the gut.

Diarrhoea is also a symptom of many other illnesses, and if it continues for longer than 48 hours you should see a doctor.

TREATING DIARRHOEA

Diarrhoea will usually go of its own accord once the bowels have settled down. Avoiding food for 24 hours may help. Prevent dehydration by drinking rehydration powders (see page 155) which prevent salt and water losses. If the diarrhoea persists, an anti-diarrhoea preparation may be helpful. Call your doctor immediately if there are any symptoms of dehydration in the elderly or the very young.

✚ **REMEDIES** see page 155

EARACHE

Earache has many different causes but the result is the same – there is marked discomfort or even pain in the ear. Sometimes this is accompanied by buzzing noises and a high temperature. Young children and babies may rub at their ears to indicate the pain.

Earache can be caused by a number of conditions. A build-up of wax in the ear can block the ear canal, making hearing harder and sometimes causing pain (see Ear Wax, below). Ear infections, such as middle ear infection (otitis media) or an infection of the ear canal (otitis externa) can cause earache. Occasionally foreign bodies in the ear, such as beads or bits of toys, can also cause earache. It is also a common symptom of colds and flu.

TREATING EARACHE

Holding a warm flannel or hot-water bottle over the affected ear may help ease the pain. If the ear is red and swollen, a cold compress may be preferable. Painkillers can help ease the throbbing and pain. If the earache does not respond to self-treatment, see your doctor to determine the cause. Earache in children should be seen by the doctor if it fails to clear quickly or if the child is in distress.

✚ REMEDIES see page 243

EAR WAX

Wax is produced by the ear to protect the ear canal from foreign objects such as dust and other airborne particles. The ear self-cleans itself by shedding the wax to prevent it building up. Sometimes, however, the wax does build up and blocks the ear canal. This may cause a partial loss of hearing or earache (see page 45).

TREATING EAR WAX

Warm some almond oil and use a dropper to gently drop the liquid into the outer ear. Do not poke the dropper into the ear canal. This should warm the wax and allow it to clear. You can also buy over-the-counter wax softening ear drops. If a plug has formed that is too solid to remove you will need to see your GP to have your ears syringed.

✚ REMEDIES see page 244

ECZEMA

Eczema describes a range of different skin conditions that cause redness, swelling, irritation and blistering. The two most common are contact eczema, which occurs when the skin reacts to an allergic substance, and atopic eczema, an inherited form of eczema. Both cause the skin to become red and itchy. The eczema can cause dry, flaky skin or wet and weeping skin. The unbearable urge to scratch can cause the sufferer to break the skin with frantic scratching, making the area bleed and increasing the chances of bacterial infection.

Contact eczema develops on people who are sensitive to an irritant or range of irritants such as wool, nylon, metals, detergents, chemicals, cosmetics and even sunlight. Certain foods can cause eczema, including eggs and fish.

Atopic eczema affects those who have a family history of allergy, including asthma, hayfever or hives (nettle rash). Children with atopic eczema often grow out of it.

TREATING ECZEMA

Try to identify any allergic substances such as soap and detergent and avoid using them. Dry, flaky eczema can be remoisturised by rubbing in emollient creams or ointments. Though they are not as pleasant to use, ointments are more effective than creams because they stay on the skin for longer. Your doctor may prescribe stronger corticosteroid creams if over-the-counter remedies do not work.

✚ REMEDIES see page 211

FATIGUE

Feeling tired is a normal reaction to excessive exertion, caused by over-exercising, over-working or just the result of leading a busy life. It can also be a symptom of illness – it is quite common to feel weak and need to sleep when suffering from many illnesses, including common ones such as colds and flu. Excessive fatigue may be due to a medical condition, such as anaemia, or some other underlying illness such as an underactive thyroid gland.

TREATING FATIGUE

Make sure that you take your holiday allocations so that you can pace yourself and not tire yourself out. Allow sufficient time for tasks so that you can fit everything in, but in a less rushed and frantic way. Allow time to just sit still and rest, have an early night or indulge in a relaxing pastime to help keep fatigue at bay.

Avoid skipping meals and eat high-energy foods such as starchy carbohydrates, which release their energy-providing sugars over several hours. Make sure you get enough vitamins and minerals from food and consider taking extra supplements.

Exercise can actually energise you, so make sure you get some fresh air combined with a walk – or go to the gym or an exercise class each week.

If none of these measures work, see your GP for tests to determine whether there is a medical reason for your persistent fatigue.

✚ REMEDIES see page 265

FEVER

Feeling hot and as if you are burning up indicates a fever. You may also feel weak, shivery and generally unwell. You may also find that you sweat a lot. Taking your temperature will confirm a fever if the reading is above the normal range of 98.4–99°F (37–37.5°C).

Fever is a symptom of many conditions such as flu, food poisoning, swollen glands, earache, to name a few. It can also be a result of heatstroke or sunstroke. Usually fever results from a bacterial or viral infection and is thought to be one of the body's ways of fighting the infection.

TREATING FEVER

The treatment for a fever depends on the underlying cause. Painkillers such as aspirin, paracetamol and ibuprofen will bring down a fever and treat many other symptoms that may be associated with the cause, such as flu. Wear light clothing, use a fan, and sponge the patient with lukewarm water.

A temperature of 105°F (41°C) or above is life-threatening and requires immediate medical attention.

✪ REMEDIES see page 134

FROZEN SHOULDER

Inflammation of the tendons that move the shoulder joint, or of the fibrous capsule of the joint, causes frozen shoulder. Occasionally, the soft sac (bursa) that cushions the joint may be the cause (see Bursitis, page 37).

The shoulder feels as if it has been frozen, because movement is impaired. Daily tasks such as brushing the hair become very difficult and painful, and reluctance to use the joint stiffens it further and makes it even more painful to use.

TREATING FROZEN SHOULDER

Over time – possibly two to three months – the joint will free itself, but the pain may make you so uncomfortable that you want to seek medical treatment. Your doctor will probably prescribe strong anti-inflammatory drugs and advise physiotherapy. Sometimes an injection into the inflamed tendon or joint may be required.

Self-treatment is with over-the-counter anti-inflammatory drugs, although long-term use of these is inadvisable. Gentle movement of the affected shoulder, if it isn't too painful, will help free it.

✪ REMEDIES see page 228

GASTRITIS

Irritation of the lining of the stomach causes gastritis. It may come on suddenly, causing acute pain, or may develop over a longer period, gradually getting worse and worse. Many things can irritate the stomach lining including drugs, alcohol, cigarette smoking, bacteria (especially Helicobacter pylon), allergies, bile acid and low levels of protective mucus in the lining. Sometimes stress can bring on an attack.

Symptoms include discomfort and/or pain in the stomach after eating, heartburn, nausea and vomiting. In acute cases the faeces may be blackened due to blood lost from the stomach. This requires immediate hospital treatment. With chronic gastritis, this slow blood loss can cause anaemia (see page 29), causing you to feel tired and breathless.

TREATING GASTRITIS

Take paracetamol rather than aspirin when treating any other ailments, as aspirin can irritate the stomach lining. Try to identify the cause of the gastritis and stop or avoid the triggers, especially alcohol.

Over-the-counter preparations containing bismuth and other antacids will help heal the stomach lining.

Sometimes gastritis produces the same symptoms as a gastric ulcer – so if your symptoms continue for more than a couple of days, or if they recur frequently, see your doctor, who may send you for tests to rule out or confirm this.

✚ **REMEDIES** see page 160

GINGIVITIS

Gingivitis is a chronic inflammation of the gums and is a major cause of tooth loss in adults, getting increasingly common with age. It often occurs due to infection, but it is usually caused by a build-up of plaque on the bases of the teeth where they meet the gums.

Bacteria within the plaque irritate the gums, making them swollen, tender and sometimes infected. Rough brushing or flossing can also irritate the gums, making them prone to infection. When infected, the gums appear an angry red-purple colour, instead of a rosy pink or light brown, and they may also bleed. Bad breath (see page 33) is a common symptom of gingivitis.

TREATING GINGIVITIS

Regular trips to the dental hygienist will ensure that plaque build-up is removed from the bases of the teeth. Regular brushing and flossing will also help.

If left untreated, gingivitis can cause loss of the teeth. This occurs because the inflammation spreads, affecting the tissues of the teeth and surrounding bone, causing the teeth to loosen and become unstable.

✚ **REMEDIES** see page 248

GOUT

Gout causes attacks of arthritis (see page 30) due to a build-up of uric crystals in the affected joint. It usually affects a single joint, especially the joint at the base of the big toe, but it can affect other joints such as the knee, ankle and foot and the wrist and the small joints of the hands.

The joint becomes red and swollen and very tender. Gout can be extremely painful and attacks may also be accompanied by a high fever – in which case there may be an infection of the joint and you should see your doctor immediately.

TREATING GOUT

Purine-containing foods can raise the level of uric acid in the blood so offal (particularly liver) should be avoided. Alcohol and some medication can also bring on an attack. You should see your GP to confirm the diagnosis. Strong non-steroidal anti-inflammatory painkillers can be given for an acute attack. Frequent attacks or very high levels of uric acid in the stool may require long-term treatment to lower the level of uric acid.

✚ **REMEDIES** see page 228

HANGNAILS

When a strip of skin tears away from the base or edges of a finger it is known as a hangnail. It can be very painful and irritating, and if the skin catches on clothing or other articles this causes further pain.

Biting the nails is a common cause of hangnails. Frequently immersing your hands in water softens the skin and nails, making hangnails more likely.

TREATING HANGNAILS

Keep your nails trimmed and use protective gloves to avoid hangnails forming. To treat a hangnail, use manicure scissors to trim the nails and then clean the area with an antiseptic or sterile wipe. Dry and then cover with a protective bandage until the area heals. Sometimes the exposed area of fleshy skin can become infected. If this occurs you should see your doctor for treatment.

✚ REMEDIES see page 217

HAYFEVER

Hayfever is an unpleasant allergy, mostly to pollen but also to other irritant substances such as fur and dust that affect the mucus membranes that line the nose. The irritant substance causes an itchy sensation in the nose followed by sneezing, a runny nose and watery, itchy and sore eyes. At the same time the eyes are often affected by conjunctivitis (see page 40).

Hayfever is most prevalent among teenagers, when up to 20 percent of young people suffer symptoms in June and July (the exam season). There is often a family history of allergy, including asthma (see page 31), eczema (see page 46) or hives (see page 51). Particular allergens can be identified by skin tests, although most sufferers will know what triggers a bout of sneezing.

TREATING HAYFEVER

Avoid allergens if at all possible. Keep bedroom and car windows shut, wear dark glasses and avoid walks in the country, especially in the afternoon when the pollen count is highest.

Bathing the eyes will help ease them and reduce inflammation, over-the-counter antihistamine preparations can alleviate the symptoms. For severe cases, stronger, prescription-only antihistamines, steriod nasal sprays or – more rarely – preventive desensitising injections can be given.

✚ REMEDIES see page 135

HEADACHES

One of the most common ailments there is, a headache can last for as little as half an hour to several hours, varying in severity from a minor ache to a severe, throbbing or stabbing ache that also affects the eyes.

Headaches are often a symptom of some other condition such as drinking too much alcohol, exposure to a stuffy environment, sinus problems, muscle tension, neck ache, emotional stress, fatigue or overwork.

TREATING HEADACHES

Headaches can be easily treated using painkillers. Various strengths are available, depending on the severity of the headache. Sometimes no treatment is needed, other than resting quietly until the headache goes.

Severe and persistent headaches may be related to fading eyesight, so having your eyes tested is advisable. If this does not prove to be the cause, you should ask your pharmacist's advice or see your GP for further investigation. Very rarely, headaches can be a symptom of other problems, including high blood pressure. If you get a sudden severe headache with vomiting you should see your doctor immediately. (See also Migraine, page 59.)

✚ **REMEDIES** see page 97

HEARTBURN

Also known as acid reflux, heartburn feels like a burning or aching sensation in the middle of the chest. It happens when the gullet goes into spasm or when stomach acid is regurgitated back up into the throat, causing a bitter taste in the mouth.

Heartburn usually occurs after eating, particularly if the food is very fatty or rich and spicy, or if it has been eaten in a hurry. It is also quite common during pregnancy. Sometimes heartburn is a symptom of hiatus hernia, when the stomach pushes upwards through the normal opening of the diaphragm and into the chest. The pain is often confused with a heart attack, particularly in middle-aged men.

TREATING HEARTBURN

Avoid foods that bring on heartburn, including alcohol. Belching seems to ease the pain. Antacids and indigestion remedies can be taken to help ease the symptoms. See your doctor if heartburn is a problem during pregnancy so that safe medication can be recommended.

In a middle-aged man, a first attack of 'heartburn' or 'indigestion', especially if it wakes him at night or is accompanied by sweating or vomiting, may be a heart attack and a doctor or ambulance should be called immediately.

✚ **REMEDIES** see page 160

HIVES

Also known as nettle rash or urticaria, hives is a swelling and irritation of the skin. It is triggered by an allergic reaction that causes the body to release histamine into the affected parts. This, in turn, makes the skin itch or tingle, and is followed by large raised yellow weals, surrounded by a red area of inflammation, appearing on the skin. Individual spots may last for only a few hours, but the rash as a whole may last for two to three days. Hives go away without scarring.

Hives can be caused by an allergic reaction to food or food additives, certain drugs such as aspirin and penicillin, exposure to heat, cold or sunlight, bites and stings, and stress.

TREATING HIVES

Self-treatment with antihistamines will ease the irritation by preventing the release of histamine. Stronger, prescription-only drugs are available if you regularly suffer from hives.

✿ REMEDIES see page 195

INDIGESTION

A commonly experienced condition, indigestion covers a wide range of symptoms, most of which are brought on by eating. They include heartburn, nausea, flatulence and a heavy feeling in the upper abdomen. Alcohol, smoking, over-eating, bolting your food, or eating spicy and rich food can all bring on indigestion.

TREATING INDIGESTION

Avoid alcohol and foods you know cause you indigestion. Taking over-the-counter antacid remedies when the symptoms occur will allow them to subside. Do not take antacid remedies on a regular basis. If you suffer from repeated indigestion, particularly if you are over 40 years old, have unexplained weight loss and vomiting, you should see your GP for further investigation.

✿ REMEDIES see page 160

INFLUENZA

Highly contagious and very debilitating, influenza is caused by a viral infection. It is spread by contaminated droplets in the air, from an infected person sneezing or coughing in your vicinity.

Influenza affects the upper respiratory system, causing the symptoms of a cold, though usually much worse. These symptoms include high fever, shivering, dry cough, sore throat and headache. In addition, influenza has other symptoms, including backache, muscle pains, fever, sweating, chills, insomnia and general lethargy. Often, influenza is accompanied by depression, which may sometimes linger long after other symptoms have cleared.

TREATING INFLUENZA

As influenza is so debilitating, you should always stay in bed when you have it. Do not try to be brave and struggle to work, because all you will do is pass it on to others. Keep warm and sleep whenever you feel like it – which will probably be most of the time.

Take paracetamol, or aspirin, or a flu remedy to bring down the temperature and relieve aching symptoms. Take care not to overdose – many remedies contain paracetamol, so you should only take one remedy at a time. Check the labels so that you know what you are taking.

Don't worry too much about not feeling hungry for the first couple of days. Instead, drink plenty of fluids to replace body fluids lost through sweating. Sugary and/or glucose drinks will help replace lost energy. Vitamin C drinks may help boost the body's immune system and help fight the illness. Warm drinks can help soothe a sore throat and cough. Steam inhalations will help clear blocked sinuses.

Call your GP if your temperature reaches 104°F (40°C), or if you fail to recover after five to seven days. The elderly may be given antibiotics to prevent any secondary respiratory infections developing, particularly pneumonia.

Once the fever has gone, you can get up and about again – but take it easy for the first few days. If you suffer from persistent depression after other flu symptoms go, try herbal remedies or see your GP.

🛠 **REMEDIES** see page 122

INFLUENZA AND 'AT RISK' GROUPS

All 'at risk' groups should see their doctor when they go down with flu. Those in this category include:

- the elderly (over 75)
- diabetics
- those with an impaired immune system (e.g. AIDS sufferers)
- those with chronic chest conditions such as bronchitis or asthma
- those with heart problems
- those with kidney problems
- those with hormone problems
- those taking steroid drugs that suppress the immune system

Each year a flu vaccine is prepared in anticipation of the virus arriving in the UK. They are 70 percent effective and are strongly advised for those who are at risk. The vaccine must be given each year, usually around October, which is just before the start of the flu season.

There is also an anti-pneumonia vaccine that is given once every ten years.

INSOMNIA

Insomnia is a significant interference with the normal sleep pattern. This may be having trouble getting to sleep, having trouble staying asleep, or waking early before the sleep cycle has been completed.

An unquiet mind is the usual cause of insomnia – excitement and exhilaration being just as disruptive to sleep as anxiety, worry and stress. However, there are many other causes. Eating a heavy meal before bedtime, or drinking stimulating drinks such as tea and coffee, or too much alcohol, can disrupt sleep and cause temporary insomnia. Although alcohol makes you sleepy, as soon as you have burnt it off you become wide awake again. Certain medications can also cause insomnia.

External factors such as too much light in the bedroom, a stuffy, airless room, or noise from neighbours or from the street – or even your partner's snoring – are all possible causes.

Insomnia can be an important symptom of anxiety and depression. Illnesses or joint and muscle pain can also interfere with getting a good night's sleep.

As we get older, we tend to need less sleep. Many elderly people think they suffer from insomnia when they are in fact getting as much sleep as they need, although it may be significantly less than they are used to.

Children may be afraid of sleeping if they have recently experienced nightmares.

TREATING INSOMNIA

Make sure your bedroom environment is conducive to sleep. Change your bed if it is uncomfortable. Try using different weights of bedding and different numbers and types of pillows. If noise is a problem, you could try earplugs – or move to a quieter bedroom, if this is possible.

Allow three hours for food to digest before going to bed. Avoid stimulating drinks and watching violent, exciting television programmes before bedtime.

A hot bath and a milky drink just before bedtime can help calm both the mind and the body. Herbal drinks of camomile, passiflora, valerian, lavender or lemon balm are all said to have calming properties. Light, recreational reading just before going to sleep can turn the mind off work problems.

If a medical condition is the cause, or if you suspect that a medication is the cause, see your GP. Some medicines, particularly over-the-counter cold and flu preparations, contain caffeine which may keep you awake. Taking your last dose three hours before bedtime may help.

Try not to cat-nap during the day, as this will only reinforce your disturbed sleep cycle. Adequate exercise during the day may help sleep.

If serious emotional or life problems are causing chronic insomnia, or if your insomnia does not improve and it is affecting daily life, see your GP. You may be prescribed a short-term course of sleeping tablets or antidepressants to help you regain a normal sleep pattern. If necessary, you may be referred for counselling.

✚ REMEDIES see page 267

IRRITABLE BOWEL SYNDROME

Irritable bowel syndrome (IBS) is a group of symptoms that cause abdominal pain and discomfort. There may be cramping pains in the abdomen, feeling full before you have finished eating, constipation, diarrhoea, back pain, excessive wind and tiredness.

IBS occurs when the muscles in the gut walls, which contract and retract to move partially digested food along the intestines, become unco-ordinated or go into spasm. For this reason, the condition is also known as spastic colon or irritable colon syndrome.

Many things can disturb the gut. Food allergies, acute or chronic anxiety and stress seem to be the most common causes.

TREATING IRRITABLE BOWEL SYNDROME
Bouts of IBS can come and go, with or without treatment. Sometimes they disappear for years, only to reappear again. To keep the gut healthy and performing properly, ensure you have enough fibre in your diet – but take care, because fibre can make some sufferers worse.

An over-the-counter remedy for IBS may help the condition. If you suspect a food intolerance, try screening out foods to see if the condition improves. But if you find that a major food group, such as dairy produce, exacerbates symptoms, take advice before cutting them out because this can lead to calcium deficiency.

If stress and anxiety are the cause of IBS, try to resolve the underlying problems by trying relaxation techniques. Exercise may improve your symptoms.

See your GP if you feel you need emotional help, if your symptoms are severe, or if there is weight loss, fever, blood in stools, severe persistent pain, or exhaustion.

✚ REMEDIES see page 169

LARYNGITIS

Laryngitis means inflammation of the larynx, the voice box. When the larynx becomes inflamed the voice becomes hoarse, or is even temporarily 'lost' and attempting to speak is painful. Often swallowing is difficult and there may be a dry, irritating cough. Acute laryngitis in children is known as croup.

Laryngitis is a symptom of colds, flu or sinus and chest infections. It can also be caused by smoking too much or by inhaling irritant substances. Over-using the voice, as in prolonged shouting or singing, can temporarily cause laryngitis.

TREATING LARYNGITIS
Resting the voice is the best remedy. Sipping warm honey and lemon drinks will help ease the throat. Avoid smoking and dusty environments, which can make the throat feel worse.

Cough suppressants can be used if the cough is irritating. Vapour rubs on the chest, or steam inhalations can help ease the airways. Painkillers such as aspirin and paracetamol can help reduce soreness.

If laryngitis lasts for more than a month, see your GP for further investigation. Laryngitis in children is potentially dangerous as their airways are smaller. Any inflammation can cause the throat to swell and obstruct breathing. Call your GP if your child has laryngitis.

✚ REMEDIES see page 144

LICE and SCABIES

Lice are small, wingless insects that are yellowish grey in colour. They live on the human body and feed by sucking human blood. The lice make the skin feel itchy and leave small red dots on the skin where they have been feeding. The female lice lay small grey or brown oval-shaped eggs on the hairshafts of the scalp or the pubic hair. Very occasionally, lice may infest beards, armpit hair and anal hair. The eggs hatch in seven days and live for several weeks.

Scabies are mites that burrow into the skin and lay their eggs. They are highly contagious and can be seen under the skin as minute blisters at the end of thin grey streaks or tracks. They are usually found between the fingers, on the wrists and around the genital area. Later on, red lumps can be seen on the trunk and limbs. Scabs can occur on the skin from repeated itching and scratching and it can become infected.

Lice and scabies usually occur where there are communities such as schools, hostels and nursing homes or where there is close physical contact. They can also be passed on through sexual contact.

TREATING LICE AND SCABIES

Lice and scabies are treated with over-the-counter preparations. For scabies, the lotion is applied to the skin to kill the mites. The whole body from the neck downward should be treated and the lotion kept on for 24 hours. After washing hands the lotion should be reapplied. For lice, the lotion is applied to the hair and left for several hours. A special nit comb (usually supplied with the preparation) is then used to comb through the hair carefully to remove any dead lice. If you do not want to use powerful chemicals, wash the hair and put on conditioner, then use the nit comb in the bath. Do this for three days in a row. The conditioner blocks the pores so that the lice cannot breathe, but does not affect the nits (eggs), which will hatch. Repeat this treatment every two weeks until the infestation clears.

Avoid catching or transmitting lice or scabies by never wearing other people's unwashed clothes or hats. Ensure you have high standards of personal hygiene and do not share hairbrushes or combs, towels or bedding. If these measures do not work, see your GP for a stronger prescription medication.

✚ REMEDIES see page 217

MEASLES (See also Mumps, page 59)

Measles is a viral infection that occurs most commonly in childhood. It is highly infectious and is spread by inhaling infected droplets sneezed or coughed by an infected child or adult. There is an eight- to 14-day incubation period before the symptoms develop. The symptoms appear in two stages: the pre-eruptive stage, which lasts three to four days, and the eruptive stage when the tell-tale red rash appears. The rash lasts for about a week, after which the spots turn a brownish colour and then fade.

Measles causes high temperature, runny nose, sore throat, sore and sometimes bloodshot eyes, coughing and generally feeling unwell. It can be dangerous. Prior to the widespread use of the Measles, Mumps and Rubella (MMR) vaccination programme, many children developed serious complications after getting the virus – pneumonia, ear infection and encephalitis.

TREATING MEASLES

Measles is much less common in children because of the widespread use of the MMR vaccine. However, if your child is aged under three and has not been vaccinated, and if exposure to measles was only in the previous five days, your GP can give an antibody injection to avert the illness developing.

If your child was not given the MMR vaccination and develops measles, your GP will monitor your child. Meanwhile, keep the child warm in bed and darken the room if the eyes are sore. Treat the symptoms and try to keep the child comfortable. If the temperature starts to go up again after the rash comes out, and the child has a bad cough or earache, they may have a secondary bacterial infection and require antibiotics.

▶ **Caution** Do not expose a child with measles to a pregnant woman. This can be highly dangerous to the unborn child and to the mother if she has not had measles herself. The woman may go into premature labour or miscarry. However, unlike the Rubella virus (German measles), ordinary measles will not cause birth defects in the child.

✚ **REMEDIES** see page 277

MENOPAUSAL PROBLEMS

The menopause is defined as not having had a menstrual period for at least two years if you are within the age range of 45–55 years. The average age for reaching the menopause is 51, but it can begin earlier than 45 years and may occur later than 55 years.

Whilst being a perfectly natural stage in life, many women are taken by surprise by the symptoms, which begin from the age of 35 years as fertility declines. This interim stage from starting symptoms to reaching menopause is known as perimenopause.

Unlike having periods, there is usually nobody to 'groom' you for menopause, as it is a little-talked-about stage in life, often surrounded in secrecy. As well as physical symptoms, there are also emotional symptoms. Many post-menopausal women are relieved that they no longer have to worry about becoming pregnant; others experience great sadness and lack of self-esteem, knowing that their childbearing days are over.

Menopausal symptoms are wide but usually include these key indicators:

• Periods become irregular, either coming more frequently or coming with larger gaps in between. They may be missed altogether for a few months, only to reappear.

• The menstrual flow changes, either becoming lighter, heavier, lasting longer or becoming shorter.

• Hot flushes occur, usually combined with night sweats. Hot flushes are a unique sensation. Quite randomly, a feeling of unpleasant or unbearable heat occurs in the body, irrespective of climatic temperature. A flush will suffuse the upper part of the body, usually the chest, back, neck and face. There may be profuse sweating and palpitations. Then, just as suddenly, the flush disappears. These flushes can occur many times a day or only occasionally. Sometimes they disappear for a few months and then reappear. When the flushes occur at night they are known as night sweats and the sensation of heat, with accompanying sweating, often causes disrupted sleep. The flushes are thought to be linked to the body's decline in oestrogen production.

• Other symptoms that may be experienced include vaginal dryness, lack of concentration, loss of libido, mood changes, anxiety, irritability, headaches, itchiness of the skin or genitals, inadequate bladder control, skin dryness and thinning hair.

TREATING MENOPAUSAL PROBLEMS

Using moisturising vaginal gels will help if sex is painful. Taking regular exercise, especially weight-bearing exercise, will help keep the bones strong and overcome the potential problems of osteoporosis (weakening of the bones) which can occur after the menopause because of the lack of oestrogen. Taking calcium supplements and eating a low-fat but calcium-rich diet will also help strengthen the bones. You need about 1.5gm of calcium daily.

Yoga or relaxation exercises will help with stress symptoms but serious emotional problems may require counselling. Western and Chinese herbalists claim to be able to help treat the symptoms, but it is advisable to see a reputable practitioner for an individual prescription.

Not every woman experiences the above symptoms, and many experience them in a mild way. However, if these measures do not help and the symptoms are disrupting your life, you should consider seeing your GP. Many of the symptoms can be treated individually – for example, insomnia and anxiety – but you may wish to consider hormone replacement therapy (HRT) which treats all the symptoms by raising the low levels of oestrogen in the body. Progesterone is also given to counteract the adverse effects of oestrogen on the lining of the womb.

✚ REMEDIES see page 182

MENSTRUAL PROBLEMS (See also Premenstrual syndrome, page 62)

The delicate hormonal balancing act that goes on within the female body governs the menstrual cycle. Sometimes the hormones cause problems. These include heavy periods, irregular periods, painful periods, absent periods and mid-cycle bleeding. The hormones can also cause a range of symptoms known as premenstrual syndrome (see page 62).

TREATING MENSTRUAL PROBLEMS

You should see your GP if you have unexplained bleeding, absent bleeding or excessive bleeding, as these may be symptoms of an underlying condition that requires treatment. Irregular periods can be regularised by drug treatment.

Uncomplicated symptoms can be eased by taking exercise, which often helps regulate the cycle and minimise pain. Cramping pains in the abdomen can be eased by holding a hot-water bottle over the area or taking anti-inflammatory painkillers such as ibuprofen or aspirin. Stress (see page 68) or weight loss can also cause irregularities in the cycle, so any relaxation or stress-relieving techniques may help. Ensure you get enough fibre in your diet, as constipation is often a problem.

✚ REMEDIES see page 178

MIGRAINE

Migraine causes severe headaches characterised by throbbing pain, usually on one side of the head. A migraine attack can often be preceded or accompanied by visual distortions, light sensitivity and nausea, vomiting and dizziness. Migraines often affect members of the same family and the majority of sufferers are women.

Attacks can be triggered by certain smells, changes in atmospheric pressure and sun glare. Foods can trigger migraine, particularly cheese, coffee, citrus fruits and chocolate, cola drinks, various smoked and processed foods and food additives such as monosodium glutamate.

Symptoms may last for several hours, and occasionally even days.

Migraine is also brought on by stress and over-work. Sometimes, there is no identifiable trigger.

TREATING MIGRAINE

If the migraine attack is severe, lying quietly in a darkened room will help ease the throbbing and nauseous sensations. Take paracetamol painkillers to dull the pain rather than aspirin, as this may upset your stomach if you feel sick. Over-the-counter painkillers which contain codeine may help ease the pain more effectively. As migraine can stop the stomach efficiently emptying, it is better to take soluble tablets.

If nausea and vomiting are a problem, an over-the-counter anti-sickness preparation may help, although it may not be absorbed if vomiting is severe.

If you suffer prolonged or frequent migraines you should see your GP for treatment as there are many effective treatments now available.

✚ REMEDIES see page 97

MUMPS *(See also Measles, page 56)*

Mumps is a viral infection that affects the salivary glands in front of the ears, causing swelling and pain. The incubation period for mumps is 14 to 21 days. Symptoms include pain in the throat, neck, face and jaw, where there is the characteristic swelling around the lower cheeks and around the jaw. There may also be a temperature. The child may go off food, finding it difficult to chew or swallow.

Once a common childhood ailment, mumps has largely been eradicated due to the widespread Measles, Mumps and Rubella (MMR) vaccination programme (see Measles, page 56).

TREATING MUMPS

Keep the child away from other children, to avoid the risk of transmitting the disease to others. Give the child doses of paracetamol to reduce fever and discomfort. Feed the child bland foods that are soft to chew and easy to swallow. Give plenty of liquids.

Warm or cold compresses around the neck may help ease the throat and reduce swelling in the glands.

▶ **Caution** It is important to offer your child MMR as viral meningitis can occur in very young children and deafness can occur at any age. In some unvaccinated male adolescents and men, mumps can cause infertility if the infection spreads to both testicles.

✚ **REMEDIES** see page 277

NAPPY RASH

Babies and young toddlers commonly get nappy rash. Their skin is very sensitive and it can become chapped by a nappy rubbing against it. This is made worse if the nappy remains unchanged when it is soiled by urine and faeces.

TREATING NAPPY RASH

Keep the baby's skin clean and change the nappy whenever it is dirty. Avoid using cleaning wipes that contain alcohol or moisturisers because the sensitive skin may react. Instead, wipe with plenty of warm water and dab dry thoroughly (don't rub). Avoid using soaps, baby lotion, baby bath preparations and talcum powder, as these may also irritate the delicate skin.

Put an emollient cream on the chapped area or where there is a rash. Whenever you can, let the air get to the skin by leaving the nappy off for as long as possible. Avoid using plastic pants as these do not allow the skin to breathe.

If the nappy rash does not clear up, you should seek your health visitor's or GP's advice as there may be a fungal infection. This appears as thick white patches in the nappy area and can be treated easily using over-the-counter remedies.

✚ **REMEDIES** see page 277

NAUSEA

Nausea is the feeling that you are about to be sick and, indeed, the sensation is often followed by vomiting. Many triggers can bring about a nauseous feeling. Car and sea sickness (see page 172), food poisoning, acute gastritis (see page 48), emotional upset and certain bacterial and viral infections can make you feel as if you are about to be sick. Sometimes nausea is a symptom of migraine (see page 59) and it is a common feature of early pregnancy.

Although the sensation of nausea is unpleasant, it does not last very long. Usually, the sensation passes or resolves itself by making you vomit. Vomiting, unpleasant though it is, is a vital reflex triggered by the brain to rid the body of unwanted substances.

TREATING NAUSEA

Once the cause has been removed, the nausea will settle. If the nausea is followed by vomiting, be sure to drink plenty of water to rehydrate the body. This is especially important for young children. Pregnant women should see their GP for advice on treating nausea. Persistent nausea may be a symptom of another condition. See your GP for investigation.

✚ **REMEDIES** see page 171

NICOTINE REPLACEMENT THERAPY

Giving up smoking is very difficult. There are substances within tobacco that are addictive, as well as substances that are carcinogenic (causing cancer). The tar in cigarettes damages your lungs and can potentially cause cancer and chronic bronchitis, but it is the nicotine that gets you addicted.

Stopping smoking requires willpower, and probably a change in lifestyle habits. Smoking is often associated with regular, pleasurable habits such as lighting up after a meal or when having a drink with friends. It can also be used to ease stressful moments. All these triggers will have to be carefully managed if giving up is to be successful.

TREATING NICOTINE ADDICTION

Complementary approaches such as acupuncture and hypnosis may help, though reputable acupuncturists will only claim to help support you as you withdraw from the nicotine, rather than claiming that they can provide an instant cure.

Self-help remedies available over-the-counter are nicotine replacement patches, inhalers and chewing gum. These deliver a measured dose of nicotine and there are various strengths available. Usually, you start with a high strength, gradually progressing to a lower strength before tailing off the treatment. It is essential to stop smoking cigarettes while taking the replacement therapy. The therapy can be supported by going to regular Stop Smoking sessions, run by many GPs at their surgeries and by some pharmacies. You can also phone Quitline (Tel: 0800 002200) for support.

✚ **REMEDIES** see page 117

OSTEOARTHRITIS

See Arthritis, page 30.

PILES

Also known as haemorrhoids, piles are swellings in the varicose veins in and around the anus. Sometimes an 'attack of piles' occurs and they swell and become hard and tender, causing much pain, especially when going to the toilet.

The veins are just under the mucus membrane lining of the lower rectum and anus. Sometimes, during defecation, the thin-walled veins bulge outside the anal canal. The veins are easily ruptured and this causes the mild bleeding usually associated with piles. Usually, the bulging veins will spring back into place but, if they don't, they have to be replaced manually.

Piles often develops during pregnancy or after childbirth because of the pressure on the veins. Constipation and straining to go to the toilet can also cause piles.

TREATING PILES

Avoid episodes of piles by ensuring you have enough fibre-containing foods in your diet such as fruit, vegetables and whole grain cereals and bread. Also make sure you drink enough liquid as this will help soften the stools. This should help overcome any problems you have with constipation. You can relieve any irritation by taking a warm salt bath or applying an icepack to the sore area.

Over-the-counter remedies include suppositories which help soften the stools during defecation and rectal ointments which ease the symptoms of inflammation and itching.

See your GP if piles are a significant problem. You may be referred for a surgical operation to remove the piles, either by tying off the affected veins to 'strangle' them, cutting of their blood supply and causing them to wither away or by injecting them to shrink the piles.

✚ **REMEDIES** see page 258

PREMENSTRUAL SYNDROME

The term premenstrual syndrome (PMS) – sometimes known as premenstrual tension (PMT) – covers a wide range of symptoms experienced by women a week or so before their monthly period begins. The symptoms are both physical and emotional. Emotionally, there may be severe mood swings, irritability, depression and tearfulness. Physically, there may be water retention, causing bloating of the body, swelling and soreness in the breasts, headaches and migraines, backache and extreme tiredness. Many women also experience clumsiness and lack of co-ordination.

All these symptoms are due to the female hormones, oestrogen and progesterone, which fluctuate in production throughout each month. The female cycle, dictated to by the pituitary gland, undergoes a delicate balancing act through the month, sending out messages to mature an egg for possible fertilisation and telling the uterus to make itself ready for receiving that fertilised egg. If the egg is not fertilised after being released, hormone production goes into decline, telling the uterus that it is not required to host the fertilised egg. This causes menstrual bleeding and it is at this point that many women cease to experience PMT – until the next cycle.

TREATING PMS

Understanding why you are behaving oddly and why you feel emotionally vulnerable plays a significant part in handling PMS. Chart your expected monthly period so that you can anticipate – and manage – these symptoms. Deferring important decisions and easing up on work and social commitments will enable you to rest and avoid becoming excited or emotional.

Exercise helps relaxation and boosts the 'happy hormones' (serotonin and endorphin), which will help counteract your emotional symptoms.

These measures, combined with taking over-the-counter herbal remedies and other preparations, work effectively for mild PMS. Severe PMS that does not respond to these measures requires advice and treatment from your GP.

✚ **REMEDIES** see page 181

RHEUMATOID ARTHRITIS

See Arthritis, page 30.

ROUNDWORMS

Roundworms live off the food that is being digested in the bowel. They lay eggs within the bowel, which are then passed out of the body during defecation.

An infestation occurs as a result of swallowing anything that has become contaminated with the roundworm's eggs. As they are usually found in soil, unwashed vegetables or not washing your hands after gardening can spread the worms. Inadequate hand-washing after using the toilet, or when changing nappies, can also spread the infection.

Often there are no symptoms, but there may be nausea, constipation, abdominal pain, coughing, coughing up blood, breathlessness and fever. Very occasionally, a large mass of worms in the intestine can block the gut, causing intestinal obstruction.

TREATING ROUNDWORMS

Anti-worm preparations can be used but the whole family has to be treated to avoid reinfection. This consists of a single dose of an anti-worm preparation, usually containing the drug piperazine, or your doctor may prescribe a three-day course of mebendazole. This dose is usually effective. However, if symptoms persist you should see your GP as there may be other bowel problems.

✚ **REMEDIES** see page 175

SCARS

After skin tissue has been damaged it heals and repairs itself. It does this very efficiently, forming scar tissue over the site of the wound. Minor, superficial wounds can heal without leaving a permanent scar, but deeper damage will leave a more noticeable scar.

Sometimes it is necessary to graft skin from one part of the body to another to cover up a serious and large wound, as the skin cannot stretch far enough over the wound for the edges to knit themselves together. This will seal the skin but leave a noticeable patch. This is often the case with serious wounds such as those caused by burn damage.

TREATING SCARS

Allow the wound to settle down. The redness will eventually fade, leaving a pale, silvery trace. If left long enough, and if only a minor scar, it will probably fade completely. After the initial healing, keep the damaged site well lubricated by moisturising regularly. For larger wounds, you should seek medical attention to minimise any subsequent scarring.

Scars caused by acne pitting or childhood chickenpox, for example, can be filled by having collagen injections into the site. This plumps up the surface of the skin, making the scars less noticeable. However, collagen is reabsorbed by the body, so the effect will only be temporary, lasting from three to six months.

Chemical peels and dermabrasion and laser techniques can be used to remove the surface of the skin, allowing new skin to form over the scar area to minimise the appearance of the scar. These remedies have to be carried out by a cosmetic surgeon or a specialist clinic.

For minor scars and blemishes, creams containing retinol can be applied to the skin. These work by removing the existing tissue and encouraging new skin growth. Mild versions of these preparations are available from a wide range of cosmetic companies. Stronger versions must be prescribed by your GP or a consultant at a clinic.

✚ **REMEDIES** see page 220

SCIATICA *(See also Back Pain, page 32)*

The sciatic nerve is the major nerve of the leg, passing down the back of the thigh from the base of the spine. Just above the knee it splits into two branches, which travel down to the foot. The commonest cause of sciatica is conditions of the spine, such as a prolapsed disc or displacement of the facet joints between the vertebrae, which can press on the nerve and cause pain, which usually spreads below the knee to the ankle.

Symptoms of damage to the sciatic nerve are wide but include muscle weakness or spasms, numbness or tingling in the legs, feet or toes, loss of adequate reflex action in the knees. Urinary incontinence in both sexes and sexual dysfunction in men is not a feature, neither is weakness of both legs. If this happens you should contact your doctor immediately.

TREATING SCIATICA

Rest helps in the acute phase when the pain is at its worst, but is not recommended for longer than is absolutely necessary. Avoid heavy lifting, and sleep on a firm mattress or put a board under the mattress.

Heat pads can help ease the pain in the muscles and anti-inflammatory drugs can help with inflammation.

Bouts of sciatic pain vary, depending on the cause of the injury. Repeated or severe bouts require stronger anti-inflammatories from your GP, who may also recommend a course of physiotherapy. If the pain does not ease, further investigations may be carried out. In extreme cases surgery may be required to remove any obstruction in the spine.

✚ **REMEDIES** see page 228

SINUSITIS

When the mucus membranes lining the air-filled spaces in the bones on each side of the nose become inflamed this is known as sinusitis. The usual cause of the inflammation is an infection. If the sinuses become blocked the mucus does not drain properly and begins to build up. Fluid replaces the air in the spaces and predisposes to infection.

Sinusitis is a common complication or consequence of upper respiratory tract infections such as colds (see page 39) and flu (see page 52). As well as infection, allergies can inflame the linings, causing mucus secretions to increase.

Symptoms include a blocked nose and sometimes pain in the sinus passages. As drainage of the sinuses is made difficult, there may be a dripping of mucus fluid into the throat from the back of the nose, or a green nasal discharge.

TREATING SINUSITIS

Nasal sprays and drops can be used to treat sinusitis. Decongestants, especially nasal decongestants, should not be used for more than five days as they can cause swelling of the lining of the nose. If the sinusitis is a symptom of a cold or flu it should be treated accordingly (see pages 39 and 52). Pain in the sinus cavities can be treated with painkillers such as aspirin, paracetamol or ibuprofen. Steam inhalation can help relieve blocked sinuses.

If sinusitis is caused by allergies these should be avoided, if at all possible. If it is caused by a bacterial infection, your GP may prescribe antibiotics. If attacks are frequent, investigations for an underlying cause are worthwhile.

✚ **REMEDIES** see page 141

SORE THROAT *(See also Tonsillitis, page 72)*

A sore throat is a very common symptom of many illnesses and conditions. It often accompanies colds (see page 39) and flu (see page 52) and is a key feature of laryngitis (see page 55).

Sore throats can also be caused by pharyngitis, an inflammation of the pharynx, which is located between the tonsils and the voice box (larynx). If there is swelling around the glands of the neck, it could be glandular fever, which usually affects teenagers and young adults. If the swelling is around the jawbone and spreads up towards the ears, it could indicate mumps (see page 59).

TREATING A SORE THROAT

If the sore throat is caused by any of the above illnesses, treat as indicated in each relevant entry. Avoid speaking if it makes the sore throat worse and avoid smoky and polluted atmospheres as this will irritate the throat further. Drink plenty of fluids to lubricate the throat. If swallowing is difficult, sip the liquids. Try sipping a hot honey and lemon drink to ease the pain. Do not smoke.

Painkillers such as aspirin and paracetamol can help ease the pain and bring down a temperature, if this is also a symptom. Gargling may also help ease the symptoms.

Usually the symptoms of sore throat pass after a day or two. Children and the elderly may need medical attention if there is an associated temperature.

A sore throat with a high fever, red and swollen tonsils with pus on them and enlarged glands in the neck is more likely to be due to a bacterial infection from the streptoccal group. This requires antibiotic treatment from your GP.

✪ **REMEDIES** see page 144

SPLINTERS

Small, sharp slivers of material such as wood, thorns and glass can lodge into the skin, usually on the hands. These splinters are painful and, unless removed and the affected area cleaned, they could cause an infection.

TREATING SPLINTERS

Douse a pair of tweezers with antiseptic and then carefully remove the splinter. Wipe the wound clean and cover with a plaster. The area should heal within a few days. If a little bit of the splinter remains and you cannot get it out with the tweezers, it usually works its own way out of the skin in a few days. However, if the area becomes swollen and painful, you should see your GP.

If the splinter occurred while gardening, check that your tetanus jabs are up to date – after the first injection you should have a booster injection every 10 years. If you have not had an injection or a booster, see your GP for an injection and, if necessary, treatment.

If the splinter lodges in the eye, you should loosely cover with a clean pad and go to the nearest Accident and Emergency Department of your local hospital for treatment.

✪ **REMEDIES** see page 217

SPRAINS and STRAINS

When a joint is stretched beyond its normal range of movement, tear damage can occur to the ligaments that stabilise the joints and the tendons which help move the joint. This is known as a sprain. Strains result from tearing or stretching of the muscle fibres when they are pulled too far beyond their normal range. Both sprains and strains cause redness and swelling in the area, sometimes accompanied by bruising.

Strains and sprains are very similar and their treatment is the same. They often occur during exercise, when the affected joint is pushed beyond its capabilities. It can also happen when falling, as the suddenness of the fall stops you from protecting yourself, thereby spraining an arm or leg. In severe cases the ligament or muscle can rip completely.

TREATING SPRAINS AND STRAINS

Treatment for sprains and strains is by RICE – Rest, Immobilise, Cool and Elevate. Avoid moving the joint as this may cause further pain. Apply a cold compress such as a bag of frozen peas to reduce the swelling and raise the limb to help ease inflammation. You can then bind the area with an elastic or crepe bandage.

While the area is healing, take care that you do not further damage the area by continuing to exercise or by lifting heavy loads. Gently begin to move the limb as soon as is possible. If there is severe pain and extensive bruising, an X-ray may be required to exclude a fracture of the joint. Severe sprains and strains require medical treatment and possibly physiotherapy.

⚕ **REMEDIES** see page 228

STIFFNESS

Stiffness in the joints and muscles is a common symptom of overuse or underuse. If the joint has been overused, you may have caused a strain (see above). If the joints have been underused the effects are not usually noticed until the following day. For example, if you are unused to exercise, you may feel stiff the next morning when you try to get out of bed.

TREATING STIFFNESS

Rest the affected part and do not repeat the activity that brought on the stiffness until the pain has gone. When you do resume the activity, do it gently and do some warm-up exercises first to loosen the muscles.

Painkillers may help ease the pain. Ibuprofen will help, particularly if it is muscular stiffness. Chronic stiffness may require stronger painkillers.

Stiffness and weakness that is worse in the mornings and is accompanied by joint pains or a feeling of being unwell – especially if it affects movements such as getting up from a chair or causes difficulty raising the arms – should be reported to your doctor so that further tests can be carried out.

⚕ **REMEDIES** see page 228

STRESS *(See also Anxiety, page 30, and Depression, page 44)*

Stress affects every aspect of our life – our behaviour, our emotional wellbeing and our physical health. Many different factors can cause it. Difficulties with personal relationships involving family, friends and work colleagues are common sources. Intimate personal relationships can give rise to marital problems that may lead to separation and divorce, which is an extremely stressful experience. Practical matters can also cause stress. These include financial problems, work pressures and redundancy. Environmental factors such as poor housing conditions and living in a location that makes you isolated from your emotional support network of friends and family can also cause you stress.

Unwanted but common life events – either happening to yourself or to someone close to you – can also cause stress. These include events such as an unwanted pregnancy, abortion, bereavement, injury, illness and disability. Stress can also occur when we are stretched beyond our ability to cope or because of deep-rooted feelings of inadequacy.

When under stress you may smoke or drink more, seek or avoid human contact, become more short-tempered, become more tearful or cry without apparent cause, or carry around with you an unidentifiable but worrying sense of doom about life.

Physical symptoms of stress are manifold – for example, anxiety, insomnia, palpitations, breathlessness, headaches, joint and muscle aches and pains, skin rashes, changes in menstrual regularity and bowel habits, and a tendency to pick up more infections than others.

TREATING STRESS

Short-term stress can be managed by taking better care of yourself. Eat well, take more exercise, try using relaxation techniques and allow yourself time to deal with the underlying causes of the stress. Talk to your partner and friends about how you feel – they may be able to take some of the burden off your shoulders for a while to give you time to recover. Physical symptoms can be eased with herbal remedies that will help calm you down and promote sleep.

Long-term or severe stress can be very damaging. You should see your GP to discuss possible drug treatment, practical help and counselling.

✿ **REMEDIES** see page 270

STYES

An infection of the outside of the eyelid is known as a stye – although it may sometimes form on the inner edge of the lid. The stye is caused by an infection from the staphyloccal bacteria that invade the sebaceous gland around the follicle of an eyelash. The infection causes a pocket of pus to form at the base of the follicle, causing the redness and swelling, but eventually it discharges and the swelling settles down.

TREATING STYES

Styes usually clear up without treatment. To ease the pain apply a compress that has been soaked in comfortably hot water and then wrung out. To stop the infection from spreading to other lashes apply an antibacterial over-the-counter ointment.

When you have a stye you should avoid rubbing or touching it, as you may spread the bacterial infection to the other lashes or the other eye.

If self-treatment does not help and the stye persists after a week, you should see your doctor.

✚ **REMEDIES** see page 247

SUNBURN

Over-exposure to the sun causes sunburn. The skin becomes red and inflamed and then peels off. Excessive exposure may also cause liquid-filled blisters to form. Sunburn can have long-term consequences as excessive exposure to the sun can cause skin cancer.

TREATING SUNBURN

Mild sunburn can be treated by applying a calamine-based lotion to the area to cool the sunburn down. If the sunburn is painful, take painkillers such as paracetamol or aspirin. If any blisters become infected, you should see your doctor for antibiotic treatment.

Once the skin flaking has gone, apply emollient moisturisers or creams to soften and moisturise the dry skin.

If sunburn is accompanied by a temperature over 104°F (40°C) and excessive thirst, nausea, drowsiness or dizziness, there may also be heatstroke or sunstroke. Call a doctor for treatment and try to keep your body temperature cool by removing clothing and applying cold compresses or sponging with tepid water.

▶ **Caution** Stay out of the sun or cover up from 11am to 3pm, the hottest part of the day. **Always** take care to protect babies and children from the sun. Apply strong sunscreens and make sure they wear T-shirts and hats to protect their delicate skin from the damaging rays of the sun. **Always** call a doctor if a child has bad sunburn or symptoms of heatstroke.

✚ **REMEDIES** see page 221

TEETHING PROBLEMS

As the first teeth push their way through the surface of the gums, the baby can experience a range of upsetting and sometimes painful symptoms, although many babies seem to have few if any problems.

Teething usually occurs around six months of age and causes the baby's gums to become swollen and red in colour. The baby's cheeks may have red patches on them and there may be dribbling and fist chewing, as the baby tries to gnaw the teeth through. Some babies become cranky and irritable and may develop diarrhoea or a slight temperature.

TREATING TEETHING PROBLEMS

Rub soothing gels or creams onto the gums. If necessary, give baby paracetamol to soothe the pain and reduce a temperature. Giving the baby something to chew on, such as a sterilised teething ring, will help calm the baby down and help the teeth come through.

▶ **Caution** If your child has a high fever, vomiting or is poorly, always call a doctor.

✚ **REMEDIES** see page 280

TENDINITIS

Tendinitis causes thickening and inflammation of the tendons. It is usually caused by overusing a limb or from injury. Commonly affected areas are the shoulder, elbow, wrist, fingers and ankle. The affected area becomes tender and sore and there may be a restricted movement of the muscle attached to the affected tendon.

TREATING TENDINITIS

Immediately after the injury, apply an icepack to the area to reduce swelling. Later on, a hot-water bottle held on the area may make the affected part more comfortable. Take anti-inflammatory painkillers.

Rest the affected part while it is too painful to move or recovery of movement will take longer, although gentle movement may be advised to prevent stiffness.

Usually tendinitis will last about two weeks. If the tendon is torn, surgery to repair the site may be required. If pain is extreme corticosteroid injections may be given. If the tendon sheath is red, swollen and painful, then antibiotics may be required.

✚ **REMEDIES** see **General Pain Relief**, page 78

TENNIS ELBOW

Tennis elbow is inflammation around the outer side of the elbow, an area in which several muscle tendons are situated. These muscles extend to the wrist and any excessive use of the muscles in this area – playing tennis is an obvious example – can cause tennis elbow. Symptoms include pain and tenderness in the area and also on the back of the forearm. The symptoms are made worse by movement.

TREATING TENNIS ELBOW

Rest the arm and avoid the activity that caused the injury until the muscles have healed. Painkillers and anti-inflammatory drugs will help ease the pain and soreness. For persistent pain, a corticosteroid injection into the site of the pain often helps.

If the injury was obtained from playing a particular sport, coaching will help improve your style.

✚ **REMEDIES** see **General Pain Relief**, page 78, and Joints and Muscles, page 226

THREADWORMS

Threadworms are tiny parasitic worms that live in the large intestine. The females lay their eggs at night in the anal area and this causes itching. If the sufferer scratches and transfers the eggs to the mouth, the cycle begins again.

The worms may be seen as short wriggling white threads in the stool, and the eggs can be detected in the stool by the lab to confirm the diagnosis.

Threadworms can be found in dust, on the fur of household pets, furniture, toys, bedding and contaminated food.

TREATING THREADWORMS

Medication can be taken in stages. Two or three doses are usually required and the whole family should be treated. If the hands are not washed, the threadworms can be ingested and the cycle can begin again. Instilling good hygiene and toilet habits in children will help prevent reinfestation.

✚ **REMEDIES** see page 175

THRUSH (ORAL)

Oral thrush is caused by the same fungal organism that causes vaginal thrush (see below). When the organism gets out of control, sore, creamy-yellow and raised patches appear in the mouth. Oral thrush is a common condition in the elderly, babies and those with a weakened immune system. Denture wearers or asthma sufferers who use steroidal puffers may also get oral thrush.

TREATING ORAL THRUSH

Over-the-counter gels, sprays and mouthwashes will help treat minor outbreaks of oral thrush in normally healthy people. If you do not respond to treatment, stronger antifungal drugs may be required from your GP.

✚ **REMEDIES** see page 255

THRUSH (VAGINAL)

Thrush is caused by a fungal organism, Candida albicans, which is always present in the body but kept under control by 'friendly' bacteria. However, when the fungus gets out of control, it produces an intense itching in the vaginal area, often accompanied by a creamy-coloured, curd-textured discharge. (The discharge should not smell. If it does, you should see your GP who may take swabs for analysis or refer you to a Genito-Urinary clinic for further investigation. You may have a sexually transmitted disease that requires treatment.)

An imbalance can be caused by taking a course of antibiotics or other drugs or by having periods of hormonal change such as during menstruation and during pregnancy. It can also develop if you have experienced severe stress or illness. Diabetes can be a cause of recurrent thrush, especially after the menopause.

Vaginal thrush can also be passed on during sexual intercourse. In men, thrush often has no symptoms, but otherwise they may have redness and soreness of the penis.

TREATING VAGINAL THRUSH

Vaginal thrush is easily treated with medication once available only on prescription but now available over-the-counter. Your partner should see his GP for a tablet treatment. Unless both partners are treated, cross-infection will keep occurring.

✚ REMEDIES see page 183

TONSILLITIS (See also Sore throat, page 65)

The tonsils lie in the folds of the throat between the tongue and the palate. Their role is to prevent infection in the body but, when they become overwhelmed by the disease organisms they are trying to fight, they become infected and tonsillitis develops. Both bacteria and viruses can cause tonsillitis, but acute tonsillitis is usually caused by streptococcal bacteria.

Symptoms include sore throat and pain when swallowing, fever, headache, vomiting and a dry cough. There will usually be pus that looks like white or yellow spots on the tonsils, and the lymph nodes in the neck may become swollen.

TREATING TONSILLITIS

Paracetamol will help relieve a fever and any discomfort. Your doctor will prescribe an antibiotic to fight the bacterial infection. Cold compresses on the neck may help ease the throat. Eating soft, easy-to-swallow foods such as yoghurt, ice cream, soup and milk puddings will help.

Those who suffer from repeated bouts of tonsillitis may have their tonsils removed. Once a popular and common procedure, it is now more rarely done.

Most cases of tonsillitis are uncomplicated, but if you are very ill or having severe difficulty swallowing you may need to have an antibiotic.

✚ REMEDIES see page 144

TOOTHACHE

Toothache is usually caused by tooth decay but it can also be caused by infection, food packing within the spaces between the teeth, sinusitis (this may mimic the pain of toothache), an abscess in the tooth (see page 28) and jaw problems.

TREATING TOOTHACHE

Clean and floss your teeth to remove any food that may have impacted between the teeth. To relieve immediate pain take painkillers. If the gums are sore, you can apply soothing gels.

Do not avoid or put off making an appointment with your dentist as the pain will usually persist until the cause has been identified and treated.

✚ REMEDIES see page 254

TRAVEL SICKNESS

Nausea, and sometimes actual vomiting, often occurs when travelling. After experiencing unaccustomed motion, the sufferer begins to have a feeling of uneasiness, sometimes escalating to distress. While the sufferer may be sick, often it is just a sensation of nausea that is experienced.

TREATING TRAVEL SICKNESS

Avoid eating before your journey and avoid alcohol, as this may enhance the effect of the sickness. There are various over-the-counter remedies that help prevent travel sickness and these should be taken before the trip begins. Some remedies may cause drowsiness and blurred vision, so avoid driving after taking them, or ask your pharmacist for advice.

✚ **REMEDIES** see page 172

ULCERS (MOUTH)

Mouth ulcers are irritating sores on the inside of the cheeks or around the inner lips. They are painful and may feel itchy.

Mouth ulcers can appear for no particular reason, although they are more likely to occur if you are run-down or feeling stressed. They can also be caused by irritation from ill-fitting dentures or bad toothbrushing techniques.

There are also more serious causes of mouth ulcers, including skin and gut disorders, viral infections and allergic reactions. Rarely they can indicate the presence of cancer.

TREATING MOUTH ULCERS

Sucking an ice cube or rinsing the mouth out with a salt-water solution can help ease the pain of a mouth ulcer. Gargling with soluble aspirin or an antiseptic mouthwash may help. Over-the-counter sprays or lozenges containing a local anaesthetic or a gel to cover and protect the area can be used.

If the ulcer becomes very itchy, painful, bleeds or causes an unpleasant taste in the mouth, see your GP so that other causes can be eliminated or treated appropriately. You may be prescribed stronger anaesthetic preparations or corticosteroid pills to relieve the pain.

✚ **REMEDIES** see page 252

VARICOSE VEINS

Varicose veins appear as twisted swollen veins just under the surface of the skin. The veins appear when weakness of the walls or defective valves within the vein allow blood to flow backwards and stagnate within the vein.

Varicose veins are quite common and usually appear on the legs. Symptoms include swollen and 'knotted' bumps along prominent purple-coloured veins, swelling in the legs, eczema, ulceration, aching legs and itchy skin around the area.

TREATING VARICOSE VEINS

Avoid becoming overweight, as this places more strain on the veins. Also, avoid long periods of standing or sitting. Lie on the floor and raise the legs up, above hip level and resting comfortably against a wall to ease the pain. Avoid crossing the legs. Taking regular exercise will help blood flow.

Support tights and stockings can be worn to prevent the blood from collecting in the veins. Over-the-counter creams and sprays can be used to relieve itching and cool the area.

Minor veins can be treated with sclerotherapy, which involves injecting the vein with substances that harden and then shrink the vein. This is suitable when the veins are disturbing for cosmetic reasons. More problematic varicose veins can be treated by tying off affected veins and allowing other healthy veins to compensate.

Sometimes a vein ruptures and bleeds heavily. Stay calm and sit on the floor with your leg up on a chair. Apply firm continuous pressure with a clean tea towel or handkerchief for a minimum of 15 to 20 minutes.

✚ REMEDIES see page 262

VERRUCA

A wart on the foot is known as a verruca, or plantar wart. Verrucae are contagious and are a result of a viral infection of the outer layer of the skin. Walking on the hard, horny skin can be very painful. Although they do not protrude very much, verrucae have a central core that penetrates into the skin, causing discomfort if pressure is placed on the area.

Verrucae are commonly acquired at swimming pools, where the infection spreads happily because of the warm, wet environment. They can also be contracted from sharing towels or bathmats – or shoes – with someone who has them.

Verrucae tend to go without treatment but this can range from a few months to several years. Often after the first verrucae infection there is an immunity to further infection.

TREATING VERRUCAE

There are various over-the-counter preparations for treating verrucae. If they do not respond, your GP may prescribe a gel and abrader kit for you to use. If this does not work, freezing with liquid nitrogen or burning them off with electrocautery under local anaesthetic may be suggested.

✚ REMEDIES see page 222

WARTS (SKIN)

Warts are raised, horny areas on the top layer of the skin. They are caused by a wide range of variations of the human papilloma virus and are spread by direct contact. You can also spread the virus to other sites of your body by touching the wart and then touching another skin area.

Warts can disappear of their own accord, but may take a couple of years to do so. Some are more persistent and, whilst not harmful, they look unpleasant.

TREATING WARTS

You can self-treat warts by using over-the-counter wart plasters or liquid preparations. Ask your pharmacist for advice about which preparation is best for the site of your wart. If these remedies do not work, your doctor may recommend freezing the warts with liquid nitrogen. This freezes the wart solid and as it thaws a blister forms and lifts the wart up off the skin. Several treatments may be required to remove the wart.

The same virus causes genital warts. These **must** be treated by a doctor. They are highly contagious and are spread through sexual contact. The patient should also be screened for other sexually transmitted diseases. Women who have had genital warts should have an annual cervical smear test as genital warts have been implicated in cervical cancer.

✚ **REMEDIES** see page 222

WOUNDS

There are many different types of wound but what they all have in common is piercing or grazing of the skin and subsequent bleeding. In all cases, check that tetanus jabs are up to date.

TREATING WOUNDS

Minor wounds can be treated by carefully removing any grit or glass, metal or gravel from the wound. Hold the affected area under running water to rinse out any contamination, then wrap the area with a clean cloth and hold upright, applying firm continuous pressure for 15 to 20 minutes until the bleeding has stopped. Dry the area with a clean cloth, apply an antiseptic cream and then cover to protect the area from damage and bacterial infection.

If there is any chance that a sliver of glass or other material is still in the wound, clean the area under running water, cover with a loose soft bandage and go to the Accident and Emergency Department to have it removed.

Severe wounds, especially those bleeding profusely, require emergency treatment from ambulance personnel or your nearest hospital's Accident and Emergency Department.

✚ **REMEDIES** see page 205

CHAPTER 3

Over-the-Counter Medicines Directory

This chapter contains a comprehensive list of widely available over-the-counter products, separated into various categories of ailments. For each of the ailments it gives an alphabetical list of the main over-the-counter medicines, along with complementary herbal and homoeopathic remedies that are available. Many of the ailments are multi-use and so you will find some of the ailments cross-referenced within each section. At the beginning of each section, you will find information on the ingredients found in the products and how they work.

Most importantly, you will also find a **warning note**. Read this very carefully. Over-the-counter medicines are safe if you use them properly, but some of them should not be used by certain groups of people, for example children under a certain age, asthmatics or diabetics or those taking certain drugs and medicines.

The alphabetical list of products contains information on what they contain and how to use them. However, for more specific information about a product, including uses, cautions and warnings, always read the product label and information leaflet inside the package. Always follow the instructions carefully. This applies to all remedies, whether orthodox or complementary. Using an over-the-counter product safely and properly, or administering it to a child, is your responsibility.

If you are receiving any medical treatment or have any medical condition (e.g. asthma, a heart condition, high blood pressure, anxiety or depression, an infection, a thyroid problem, diabetes or kidney or liver problems) **always check with a pharmacist or your GP** before taking any over-the-counter medicine. Remember – you cannot be too careful. You should also be particularly careful about taking remedies if you are pregnant or breast-feeding.

Always check with a pharmacist whether a product is suitable for you or your child's individual symptoms. Many may not be.

In addition, do not take any over-the-counter remedy if you are already taking prescription medication or another over-the-counter remedy. This is because many medicines interact and can cause harmful effects. This is equally important if you are taking complementary remedies.

Entries with a ⛺ symbol denote remedies specifically designed for children. Complementary products are also clearly identified with a ❀.

GENERAL PAIN RELIEF

This section contains a list of over-the-counter products for general pain relief. It includes information on the main ingredients in each product, as well as how to take them. Unless otherwise stated, the doses given are suitable only for adults and children over 12 years. If the product is suitable for a child under 12, this will be identified.

There are three main ingredients in over-the-counter painkillers. These are aspirin, ibuprofen and paracetamol, either on their own, or in combination with other painkillers, such as aloxiprin, codeine and dihydrocodeine. Some products also contain an antihistamine, such as diphenhydramine or doxylamine, which may help you to sleep, particularly if you experience pain at night. Some products also contain caffeine, which may help to promote a general feeling of wellbeing. Information is also provided on whether the product is available in tablet, capsule or powder form. There are also soluble versions that can be dissolved in water or other fluid to make a drink.

All painkillers are effective for a wide variety of painful conditions, including headache, migraine, backache, lumbago, sciatica, period pain, muscular aches, pains and swelling, arthritic and rheumatic pain and swelling, joint swelling and stiffness, fibrositis, toothache, neuralgia, sore throat, fever and symptoms of colds and flu. The main difference between them is that products containing aspirin and ibuprofen help to relieve pain, reduce fever and reduce inflammation. Paracetamol helps to relieve pain and reduce fever, but has little effect on inflammation, so is sometimes less useful for muscular problems. Both aspirin and ibuprofen can cause irritation of the stomach, so products containing them are best taken with or after food or milk.

WARNING NOTE

Aspirin

The following precautions apply to all aspirin and remedies containing aspirin listed in this book:

- If you are asthmatic or allergic to aspirin or other anti-inflammatories, e.g. ibuprofen, check that the product you select does not contain aspirin. For a list of all aspirin ingredients, check the ingredients box on the packet. When you buy a remedy, always read the labels to ensure that the product you select does not contain aspirin.

- **Aspirin is not suitable for children under 12 years.**

- Pregnant and breast-feeding women should not take aspirin or products containing aspirin without first checking with their GP or pharmacist.

- Those with stomach ulcers and stomach problems should not take products containing aspirin unless advised by their GP.

- Those with blood coagulation problems, including those taking medicines to reduce clotting of the blood, kidney problems and liver problems should not take products containing aspirin, unless advised by their GP.

- Do not combine aspirin with other over-the-counter or prescription medications containing aspirin or you risk overdosing. Always check the labels and if you have any doubts, check with your pharmacist or GP.

Paracetamol

The following precautions apply to all paracetamol and remedies containing paracetamol listed in this book:

- Those with liver and kidney problems should not take paracetamol, unless advised by their GP.

- Do not combine paracetamol with other over-the-counter or prescription medications containing paracetamol or you risk overdosing. Always check the labels and if you have any doubts, check with your pharmacist or GP.

- Some paracetamol products listed here are suitable for children under 12 years. These are indicated. Do not give products containing paracetamol to children under 12 years unless a dosage is specifically listed.

Ibuprofen

The following cautions apply to all ibuprofen and remedies containing ibuprofen listed in this book:

- If you are asthmatic or allergic to aspirin, do not use ibuprofen products. For a list of all ibuprofen ingredients, check the ingredients box. When you buy a remedy, always read the labels to ensure that the product you select does not contain ibuprofen.

- Pregnant and breast-feeding women should not take ibuprofen or products containing ibuprofen without first checking with their GP.

- Those with stomach ulcers and stomach problems should not take ibuprofen-containing products unless advised by their GP.

- Those with blood coagulation problems, including those taking medicines to reduce clotting of the blood, kidney problems and liver problems should not take products containing ibuprofen, unless advised by their GP.

- Do not combine ibuprofen with other over-the-counter or prescription medications containing ibuprofen or you risk overdosing. Always check the labels and if you have any doubts, check with your pharmacist or GP.

- Some soluble tablets and powders contain sodium. If you are on a sodium-restricted diet for any reason, if you have liver or kidney problems, if you are pregnant or have heart disease, ask your GP or pharmacist before taking a soluble product.

For specific uses, cautions and warnings for each individual product, read the product label and the information leaflet.

Advil Ibuprofen

Description: An analgesic tablet. Contains ibuprofen 200mg.
Dose: 1–2 tablets, with or just after food, every 4–6 hours. Maximum 6 tablets in 24 hours. Not suitable for children under 12 years.

Advil Extra Strength Ibuprofen

Description: An analgesic tablet Contains ibuprofen 400mg.
Dose: 1 tablet to be taken up to 3 times a day. Maximum 3 tablets in 24 hours. Not suitable for children under 12 years.

Alka-Seltzer

Description: An analgesic and antacid effervescent tablet for headache and upset stomach caused by overeating and excess alcohol consumption. Contains aspirin 324mg, sodium bicarbonate and citric acid.
Dose: 2 tablets dissolved in water every 4 hours. Maximum 8 tablets in 24 hours. Not suitable for children under 12 years.

Alka-Seltzer XS

Description: An analgesic and antacid effervescent tablet to relieve general pain, especially after over-indulgence of food and alcohol. Contains aspirin 267mg, paracetamol 133mg, caffeine, sodium bicarbonate and citric acid.
Dose: 1–2 tablets dissolved in water. Maximum 8 tablets in 24 hours. Not suitable for children under 12 years.

Anadin

Description: An analgesic tablet. Contains aspirin 325mg and caffeine.
Dose: 1–2 tablets every 4 hours. Maximum 12 tablets in 24 hours. Not suitable for children under 12 years.

Anadin Maximum Strength

Description: An analgesic capsule. Contains aspirin 500mg and caffeine.
Dose: 1–2 capsules every 4 hours. Maximum 8 capsules in 24 hours. Not suitable for children under 12 years.

Anadin Extra*

Description: An analgesic tablet. Contains aspirin 300mg and paracetamol 200mg
Dose: 2 tablets every 4 hours. Maximum 8 tablets in 24 hours. Not suitable for children under 12 years.
* Also available as soluble tablets with the addition of caffeine.

Anadin Ibuprofen

Description: An analgesic tablet. Contains ibuprofen 200mg.
Dose: 1–2 tablets 2–3 times a day. Maximum 6 tablets in 24 hours. Not suitable for children under 12 years.

Anadin Paracetamol

Description: An analgesic tablet. Contains paracetamol 500mg.
Dose: Adults: 2 tablets every 4 hours. Maximum 8 tablets in 24 hours. Children 6–12 years: Half to 1 tablet every 4 hours. Not suitable for children under 6 years.

Askit Powders

Description: An analgesic dissolvable powder. Contains aspirin 530mg, caffeine and aloxiprin.
Dose: 1 powder mixed with water every 4 hours. Maximum 6 powders in 24 hours. Not suitable for children under 12 years.

Aspro Clear

Description: An analgesic effervescent tablet. Contains aspirin 300mg.
Dose: 2–3 tablets dissolved in water every 3 hours. Maximum 13 tablets in 24 hours. Not suitable for children under 12 years.

Bayer Aspirin

Description: An analgesic tablet. Contains aspirin 300mg.
Dose: 1–3 tablets every 4 hours. Maximum 12 tablets in 24 hours. Not suitable for children under 12 years.

Caprin

Description: An analgesic tablet. Contains aspirin 300mg.
Dose: 1–3 tablets 3–4 times a day. Maximum 12 tablets in 24 hours. Not suitable for children under 12 years.

Codis 500

Description: A soluble analgesic tablet. Contains aspirin 500mg and codeine phosphate 8mg.
Dose: 1–2 tablets dissolved in water every 4 hours, as required. Maximum 8 tablets in 24 hours. Not suitable for children under 12 years.

Cojene

Description: An analgesic tablet. Contains aspirin 300mg, codeine phosphate 8mg and caffeine.
Dose: 1–2 tablets every 4 hours. Maximum 6 tablets in 24 hours. Not suitable for children under 12 years.

Cuprofen

Description: An analgesic tablet. Contains ibuprofen 200mg.
Dose: 2 tablets after food and 1–2 tablets every 4 hours if required. Maximum 6 tablets in 24 hours. Not suitable for children under 12 years.

Cuprofen Maximum Strength

Description: An analgesic tablet. Contains ibuprofen 400mg.
Dose: 1 tablet every 8 hours with food. Maximum 3 tablets in 24 hours. Not suitable for children under 12 years.

Disprin

Description: A soluble analgesic tablet. Contains aspirin 300mg.
Dose: 2–3 tablets every 4 hours. Maximum 13 tablets in 24 hours. Not suitable for children under 12 years.

Disprin Direct

Description: An analgesic tablet which dissolves in the mouth without water. Contains aspirin 300mg.
Dose: 1–3 tablets (without water) every 4 hours, as required. Maximum 13 tablets in 24 hours. Not suitable for children under 12 years.

Disprin Extra

Description: A soluble analgesic tablet. Contains aspirin 300mg and paracetamol 200mg.
Dose: 1–2 tablets dissolved in water every 4 hours, as required. Maximum 6 tablets in 24 hours. Not suitable for children under 12 years.

Fynnon Calcium Aspirin

Description: A soluble analgesic tablet. Contains aspirin 500mg.
Dose: 1–2 tablets dissolved in water every 4 hours. Maximum 8 tablets in 24 hours. Not suitable for children under 12 years.

Hedex

Description: An analgesic tablet. Contains paracetamol 500mg.
Dose: Adults: 2 tablets up to 4 times a day. Maximum 8 tablets in 24 hours. Children aged 6–12 years: Half of 1 tablet every 4 hours. Maximum 4 tablets in 24 hours. Not suitable for children under 6 years.

Hedex Extra

Description: An analgesic tablet Contains paracetamol 500mg and caffeine.
Dose: 2 tablets up to 4 times a day. Maximum 8 tablets in 24 hours. Not suitable for children under 12 years.

Hedex Ibuprofen

Description: An analgesic tablet. Contains 200mg ibuprofen.
Dose: 1–2 tablets up to 3 times a day. Maximum of 6 tablets in 24 hours. Not suitable for children under 12 years.

Maximum Strength Aspro Clear

Description: An effervescent analgesic tablet. Contains aspirin 500mg.
Dose: 1–2 tablets dissolved in water every 4 hours. Maximum 8 tablets in 24 hours. Not suitable for children under 12 years.

Nurofen

Description: An analgesic tablet. Contains ibuprofen 200mg.
Dose: 2 tablets. If necessary, a further 1–2 tablets every 4 hours. Maximum 6 tablets in 24 hours. Not suitable for children under 12 years.

Nurofen Advance

Description: An analgesic tablet. Contains ibuprofen 200mg.
Dose: 2 tablets with water. If necessary, a further 1–2 tablets every 4–6 hours. Maximum 6 tablets in 24 hours. Not suitable for children under 12 years.

Nurofen 400

Description: An analgesic tablet. Contains ibuprofen 400mg.
Dose: 1 tablet. If necessary, 1 further tablet every 4 hours. Maximum 3 tablets in 24 hours. Not suitable for children under 12 years.

Nurofen Micro-Granules

Description: Effervescent analgesic granules in sachets. Each sachet contains ibuprofen 400mg.
Dose: 1 sachet dissolved in water. If necessary, 1 further sachet every 4 hours. Maximum 3 sachets in 24 hours. Not suitable for children under 12 years.

Nurofen Plus

Description: An analgesic tablet. Contains ibuprofen 200mg and codeine phosphate 12.5mg.
Dose: 2 tablets. If necessary, further 1–2 tablets every 4–6 hours. Maximum 6 tablets in 24 hours. Not suitable for children under 12 years.

Nurse Sykes Powders

Description: An analgesic powder. Contains aspirin 165.3mg, paracetamol 120mg and caffeine.
Dose: 1 powder dissolved in water every 4 hours. Maximum 6 powders in 24 hours. Not suitable for children under 12 years.

Pacifene

Description: An analgesic tablet. Contains ibuprofen 200mg.
Dose: 1–2 tablets 3 times a day as required. Maximum 6 tablets in 24 hours. Not suitable for children under 12 years.

Pacifene Maximum Strength

Description: An analgesic tablet. Contains ibuprofen 400mg.
Dose: 1 tablet every 4 hours. Maximum 3 tablets in 24 hours. Not suitable for children under 12 years.

Panadeine

Description: An analgesic tablet. Contains paracetamol 500mg and codeine phosphate 8mg.
Dose: Adults: 2 tablets up to 4 times a day. Maximum 8 tablets in 24 hours. Children aged 7–12 years: Half to 1 tablet every 4 hours. Maximum 4 tablets in 24 hours. Not suitable for children under 7 years.

Panadol

Description: An analgesic tablet. Contains paracetamol 500mg.
Dose: Adults: 2 tablets every 4 hours as required. Maximum 8 tablets in 24 hours. Children aged 6–12 years: Half to 1 tablet every 4 hours as required. Maximum 4 tablets in 24 hours. Not suitable for children under 6 years.

Panadol Capsules

Description: An analgesic capsule. Contains paracetamol 500mg.
Dose: 2 capsules every 4 hours as required. Maximum 8 capsules in 24 hours. Not suitable for children under 12 years.

Panadol Extra

Description: An analgesic tablet. Contains paracetamol 500mg and caffeine.
Dose: 2 tablets every 4 hours as required. Maximum 8 tablets in 24 hours. Not suitable for children under 12 years.

Panadol Extra Soluble

Description: An effervescent analgesic tablet. Contains paracetamol 500mg and caffeine.
Dose: 2 tablets dissolved in water every 4 hours as required. Maximum 8 tablets in 24 hours. Not suitable for children under 12 years.

Panadol Night

Description: An analgesic capsule. Contains paracetamol 500mg and diphendydramine (an antihistamine).
Dose: 2 tablets 20 minutes before bedtime. Not suitable for children under 12 years.

Panadol Soluble

Description: An effervescent tablet. Contains paracetamol 500mg.
Dose: Adults: 2 tablets dissolved in water every 4 hours as required. Maximum 8 tablets in 24 hours. Children aged 6–12 years: Half to 1 tablet dissolved in water every 4 hours as required. Maximum 4 tablets in 24 hours. Not suitable for children under 6 years.

Panadol Ultra

Description: An analgesic tablet. Contains paracetamol 500mg and codeine phosphate 12.8mg.
Dose: 2 tablets up to 4 times a day as required. Maximum 8 tablets in 24 hours. Not suitable for children under 12 years.

Paracets

Description: An analgesic tablet. Contains paracetamol 500mg.
Dose: Adults: 2 tablets up to 4 times a day as required. Maximum 8 tablets in 24 hours. Children aged 6–12 years: Half to 1 tablet up to 4 times a day as required. Maximum 4 tablets in 24 hours. Not suitable for children under 6 years.

Paracets Capsules

Description: An analgesic capsule. Contains paracetamol 500mg.
Dose: Adults: 1–2 capsules every 6 hours. Maximum 8 capsules in 24 hours. Children aged 6–12 years: 1 capsule every 6 hours. Maximum 4 capsules in 24 hours. Not suitable for children under 6 years.

Paraclear

Description: An effervescent analgesic tablet. Contains paracetamol 500mg.
Dose: Adults: 1–2 tablets dissolved in water every 4 hours. Maximum 8 tablets in 24 hours. Children aged 6–12 years: Half to 1 tablet every 4 hours. Maximum 4 tablets in 24 hours. Not suitable for children under 6 years.

Paraclear Extra Strength

Description: An analgesic tablet. Contains paracetamol 500mg and caffeine.
Dose: 1–2 tablets every 4–6 hours. Maximum 8 tablets in 24 hours. Not suitable for children under 12 years.

Paracodol*

Description: An analgesic capsule. Contains paracetamol 500mg and codeine phosphate 8mg.
Dose: 1–2 capsules every 4–6 hours. Maximum 8 capsules in 24 hours. Not suitable for children under 12 years.
* Also available as soluble tablets.

Paramol

Description: An analgesic tablet. Contains paracetamol 500mg and dihydrocodeine tartrate 7.46mg.
Dose: 1–2 tablets during or after meals, every 4–6 hours as required. Maximum 8 tablets in 24 hours. Not suitable for children under 12 years.

Phensic

Description: An analgesic tablet. Contains aspirin 325mg and caffeine 22mg.
Dose: 2 tablets every 3–4 hours as required. Maximum 12 tablets in 24 hours. Not suitable for children under 12 years.

Proflex

Description: An analgesic tablet. Contains ibuprofen 200mg.
Dose: 1–2 capsules 3 times a day. Maximum 6 capsules in 24 hours. Not suitable for children under 12 years.

Proflex Sustained Relief Capsules

Description: An analgesic capsule. Contains ibuprofen 300mg.
Dose: 2 capsules twice a day. Maximum 4 capsules in 24 hours. Not suitable for children under 12 years.

Propain

Description: An analgesic tablet. Contains paracetamol 400mg, codeine phosphate 10mg, diphenhydramine 5mg (an antihistamine) and caffeine.
Dose: 1–2 tablets every 4 hours. Maximum 10 tablets in 24 hours. Not suitable for children under 12 years.

Relcofen*

Description: An analgesic tablet. Contains ibuprofen 200mg.
Dose: 1–2 tablets 3 times a day. Maximum 6 tablets in 24 hours. Not suitable for children under 12 years.
* Also available containing ibuprofen 400mg.

Solpadeine*

Description: An analgesic tablet. Contains paracetamol 500mg, codeine phosphate 8mg and caffeine.
Dose: 2 tablets up to 4 times a day. Maximum 8 capsules in 24 hours. Not suitable for children under 12 years.
* Also available as soluble tablets.

Solpadeine Capsules

Description: An analgesic capsule. Contains paracetamol 500mg, codeine phosphate 8mg and caffeine 30mg.
Dose: 2 capsules up to 4 times a day. Maximum 8 capsules in 24 hours. Not suitable for children under 12 years.

Solpadeine Max

Description: An analgesic tablet. Contains paracetamol 500mg and codeine phosphate hemihydrate 12.8mg.
Dose: 2 tablets every 4 hours. Maximum 8 tablets in 24 hours. Not suitable for children under 12 years.

Solpaflex

Description: An analgesic tablet. Contains ibuprofen 200mg and codeine phosphate hemihydrate 12.8mg.
Dose: 1–2 tablets every 4–6 hours as required. Maximum 6 tablets in 24 hours. Not suitable for children under 12 years.

Syndol

Description: An analgesic tablet. Contains paracetamol 450mg, codeine phosphate 10mg and caffeine 30mg and doxylamine succinate (an antihistamine).
Dose: 1–2 tablets every 4–6 hours as required. Maximum 8 tablets in 24 hours. Not suitable for children under 12 years.

Tramil

Description: An analgesic capsule. Contains paracetamol 500mg.
Dose: 2 capsules every 4 hours as required. Maximum 8 capsules in 24 hours. Not suitable for children under 12 years.

Veganin

Description: An analgesic tablet. Contains paracetamol 250mg, aspirin 250mg and codeine phosphate 6.8mg.
Dose: 1–2 tablets every 3–4 hours as required. Maximum 8 tablets in 24 hours. Not suitable for children under 12 years.

COMPLEMENTARY PRODUCTS

There are no direct complementary equivalents of orthodox painkillers. However, there are numerous remedies that may help to alleviate specific symptoms, although if the pain persists you should always consult your pharmacist or doctor. For details of complementary remedies, see under individual conditions, for example headache, muscular aches and pains, sore throat, etc.

GENERAL PAIN RELIEF FOR CHILDREN

This section contains a list of over-the-counter products for general pain relief in children. It includes information on the main ingredients in each product, as well as to how they should be taken. Most painkillers for children contain paracetamol or occasionally ibuprofen. Products for children under the age of 12 years do not contain aspirin. This is because aspirin should never be given to this age group. Children's painkillers can be used to treat a wide range of painful and feverish conditions in children, including earache, toothache and teething, sore throat, headache, fever, colds, mumps, measles and reactions to vaccination and immunisation.

Doses are given for separate age ranges. If the child is younger than the age range stated, do not give the product without the advice of your pharmacist or GP. None of the products listed is suitable for children under the age of 3 months without a doctor's advice. However, some children's painkillers are specially formulated for children between the ages of 6 and 12 years. These products should therefore not be given to children under the age of 6 years. Always read labels carefully.

WARNING NOTE

- Check age ranges and doses very carefully. If your child is younger than the age range stated, do not give the product without the advice of a pharmacist or GP.

- Never give any product containing aspirin to a child under 12 years.

- Do not give painkillers to children for more than 3 days unless advised by GP.

- Products in this section are generally not suitable for infants and children with severe liver and kidney conditions, unless advised by GP.

For specific uses, cautions and warnings for each individual product, read the product label and the information leaflet.

⚐ Calpol Infant Suspension*

Description: A strawberry-flavoured analgesic liquid. Contains paracetamol 120mg in 5ml.
Dose: Maximum 4 doses in 24 hours. Babies aged 3–12 months: 2.5–5ml at 4-hourly intervals. Maximum 20ml in 24 hours. Children aged 12 months–under 6 years: 5–10ml at 4-hourly intervals. Not suitable for babies under 3 months, but if advised by GP, a 2.5ml dose may be given if fever follows vaccination at 2 months.
*Calpol Sugar-Free Infant Suspension also available.

⚰ Calpol Six Plus Suspension*

Description: A strawberry-flavoured sugar- and colour-free analgesic liquid. Contains paracetamol 250mg in 5ml.
Dose: Maximum 4 doses in 24 hours. Children aged 6–12 years: 5–10ml at 4–hourly intervals. For children under 6 years, use Calpol Infant.
* Also available as Calpol Six Plus Sugar- and Colour-free Suspension.

⚰ Disprol Paracetamol Suspension

Description: A banana-flavoured, sugar-free analgesic liquid. Contains 120mg paracetamol in 5ml.
Dose: Maximum 4 doses in 24 hours. Babies aged 3–12 months: 2.5–5ml at 4–hourly intervals. Children aged 12 months–6 years: 5–10ml at 4–hourly intervals. Not suitable for babies under 3 months, but, if advised by GP, a 2.5ml dose may be given if fever develops following vaccination at 2 months.

⚰ Fennings Children's Cooling Powders

Description: An analgesic powder. Contains paracetamol 50mg in 1ml.
Dose: Dissolve powder in water. Maximum 4 doses in 24 hours. Babies aged 3–12 months: 1 powder. Children aged 12 months–6 years: 2 powders. Children aged 6–12 years: 4 powders. Not suitable for babies under 3 months.

⚰ Infadrops

Description: An analgesic liquid with measuring pipette. Contains paracetamol 100mg.
Dose: Using measuring pipette, the following doses can be given 3–4 times a day. Maximum 4 doses in 24 hours. Babies aged 3–12 months: 0.8ml. Babies aged 12 months–2 years: 1.2ml. Children aged 2–3 years: 1.6ml. Not suitable for babies under 3 months, but if advised by a GP, a 0.6ml dose may be given if fever develops following vaccination at 2 months.

⚰ Junior Disprol Soluble Paracetamol Tablets

Description: A lime-flavoured soluble analgesic tablet. Contains paracetamol 120mg. Dissolve in water.
Dose: Maximum 4 doses in 24 hours. Children aged 12 months–6 years: 1–2 tablets every 4 hours. Children aged 6–12 years: 2–4 tablets every 4 hours. Not suitable for babies under 12 months.

✗ Medinol Over 6 Paracetamol Oral Suspension

Description: A strawberry-flavoured sugar- and colour-free analgesic liquid. Contains paracetamol 250mg in 5ml.
Dose: Maximum 4 doses in 24 hours. Children aged 6–12 years: 5–10ml at 4-hourly intervals. For children under 6 years, use Medinol Under 6.

✗ Medinol Under 6 Paracetamol Oral Suspension

Description: A strawberry-flavoured sugar- and colour-free analgesic liquid. Contains paracetamol 120mg in 5ml.
Dose: Maximum 4 doses in 24 hours. The following doses can be given at 4-hourly intervals. Babies aged 3–12 months: 2.5–5ml. Children aged 12 months–5 years: 10ml. Children over 5 years: 15–20ml. Not suitable for babies under 3 months, but if advised by a GP, a 2.5ml dose can be given if fever develops following vaccination at 2 months.

✗ Medised*

Description: A blackcurrant-flavoured analgesic liquid. Contains paracetamol 120mg in 5ml and promethazine hydrochloloride (an antihistamine).
Dose: Maximum 4 doses in 24 hours. The following doses can be given at 4-hourly intervals. Maximum 4 doses in 24 hours. Children aged 12 months–6 years: 10ml. Children aged 6–12 years: 20ml. Not suitable for babies under 12 months.
* Also available in colour- and sugar-free version.

✗ Nurofen for Children

Description: An orange-flavoured, sugar- and colour-free analgesic liquid. Contains ibuprofen 100mg in 5ml.
Dose: The following doses can be given 3–4 times a day. Maximum 4 doses in 24 hours. Babies aged 12 months–2 years: 2.5ml. Children aged 3–7 years: 5 ml. Children aged 8–12 years: 10 ml. For babies aged 6 months–12 months: 2.5ml up to 3 times in 24 hours. Not suitable for babies under 6 months.

✗ Placidex Syrup

Description: An analgesic liquid. Contains 120mg paracetamol.
Dose: Maximum 4 doses in 24 hours. The following doses can be given at 4-hourly intervals. Maximum 4 doses in 24 hours: Babies 3–12 months: 2.5–5ml. Not suitable for babies under 3 months, but if advised by a GP, a 2.5ml dose can be given if fever develops following vaccination at 2 months.

COMPLEMENTARY PRODUCTS

HOMOEOPATHIC REMEDIES

❀ 🐎 Weleda Camomilla

Description: A homoeopathic remedy for children with irritability and restlessness, toothache and teething, babies who cry constantly and want to be carried, colic and earache.
Dose: 3x and 30c.

ANTISEPTICS

Antiseptics are a key ingredient in many over-the-counter remedies and their uses vary widely, including the cleaning of cuts and grazes, soothing bites and stings, acne, sore throats, chapped hands, nappy rash, minor burns and scalds and general first aid.

This section covers those antiseptics not covered in other sections (see also Skin Problems, page 185, Respiratory Conditions, page 101, Burns, page 200, Bites and Stings, page 195, Cuts and Wounds, page 205).

There are several antiseptics, including benzalkonium chloride, cetrimide, chlorhexidine chloroxylenol, phenols and povidone iodine. Other healing and soothing ingredients such as menthol, methyl salicylate, thymol, titanium dioxide and zinc oxide may be included, and some products contain a mild local anaesthetic. For general antiseptic purposes, there is little to choose between the different ingredients.

WARNING NOTE

• Most liquid antiseptics should be diluted, depending on their intended use. Always check the label before you use the product.

• Cream antiseptics are applied directly to the affected part.

• Stop using an antiseptic preparation if you experience an adverse skin reaction unrelated to the condition, such as reddening, irritation or a rash.

• A few products contain lanolin. Do not use these products if you are allergic to this ingredient.

• Take care not to get any antiseptic into the eyes. If this occurs, rinse out with copious amounts of clean water.

• Products containing povidone iodine should not be used by pregnant and breast-feeding women, those with thyroid problems and those taking lithium.

For specific uses, cautions and warnings for each individual product, read the product label and the information leaflet.

Cetrimide Cream

Description: An antiseptic cream. Contains cetrimide.
Dose: Apply to the affected area or onto a dressing.

Dettol Cream

Description: An antiseptic cream. Contains triclosan, chloroxylenol, edetic acid.
Dose: Apply cream thinly to affected area as required.

Dettol Antiseptic Pain Relief Spray

Description: A liquid antiseptic and mild anaesthetic in spray form. Contains benzalkonium chloride and lidocaine hydrochloride (a mild anaesthetic).
Dose: Spray liquid onto the affected area. Repeat as required.

Dettol Fresh

Description: A liquid antiseptic/disinfectant. Contains benzalkonium chloride.
Dose: Dilute in proportion of 50ml in 1 litre of water and apply to affected area.

Dettol Liquid

Description: A liquid antiseptic/disinfectant. Contains chloroxylenol.
Dose: Dilute with water, as appropriate for intended use.

DDD Medicated Cream

Description: A medicated cream used as an antiseptic. Contains thymol, menthol, methyl salicylate, chlorbutol and titanium dioxide.
Dose: Apply morning and evening until problem has cleared.

DDD Medicated Lotion

Description: A medicated lotion used as an antiseptic. Contains thymol, menthol, salicylic acid, chlorbutol, methyl salicylate, glycerin and ethanol.
Dose: Apply to clean skin as necessary.

Germolene Antiseptic Wipes

Description: A cleansing wipe impregnated with antiseptic. Contains benzalkonium chloride and chlorohexidine gluconate.
Dose: Use to clean wounds as required.

Germolene Cream

Description: An antiseptic cream. Contains phenol and chlorohexidine gluconate.
Dose: Clean affected area, apply cream and gently rub in. If required, cover with a clean dressing.

Germolene Ointment

Description: An antiseptic ointment. Contains zinc oxide, methyl salicylate, phenol, lanolin and octaphonium chloride.
Dose: Apply directly to affected area or onto a dressing.

Savlon Antiseptic Cream

Description: An antiseptic cream. Contains cetrimide and chlorhexidine gluconate.
Dose: Apply cream to affected part as required.

Savlon Antiseptic Wound Wash

Description: A liquid spray antiseptic. Contains chlorhexidine gluconate.
Dose: Spray onto affected area to flood the wound and wash away any dirt or debris. Wipe away excess dirt if necessary.

Savlon Concentrated Antiseptic

Description: A liquid antiseptic. Contains chlorhexidine gluconate and cetrimide.
Dose: Dilute with water in proportions directed for each condition.

Savlon Dry Antiseptic

Description: An antiseptic aerosol spray powder. Contains povidone iodine.
Dose: Spray onto affected area until a light dusting of powder covers wound.

TCP Antiseptic Ointment

Description: An antiseptic ointment. Contains iodine, methyl salicylate, sulphur, tannic acid, camphor, salicylic acid and TCP liquid antiseptic (see below).
Dose: Apply to affected area after cleaning, as required.

TCP First Aid Antiseptic Cream

Description: An antiseptic cream. Contains chloroxylenol, triclosan, sodium salicylate and TCP liquid antiseptic (see below).
Dose: Apply to affected area after cleaning, as required.

TCP Liquid

Description: A liquid antiseptic. Contains phenol and halogenated phenols.
Dose: Dilute as appropriate for a gargle, mouthwash or first aid cleanser. Apply undiluted to spots and mouth ulcers.

COMPLEMENTARY PRODUCTS

HERBAL REMEDIES

❋ Lanes Tea Tree and Witch Hazel Cream

Description: For the relief of minor skin conditions, including dry, chapped skin, nappy rash and sunburn. Also for the treatment of minor cuts, burns and wounds. Contains tea tree and witch hazel, as well as eucalyptus oil, camphor and melaleuca oil.
Dose: Apply generously several times a day as required and at bedtime.

❋ Nelsons Tea Tree Cream

Description: A cream containing tea tree, which has antiseptic properties, for cleaning minor cuts, wounds and abrasions, and insect bites and stings.
Dose: Apply to the affected area.

HEADACHE AND MIGRAINE

HEADACHE

All over-the-counter painkillers are suitable for the relief of headache. See **General Pain Relief**, page 78, and **General Pain Relief for Children**, page 89. Make sure you read the cautions and warnings in those sections before using the products.

This section lists some homoeopathic remedies which you may wish to consider for the relief of headache. The warnings concerning general pain relief products also apply for complementary products.

COMPLEMENTARY PRODUCTS

HOMOEOPATHIC REMEDIES

❀ Actaea racemosa

Description: A homoeopathic remedy for headache with severe pains starting at the back of the head and spreading upwards.
Dose (and manufacturers): Nelsons 6c, Weleda 6c.

❀ Belladonna

Description: A homoeopathic remedy for severe, throbbing headache.
Dose (and manufacturers): Ainsworths 30c, Nelsons 6c, Weleda 6c.

❀ Calcarea phosphorica

Description: A homoeopathic remedy for headache brought on by overstudying.
Dose (and manufacturers): Nelsons 6c, New Era 6x, Weleda 6c.

❀ Coffea

Description: A homoeopathic remedy for one-sided, nervous headache.
Dose (and manufacturer): Weleda 6c.

❀ Gelsemium

Description: A homoeopathic remedy for general headache and those brought on by colds and flu.
Dose (and manufacturers): Ainsworths 30c, Nelsons 6c, Weleda 6c.

❀ Ignatia

Description: A homoeopathic remedy for piercing headache.
Dose (and manufacturers): Nelsons 6c, Weleda 6c or 30c.

❀ Kalium phosphoricum

Description: A homoeopathic remedy for headache with humming in the ears and headache brought on by stress.
Dose (and manufacturers): Nelsons 6c, New Era 6x, Weleda 6c.

❀ Lachesis

Description: A homoeopathic remedy for throbbing headache.
Dose (and manufacturer): Weleda 6c.

❀ Natrum muriaticum

Description: A homoeopathic remedy for severe headache.
Dose (and manufacturers): Ainsworths 30c, Nelsons 6c, New Era 6x, Weleda 6c and 30c.

❀ Nux vomica

Description: A homoeopathic remedy for headache accompanied by nausea, sickness or dizziness.
Dose (and manufacturers): Nelsons 6c, Weleda 6c and 30c.

❀ Thuja

Description: A homoeopathic remedy for severe headache.
Dose (and manufacturers): Nelsons 6c, Weleda 6c.

MIGRAINE

All over-the-counter painkillers are suitable for the relief of headache. See **General Pain Relief**, page 78. Make sure you read the cautions and warnings in those sections before using the products. However, this section lists some over-the-counter products which are specifically used for migraine and its associated symptoms, together with complementary products.

WARNING NOTE

• The products in this section are not suitable for children under 10 years.

• Those containing an antihistamine may cause drowsiness due to a sedative action.

- They should not be taken for extended periods of time, unless advised by your GP.

- Do not combine with other paracetamol remedies because of the risk of overdosing.

- Pregnant and breast-feeding women should check with their GP before using.

For specific uses, warnings and cautions, always read the product label and patient information leaflet.

Migraleve 1 (Pink)

Description: A pink tablet for the relief of migraine that features symptoms of nausea and vomiting. Contains paracetamol 500mg, codeine phosphate 8mg and buclizine hydrochloride 6.25mg (a sedative antihistamine).
Dose: Adults: 2 tablets as soon as an attack starts or is anticipated. Maximum 2 tablets in 24 hours. Children aged 10–14 years: 1 tablet. Maximum 1 tablet in 24 hours. Not suitable for children under 10 years.

Migraleve 2 (Yellow)

Description: A yellow tablet containing paracetamol 500mg and codeine phosphate 8mg. For the later stages of a continuing migraine attack after Migraleve 1 has been taken.
Dose: Adults: 2 tablets every 4 hours. Maximum 6 tablets in 24 hours. Children aged 10–14 years: 1 tablet every 4 hours. Maximum 3 tablets in 24 hours. Not suitable for children under 10 years.

Migraleve Duo

Description: Pink and yellow tablets for complete migraine attack. Pink tablet contains 500mg paracetamol, 8mg of codeine phosphate and 6.25mg of buclizine hydrochloride (a sedative antihistamine). Yellow tablet contains paracetamol 500mg and codeine phosphate 8mg.
Dose: Adults: 2 pink tablets at onset. If later required, 2 yellow tablets every 4 hours. Maximum 2 pink and 6 yellow tablets in 24 hours. Children aged 10–14 years: 1 pink tablet at onset. If later required, 1 yellow tablet every 4 hours. Maximum 1 pink and 3 yellow tablets in 24 hours. Not suitable for children under 10 years.

COMPLEMENTARY PRODUCTS

HOMOEOPATHIC REMEDIES

❀ Feverfew

Description: A homoeopathic remedy for reducing the frequency and severity of migraine headaches.
Dose (and manufacturer): Weleda 6x.

❀ Kalium bichromicum

Description: A homoeopathic remedy for migraine with blurred vision that precedes an attack.
Dose (and manufacturers): Nelsons 6c, Weleda 6c and 30c.

❀ New Era Combination F

Description: A combination of kali phos, mag phos, nat mur and silica for the treatment of migraine.
Dose: 1 tablet containing 6x of each of above ingredients.

❀ Silica

Description: A homoeopathic remedy for migraine.
Dose (and manufacturers): Ainsworths 30c, Nelsons 6c, New Era 6x, Weleda 6c and 30c.

❀ Thuja

Description: A homoeopathic remedy for migraine.
Dose (and manufacturers): Nelsons 6c, Weleda 6c.

RESPIRATORY CONDITIONS

• Asthma • Bronchitis and Coughs • Catarrh • Colds and Flu
• Hayfever • Sinusitis • Sore Throat

ASTHMA

Asthma should always be treated by a GP. Never attempt to treat it yourself without advice from your doctor. No over-the-counter remedies are suitable for asthma treatment. However, there are some complementary remedies which have traditionally been used to assist asthma sufferers. These are listed below. However, read the Warning Note before considering taking any remedy.

COMPLEMENTARY PRODUCTS

WARNING NOTE

• The following remedies should not be used as a substitute for conventional treatments.

• Do not take remedies without first checking with your GP.

• Some homoeopaths advise the following remedies for asthma. However, the remedies listed may not in general be recommended specifically for asthma on the packaging.

HOMOEOPATHIC REMEDIES

❀ Calcarea phosphorica

Description: A homoeopathic remedy for bronchial asthma.
Dose (and manufacturers): Nelsons 6c, New Era 6x, Weleda 6c and 30c.

❀ Kalium phosphoricum

Description: For nervous asthma or asthma with laboured breathing.
Dose (and manufacturers): Nelsons 6c, New Era 6x, Weleda 6c and 30c.

❀ Kalium sulphuricum

Description: For asthma accompanied by bronchitis.
Dose (and manufacturer): New Era 6x.

BRONCHITIS AND COUGHS

See also Catarrh, page 119, and Colds and Flu, page 122.

Products for cough fall into two basic categories, those for loose, chesty or productive cough, and those for dry, barking, ticklish or non-productive cough. The main ingredients found in products for productive cough are known as expectorants, because they help the removal of phlegm and mucus. Examples of these ingredients include ammonium chloride, creosote, guaiphenesin, ipecacuanha, squill and sodium citrate.

The main ingredients in products for non-productive cough are known as cough suppressants, because they help to suppress the coughing reflex. Examples include codeine, pholcodine and dextromethorphan. These ingredients can cause constipation.

Many cough remedies contain additional ingredients, including antihistamines, decongestants and soothing substances such as glucose, glycerol, honey, syrup and treacle. Menthol and various oils are sometimes included to relieve nasal stuffiness and help breathing.

Antihistamines help to dry up bronchial and nasal phlegm and they may also help you to sleep. Beware of using products containing antihistamines during the day because they can make you drowsy and affect your ability to drive or operate machinery. Examples of antihistamines used in cough mixtures include brompheniramine, chlorpheniramine, diphenhydramine, promethazine and triprolidine. Some people should not take products containing antihistamines. For warnings about antihistamines see page 103.

Decongestants help to open up the airways and are therefore useful where the respiratory tract is congested. Examples include ephedrine, pseudoephedrine, phenylpropanolamine and theophylline. Some people should not take products containing decongestants. For detailed warnings about decongestants, see page 103.

Products containing both a cough suppressant and a decongestant are useful for a dry cough with congestion. Products containing an expectorant and a decongestant are useful for a chesty, productive cough with congestion.

This section contains a list of products for cough with their main ingredients and how to take them. For specific uses, cautions and warnings, read product labels and patient information leaflets. If treating children, always check age ranges and doses very carefully. If your child is younger than the age range stated, do not give the product without the advice of a pharmacist or GP.

WARNING NOTE

Paracetamol

• Several products listed in this section contain paracetamol. These include painkillers, bronchitis and cough remedies, and colds and flu remedies. Always check the label to see if a product contains paracetamol. If it does, do not take any other product containing paracetamol at the same time.

• If you have a liver or kidney problem, do not take any product containing paracetamol without asking your pharmacist or GP.

Aspirin and ibuprofen

• Do not give products containing aspirin to children under 12 years.

• Do not take products containing aspirin and ibuprofen if you are asthmatic, allergic to aspirin or have stomach problems, for example ulcers.

• Those with blood coagulation problems, including those taking medicines to reduce clotting of the blood, and those with kidney problems and liver problems, should not take products containing aspirin or ibuprofen without asking their pharmacist or GP.

• Do not combine aspirin or ibuprofen with other over-the-counter or prescription medications containing aspirin or ibuprofen. This is because you risk overdosing. Always check the labels and if you have any doubts, check with your pharmacist or GP.

Antihistamines

• Remedies containing antihistamines may cause drowsiness. Even those labelled 'non-drowsy' can cause drowsiness in certain people.

• Do not combine with other sedative drugs, such as antidepressants and sleeping tablets; or with alcohol, as this will increase the drowsiness. Do not drive or operate machinery if the remedy makes you drowsy.

• Do not use in pregnancy or if you have prostate enlargement, urinary retention, liver disease or glaucoma.

Decongestants

• Over-the-counter remedies containing decongestants should not be used if you are taking Monoamine Oxidase Inhibitor drugs (MAOIs), or for 2 weeks after finishing MAOI therapy, if you are diabetic, have an over-active thyroid, have high blood pressure, or any heart problems or conditions.

  In addition, patients with asthma should take special care with remedies containing theophylline as it may interact with medication they are already taking for their condition.

Actifed Compound Linctus

Description: A liquid cough remedy containing dextromethorphan (a cough suppressant), pseudoephedrine (a decongestant) and triprolidine (an antihistamine).
Dose: Maximum 4 doses in 24 hours. Adults: 10ml dose every 4–6 hours. Children aged 6–12 years: 5ml every 4–6 hours. Children aged 2–5 years: 2.5ml every 4–6 hours. Not suitable for children under 2 years.

Actifed Expectorant

Description: A liquid cough remedy containing guaiphenesin (an expectorant), pseudoephedrine (a decongestant) and an antihistamine.
Dose: Adults: 10ml every 4–6 hours. Children aged 6–12 years: 5ml every 4–6 hours. Children aged 2–5 years: 2.5ml every 4–6 hours. Not suitable for children under 2 years.

Adult Meltus Dry Cough Elixir

Description: A liquid cough remedy containing dextromethorphan (a cough suppressant) and pseudoephedrine (a decongestant).
Dose: 5–10ml 4 times a day. Not suitable for children under 12 years.

Adult Meltus Expectorant

Description: A liquid cough remedy containing guaiphenesin (an expectorant), cetylpyridium (an antiseptic), and sucrose and purified honey.
Dose: 5–10ml every 3–4 hours. Not suitable for children under 12 years.

Adult Meltus Expectorant with Decongestant

Description: A liquid cough remedy containing guaiphenesin (an expectorant) and pseudoephedrine (a decongestant).
Dose: 10ml 4 times a day. Not suitable for children under 12 years.

⚰ Baby Meltus Cough Linctus

Description: A liquid cough remedy containing acetic acid (a soothing ingredient).
Dose: Babies aged 3–12 months: 2.5ml every 2–3 hours. Babies aged 13–30 months: 5ml every 2–3 hours. Babies over 30 months: 10ml every 2–3 hours. Not suitable for babies under 3 months.

Benylin Chesty Coughs*

Description: A liquid cough remedy containing diphenhydramine (an antihistamine) and menthol.
Dose: Adults: 10ml 4 times a day. Children aged 6–12: 5ml 4 times a day. Not suitable for children under 6 years.
* A non–drowsy version is available.

⚰ Benylin Children's Chesty Coughs

Description: A liquid cough remedy containing guaiphenesin (an expectorant).
Dose: Children aged 6–12 years: 10ml 4 times a day. Maximum 4 doses a day. Children aged 12 months–5 years: 5ml 4 times a day. Maximum 4 doses a day. Not suitable for babies under 12 months.

⚞ Benylin Children's Dry Coughs

Description: A liquid cough remedy containing pholcodine (a cough suppressant).
Dose: Children aged 6–12 years: 10–15ml 3 times a day. Children aged 12 months–5 years: 5ml 3 times a day. Not suitable for babies under 12 months.

⚞ Benylin Children's Night Coughs

Description: A cough remedy containing diphenhydramine (an antihistamine) and menthol.
Dose: Children aged 6 years and over: 10ml 4 times a day. Maximum 4 doses a day. Children aged 12 months–5 years: 5ml 4 times a day. Maximum 4 doses a day. Not suitable for babies under 12 months.

⚞ Benylin Children's Coughs and Colds

Description: Sugar- and colour-free liquid containing dextromethorphan (a cough suppressant) and triprolidine (an antihistamine).
Dose: Babies aged 12 months–2 years: 2.5ml 3–4 times a day. Children aged 2–5 years: 5ml 3–4 times a day. Children aged 6–12 years: 10ml 3–4 times a day. Not suitable for babies under 12 months.

Benylin Cough and Congestion

Description: A liquid cough remedy containing diphenhydramine (an antihistamine), dextromethorphan (a cough suppressant), pseudoephedrine (a decongestant) and menthol.
Dose: Adults: 10ml 4 times a day. Maximum 4 doses a day. Children aged 6–12 years: 5ml 4 times a day. Maximum 4 doses a day. Not suitable for children under 6 years.

Benylin Dry Coughs*

Description: A liquid cough remedy containing dextromethorphan (a cough suppressant), diphenhydramine (an antihistamine) and menthol.
Dose: Adults: 10ml 4 times a day. Children aged 6–12 years: 5ml 4 times a day. Not suitable for children under 6 years.
* A non-drowsy version is also available.

Benylin with Codeine

Description: A liquid cough remedy containing codeine (a cough suppressant) and diphenhydramine (an antihistamine).
Dose: Adults: 10ml 4 times a day. Children aged 6–12 years: 5ml 4 times a day. Not suitable for children under 6 years.

Bronalin Dry Cough Elixir

Description: A liquid cough remedy containing dextromethorphan (a cough suppressant) and pseudoephedrine (a decongestant).
Dose: Adults: 5–10ml 4 times a day. Children aged 6–12 years: 2.5ml. Not suitable for children under 6 years.

Bronalin Expectorant Linctus

Description: A liquid cough remedy containing diphenhydramine (an antihistamine) and sodium citrate and ammonium bicarbonate (both expectorants).
Dose: Adults: 5–10ml up to 4 times a day. Children aged 6–12 years: 5ml. Not suitable for children under 6 years.

⚲ Bronalin Junior Linctus

Description: A liquid cough remedy containing diphenhydramine (an antihistamine) and sodium citrate (an expectorant).
Dose: 5–10ml, according to age, 3 times a day. Read label. Not suitable for babies under 12 months.

Buttercup Syrup (Original)*

Description: A liquid cough remedy containing squill and capsicum (expectorants).
Dose: Adults: 10ml 3 times a day and at bedtime. Children over 2 years: 5ml. Not suitable for children under 2 years.
* Also available in honey and lemon flavour.

⚲ Buttercup Infant Cough Syrup

Description: A liquid cough remedy containing ipecacuanha (an expectorant), with liquid glucose and menthol.
Dose: Children aged 12 months–5 years: 5ml 3–4 times a day. Not suitable for babies under 12 months.

Cabdriver's Cough Linctus

Description: A liquid cough remedy containing dextromethorphan (a cough suppressant), with terpin, menthol, pumilio pine oil and eucalyptus oil.
Dose: 5ml every 4 hours. Not suitable for children under 12 years.

Copholco

Description: A liquid cough remedy containing pholcodine (a cough suppressant) with terpin, menthol and cineole.
Dose: Adults: 10ml 4–5 times a day. Children over 8 years: 5ml. Not suitable for children under 8 years.

Covonia Bronchial Balsam

Description: A liquid cough remedy containing dextromethorphan (a cough suppressant) with menthol.
Dose: Adults: 10ml every 4 hours. Elderly: check the dosage with a pharmacist. Children aged 6–12 years: 5ml every 4 hours. Not suitable for children under 6 years.

⚘ Covonia for Children

Description: A liquid cough remedy containing dextromethorphan (a cough suppressant) with benzoic acid.
Dose: Children: 5–10ml, according to age, every 4–6 hours as required. Not suitable for children under 2 years.

Covonia Mentholated Cough Mixture

Description: A liquid cough remedy containing menthol, with liquorice and squill (expectorants).
Dose: Adults: 5–10ml every 4 hours. Children 5–12 years: 5ml every 4 hours. Not suitable for children under 5 years.

Covonia Night Time Formula

Description: A liquid cough remedy containing dextromethorphan (a cough suppressant) and diphenhydramine (an antihistamine).
Dose: 15ml before bedtime. Not suitable for children under 5 years.

Dimotane Co*

Description: A liquid cough remedy containing brompheniramine (an antihistamine), pseudoephedrine (a decongestant) and codeine (a cough suppressant) with ethanol (alcohol).
Dose: Adults: 5–10ml up to 4 times a day. Children 4–12 years: 5–7.5ml 3 times a day, depending on age. Read label. Not suitable for children under 4 years.
* Also available in children's formula.

Do-Do ChestEze

Description: Tablets containing ephedrine (a decongestant), theophylline (a bronchodilator) and caffeine.
Dose: Adults: Maximum of 1 tablet in 4 hours. Maximum of 4 tablets in 24 hours. Children over 12 years: Maximum of 3 tablets in 24 hours. Not suitable for children under 12 years.

Do-Do Chesteze Expectorant Syrup

Description: A liquid cough remedy containing guaiphenesin (an expectorant).
Dose: 5–10ml every 2–4 hours. Not suitable for children under 12 years.

Ecdylin Syrup

Description: A liquid cough remedy containing diphenhydramine (an antihistamine) and ammonium chloride (an expectorant).
Dose: Adults: 5–10ml every 2–3 hours. Children aged 12 months–12 years: 2.5–5ml every 3–4 hours, depending on age. Read label. Not suitable for babies under 12 months.

Expulin Cough Linctus*

Description: A liquid cough remedy containing pholcodine (a cough suppressant) and chlorpheniramine (an antihistamine) and pseudoephedrine (a decongestant).
Dose: Adults: 10ml 4 times a day. Children aged 2–12 years: 2.5–10ml a day, depending on age. Read label. Not suitable for children under 2 years.
* Children's version also available.

Expulin Chesty Cough Linctus

Description: A liquid cough remedy containing guaiphenesin (an expectorant).
Dose: Adults: 10ml every 2–3 hours. Children aged 3–12 years: 5ml every 2–3 hours. Not suitable for children under 3 years.

Expulin Dry Cough Linctus

Description: A liquid cough remedy containing pholcodine (a cough suppressant).
Dose: 5ml 3–4 times a day. Not suitable for children under 12 years.

Famel Expectorant

Description: A liquid cough remedy containing guaiphenesin (an expectorant).
Dose: Adults: 20ml every 2–4 hours, as required. Children aged 12 months-12 years: 5–10ml, depending on age. Read label. Not suitable for babies under 12 months.

Famel Original

Description: A liquid cough remedy containing codeine (a cough suppressant) with creosote.
Dose: 10–15ml 3 times a day. Not suitable for children under 12 years.

Fedril Expectorant

Description: A liquid cough remedy containing diphenhydramine (an antihistamine), ammonium chloride (an expectorant) and menthol.
Dose: Adults: 5–10ml 3–4 times a day. Children aged 2–12 years: 2.5–5ml, depending on age. Read label. Not suitable for children under 2 years.

Fedril Tickly Cough

Description: A liquid cough remedy containing cetylpyridium (an antiseptic), ipecacuanha and ammonium chloride (both expectorants), with lemon oil, purified honey, glycerin and citric acid.
Dose: Adults: 15ml every 2–3 hours. Children aged 2–12 years: 5–10ml, depending on age. Read label. Not suitable for children under 2 years.

Fennings Little Healers

Description: A tablet containing ipecacuanha (an expectorant).
Dose: Adults: 2 tablets 3 times a day. Children aged 5–12 years: 1 tablet. Not suitable for children under 5 years.

Galenphol Adult Linctus

Description: A liquid cough remedy containing pholcodine (a cough suppressant).
Dose: Adults: 10–15ml 3–4 times a day. Children aged 6–12 years: 5–10ml. Not suitable for children under 6 years.

⚰ Galenphol Paediatric

Description: A liquid cough remedy containing pholcodine (a cough suppressant).
Dose: Children aged 12 months–5 years: 5–10ml 3 times a day. Babies aged 3–12 months: 2.5ml. Not suitable for babies under 3 months.

Galloway's Cough Syrup

Description: A liquid cough remedy containing ipecacuanha and squill (both expectorants).
Dose: Adults: 10ml 3–4 times a day. Children under 10 years: Half adult dose. Read label.

Hill's Balsam Chesty Cough Liquid

Description: A liquid cough remedy containing guaiphenesin (an expectorant).
Dose: 5–10ml every 2–4 hours. Maximum 60ml in 24 hours. Not suitable for children under 12 years.

⚰ Hill's Balsam Chesty Cough Liquid for Children (Sugar-free)

Description: A liquid sugar-free cough remedy containing ipecacuanha, citric acid, capsicum (expectorants), with benzoin, saccharin and orange oil.
Dose: 2.5–5ml 3 times a day and at bedtime, according to age. Read label.

Hill's Balsam Dry Cough Liquid

Description: A liquid cough remedy containing pholcodine (a cough suppressant).
Dose: 5ml 3–4 times a day. Not suitable for children under 12 years.

Jackson's All Fours

Description: A liquid cough remedy containing guaiphenesin (an expectorant).
Dose: 10–20ml at bedtime or every 4 hours. Not suitable for children under 12 years.

⚰ Junior Meltus Expectorant*

Description: A liquid cough remedy containing guaiphenesin (an expectorant) with cetylpyridium (an antiseptic) and purified honey and sucrose.
Dose: Children over 6 years: 10ml 3–4 times a day. Children aged 12 months–6 years: 5ml 3–4 times a day. Not suitable for babies under 12 months.
* Sugar- and colour-free version also available.
* Dry cough formula also available.

Lemsip Chesty Cough

Description: A liquid cough remedy containing guaiphenesin (an expectorant).
Dose: Adults: 10–20ml 3–4 times a day. Children aged 2–12 years: 5–10ml, according to age. Read label. Not suitable for children under 2 years.

Lemsip Dry Cough

Description: A liquid cough remedy containing honey, lemon oil, glycerol and citric acid.
Dose: Adults: 10ml 3–4 times a day. Children under 12 years: 5ml 3–4 times a day. Read label.

Liqufruta Garlic

Description: A liquid cough remedy containing guaiphenesin (an expectorant).
Dose: Adults: 10–15ml 3 times a day and at bedtime. Children aged 3–12 years: 10ml. Children aged 12 months–3 years: 5ml. Not suitable for babies under 12 months.

Nurse Sykes Bronchial Balsam

Description: A liquid cough remedy containing guaiphenesin (an expectorant).
Dose: 5–10ml at bedtime or every 4 hours. Not suitable for children under 12 years.

Pavacol D

Description: A liquid sugar-free cough remedy containing pholcodine (a cough suppressant).
Dose: Adults: 5–10ml up to 4 times a day. Children aged 12 months–12 years: 2.5–5ml 3-5 times a day, according to age. Read label. Not suitable for babies under 12 months.

Phensedyl Plus Linctus

Description: A liquid cough remedy containing promethazine (an antihistamine), pholcodine (a cough suppressant) and pseudoephedrine (a decongestant).
Dose: 5–10ml 3–4 times a day. Not suitable for children under 12 years.

Pulmo Bailly

Description: A liquid cough remedy containing guaicol (an expectorant) and codeine (a cough suppressant).
Dose: Adults: up to 10ml diluted in water and taken before food. Maximum 3 doses in 24 hours. Children aged 5–15 years: 5ml. Not suitable for children under 5 years.

Robitussin Chesty Cough Medicine

Description: A liquid cough remedy containing guaiphenesin (an expectorant).
Dose: Adults: 10ml 4 times a day. Children aged 12 months–12 years: 2.5–5ml, according to age. Read label. Not suitable for babies under 12 months.

Robitussin for Chesty Coughs with Congestion

Description: A liquid cough remedy containing guaiphenesin (an expectorant) with pseudoephedrine (a decongestant).
Dose: Adults: 10ml 4 times a day. Children aged 2–12 years: 2.5-5ml, according to age. Not suitable for children under 2 years.

⚰ Robitussin Dry Cough*

Description: A liquid cough remedy containing dextromethorphan (a cough suppressant).
Dose: Adults: 10ml 4 times a day. Children aged 6–12 years: 5ml 4 times a day. Not suitable for children under 6 years.
*Junior version also available.

Robitussin Night Time

Description: A liquid sugar-free cough remedy containing brompheniramine (an antihistamine), pseudoephedrine (a decongestant) and codeine (a cough suppressant).
Dose: Adults: 5–10ml up to 4 times a day. Children aged 4–12 years: 5–7.5ml 3 times a day, according to age. Read label. Not suitable for children under 4 years.

Sudafed Expectorant

Description: A liquid cough remedy containing guaiphenesin (an expectorant) and pseudoephedrine (a decongestant).
Dose: Adults: 10ml 4 times a day. Children aged 6–12 years: 5ml. Children aged 2–5 years: 2.5ml. Not suitable for children under 2 years.

Sudafed Linctus

Description: A liquid cough remedy containing dextromethorphan (a cough suppressant) and pseudoephedrine (a decongestant).
Dose: Adults: 10ml 4 times a day. Children aged 6–12 years: 5ml. Children aged 2–5 years: 2.5ml. Not suitable for children under 2 years.

⚰ Tancolin

Description: A liquid cough remedy containing dextromethorphan (a cough suppressant) with vitamin C.
Dose: Children 6 months–12 years: 2.5–15ml, according to age, up to 3 times a day. Read label. Not suitable for babies under 6 months.

⚰ Tixylix Chesty Cough

Description: A liquid cough remedy containing guaiphenesin (an expectorant).
Dose: Children: 2.5–10ml, according to age. Read label. Not suitable for babies under 12 months.

⚰ Tixylix Daytime*

Description: A liquid cough remedy containing pholcodine (a cough suppressant).
Dose: Children: 2.5–10ml every 6 hours, according to age. Read label. Not suitable for babies under 12 months.
* Night time version also available; contains promethazine (an antihistamine).

Veno's Dry Cough

Description: A liquid cough remedy containing glucose and treacle.
Dose: Adults: 10ml every 2–3 hours. Children aged 3–12 years: 5ml. Not suitable for children under 3 years.

Veno's Expectorant

Description: A liquid cough remedy containing guaiphenesin (an expectorant) with glucose and treacle.
Dose: Adults: 10ml every 2–3 hours. Children aged 3–12 years: 5ml every 2–3 hours. Not suitable for children under 3 years.

Veno's Honey and Lemon

Description: A liquid cough remedy containing lemon, glucose and treacle.
Dose: Adults: 10ml every 2–3 hours. Children aged 3–12 years: 5ml. Not suitable for children under 3 years.

Vicks Original Cough Syrup (Chesty cough)

Description: A liquid cough remedy containing guaiphenesin and sodium citrate (both expectorants), cetylpyridium (an antiseptic).
Dose: Adults: 10ml every 3 hours, as required. Children aged 6–12 years: 5ml. Not suitable for children under 6 years.

Vicks Medinite

Description: A liquid cough remedy containing dextromethorphan (a cough suppressant), ephedrine (a decongestant) doxylamine (an antihistamine) and paracetamol.
Dose: Adults: 30ml at bedtime. Children aged 10–12 years: 15ml. Not suitable for children under 10 years.

Vicks Vaposyrup for Chesty Coughs

Description: A liquid cough remedy containing guaiphenesin (an expectorant).
Dose: Adults: 15ml up to 6 times a day. Children aged 6–11 years: 10ml. Children aged 2–5 years: 5ml. Not suitable for children under 2 years.

Vicks Vaposyrup for Dry Coughs

Description: A liquid cough remedy containing dextromethorphan (a cough suppressant).
Dose: Adults: 15ml up to 4 times a day. Children aged 6–11 years: 5ml. Children aged 2–5 years: 2.5ml. Not suitable for children under 2 years.

Vicks Vaposyrup for Tickly Coughs

Description: A liquid cough remedy containing menthol.
Dose: Adults: 10ml every 3–4 hours. Maximum 6 doses in 24 hours. Children 6–12 years: Half adult dose. Not suitable for children under 6 years.

COMPLEMENTARY PRODUCTS

HERBAL REMEDIES

The following herbal remedies are suitable for relief of cough and associated symptoms such as catarrh and sore throat.

WARNING NOTE

- If you are pregnant or breast-feeding, do not take any of these remedies without checking with a pharmacist or GP.

- For specific uses, cautions and warnings, read product labels and patient information leaflets. If treating children, always check age ranges and doses very carefully. If your child is younger than the age range stated, do not give the product without the advice of a pharmacist or GP.

❀ Bio-Strath Thyme Formula

Description: A liquid herbal cough remedy. Contains primula, thyme and yeast.
Dose: 20 drops in water 3 times a day before meals.

❀ Cough Eeze

Description: A tablet herbal cough remedy with an expectorant. Contains horehound, inula and ipecacuanha.
Dose: Adults: 2 tablets 3 times a day. Children aged 8–12 years: 1 tablet.

❀ ⚓ Ernest Jackson's Children's Cough Pastilles*

Description: A pastille herbal remedy used as an expectorant for children's coughs. Contains citric acid, honey, ipecacuanha and squill.
Dose: 1 pastille dissolved in the mouth. Number to be used in 24 hours depends on age of child. Read label.
* Night cough pastilles also available.

❀ Heath & Heather Balm of Gilead Cough Pastilles

Description: A pastille herbal cough remedy used as an expectorant. Contains balm of Gilead, lobelia and squill.
Dose: 1 pastille dissolved in the mouth as required. Maximum 12 pastilles in 24 hours.

❀ Lanes Honey and Molasses Cough Mixture

Description: A liquid herbal expectorant remedy. Contains horehound, ipecacuanha and squill.

Dose: Adults: 5ml 3 times a day. Children aged 2–14 years: 2.5ml. Number of doses per day vary, according to age. Read label.

❀ Lobelia Compound

Description: A tablet herbal remedy to act as an anti-spasmodic, expectorant and respiratory stimulant. Contains gum ammoniacum, lobelia and squill.
Dose: 1 tablet 3 times a day.

❀ Potter's Antibron

Description: A tablet herbal remedy used as an expectorant, anti-spasm, soothing and sedative cough treatment. Contains coldsfoot, euphorbia, lobelia, pleurisy root, senega and wild lettuce.
Dose: Adults: 2 tablets 3 times a day. Children over 7 years: 1 tablet.

❀ Potter's Balm of Gilead

Description: A liquid herbal expectorant to relieve cough symptoms. Contains balm of Gilead, lobelia, lungwort and squill.
Dose: Adults: 10ml diluted in water 3–4 times a day. Children over 5 years: 5ml.

❀ Potter's Chest Mixture

Description: A liquid herbal expectorant cough remedy. Contains horehound, lobelia, pleurisy root, senega and squill.
Dose: 5ml every 3 hours.

❀ Potter's Lightning Cough Remedy

Description: A liquid herbal cough remedy. Contains anise and liquorice.
Dose: Adults: 10ml 3–4 times a day. Children over 5 years: 5ml every 5–6 hours.

❀ Potter's Vegetable Cough Remover

Description: A liquid herbal remedy that acts as an expectorant and antispasmodic to relieve cough symptoms. Contains black cohosh, elecampane, horehound, hyssop, ipecacuanha, lobelia, pleurisy root and scullcap.
Dose: Adults: 10ml 3–4 times a day. Children over 8 years: 5ml 3 times a day. Children aged 5–7 years: 5ml twice a day.

❀ Weleda Cough Drops

Description: A liquid herbal cough remedy. Contains angelica, aqua cherry laurel, cinnamon, clove, coriander, lemon balm, lemon oil and nutmeg.
Dose: 10–20 drops in warm water every 2 hours.

❁ Weleda Herb and Honey Cough Elixir

Description: A liquid herbal cough remedy. Contains aniseed, elderflowers, horehound, Iceland moss, marshmallow and thyme.
Dose: Adults: 10ml diluted in water every 3–4 hours. Maximum 4 doses in 24 hours. Children over 6 years: Half adult dose.

HOMOEOPATHIC REMEDIES

❁ Aconite

Description: A homoeopathic remedy for dry, barking cough.
Dose (and manufacturers): Ainsworths 30c, Nelsons 6c, Weleda 6c and 30c.

❁ Bryonia

Description: A homoeopathic remedy for dry, irritating coughs.
Dose (and manufacturers): Ainsworths 30c, Nelsons 6c, Weleda 6c and 30c.

❁ Calcarea fluorica

Description: A homoeopathic remedy for coughs with yellow mucus.
Dose (and manufacturers): Nelsons 6c, New Era 6 x, Weleda 6c and 30c.

❁ Carbo vegetabilis

Description: A homoeopathic remedy for violent coughing.
Dose (and manufacturers): Nelsons 6c, Weleda 6c and 30c.

❁ Drosera

Description: A homoeopathic remedy for tickly coughs, violent attacks of coughing which may end in vomiting or barking coughs.
Dose (and manufacturers): Ainsworths 30c, Nelsons 6c, Weleda 6c and 30c.

❁ Euphrasia

Description: A homoeopathic remedy for daytime coughing that produces mucus.
Dose (and manufacturers): Ainsworths 30c, Nelsons 6c, Weleda 6c and 30c.

❁ Hepar sulphuris

Description: For coughing made worse by cold air.
Dose (and manufacturers): Ainsworths 30c, Nelsons 6c, Weleda 6c and 30c.

❀ Ignatia

Description: A homoeopathic remedy for irritating coughs.
Dose (and manufacturers): Nelsons 6c, Weleda 6c and 30c.

❀ Nux vomica

Description: A homoeopathic remedy for violent coughs.
Dose (and manufacturers): Ainsworths 30c, Nelsons 6c, Weleda 6c and 30c.

❀ Phosphorus

Description: For coughing that causes breathing difficulties.
Dose (and manufacturers): Ainsworths 30c, Nelsons 6c, Weleda 6c and 30c.

Nicotine replacement therapy

Nicotine replacement therapy helps smokers to give up by providing nicotine, although at a lower level of nicotine than that provided by cigarettes. This helps to overcome the withdrawal symptoms and craving associated with quitting.

Products are available in the form of patches, chewing gum, lozenges and an inhaler. Nicotine patches are placed on the skin and release nicotine into the bloodstream. A fresh patch should be put on to an area of clean, dry, non-hairy skin such as the upper arm or upper leg every 16–24 hours (depending on the product). The part of your body you use for the patch should vary each time you apply a new patch. The product should be used over a period of 10–12 weeks in a gradually decreasing strength until nicotine intake is reduced to zero.

Nicotine gum releases nicotine into the bloodstream from the mouth. A piece of gum should be put in the mouth whenever you get the urge to smoke. This mimics smoking both in terms of nicotine intake and also in behaviour, simply because you are putting something in your mouth. The gum is most effective if you chew it until you experience a strong taste and then put it between your gum and teeth until the taste has gone. With lozenges, on the other hand, it is important that you allow them to dissolve slowly in your mouth and not to chew, suck or swallow them.

The nicotine inhaler is suitable for people wanting to quit, but who particularly need something to do with their hands.

WARNING NOTE

• Do not continue to smoke while using one of these products.

• Do not use any other nicotine-containing products.

• With patches, stop using if you experience any kind of rash or swelling at the part of the body where you put on the patch.

- If you are pregnant or breast-feeding, and want to stop smoking see your pharmacist or GP.

- Do not use one of these products without advice from the pharmacist.

- If you suffer from a heart or circulatory problem, any other medical condition, or are taking any medication, ask your pharmacist or GP before using one of these products.

Nicorette*

Description: Chewing gum treatment for nicotine dependence. Contains 2mg of nicotine per gum piece. This is the strength for those who smoke less than 20 cigarettes per day.
Dose: Chew 1 piece of gum for 30 minutes. Maximum 15 pieces in 24 hours. After 3 months gradually reduce dose.
* Nicorette Plus is also available, containing 4mg of nicotine.

Nicorette Inhalator

Description: Cartridges for inhalation treatment for nicotine dependence. 10mg of nicotine per cartridge. This is the strength for those who smoke more than 20 cigarettes per day.
Dose: Insert cartridge into the inhaler and suck as and when the urge to smoke occurs. Replace cartridge after approximately 20 minutes when nicotine is low. Maximum 12 cartridges in 24 hours, reducing in amount over 3-month period.

Nicorette Patch (3 strengths)

Description: Skin patch treatment for nicotine dependence.
Dose: Available in 5mg, 10mg and 15mg strengths. Apply one patch to arm on waking and remove 16 hours later. Gradually reduce dosage by using lower dose patches.

Nicotinell Chewing Gum*

Description: Chewing gum treatment for nicotine dependence. Contains 2mg of nicotine per gum piece.
Dose: Chew 8–12 pieces per day. Maximum 25 pieces in 24 hours. Gradually reduce number of pieces chewed over 3-month period.
* Also available containing 4mg of nicotine.

Nicotinell TTS (patch)

Description: Skin patch treatment for nicotine dependence.
Dose: 3 dose strengths available, according to cigarette consumption. Check with pharmacist for the dose that suits your smoking habit. Gradually reduce dosage by using lower dose patches.

COMPLEMENTARY PRODUCTS

❀ Potter's Antismoking Tablets

Description: A herbal remedy providing similar effects to nicotine designed to help reduce nicotine addiction. Contains lobelia.
Dose: 1 tablet every hour. Maximum 10 tablets in 24 hours.

❀ Resolution

Description: Lozenges used as an aid for nicotine dependence. Contains vitamins A, C and E and nicotine.
Dose: 1 lozenge to be dissolved in mouth as a substitute for smoking a cigarette.

❀ Stoppers

Description: Lozenges used as an aid for nicotine dependence. Contains nicotine.
Dose: 1 lozenge to be dissolved in mouth as a substitute for smoking a cigarette.

CATARRH

See also Bronchitis and Coughs, page 102, and Colds and Flu, page 122.

This section contains a list of products for catarrh with their main ingredients and how to use them. However, there is a great deal of overlap between products for catarrh, coughs and colds and flu, simply because these three ailments often occur together at the same time. For specific uses, cautions and warnings, read the product label.

Catarrh-Ex

Description: A capsule containing phenylephrine (a decongestant), paracetamol and caffeine.
Dose: 1–2 capsules every 4–6 hours. Maximum 8 capsules in 24 hours.

⚑ Cupal Baby Chest Rub

Description: An aromatic ointment to treat catarrh and congestion in babies and young children over the age of 3 months. Contains menthol and eucalyptus oils.
Dose: Rub gently onto chest, throat and back twice a day.

⚹ Tixylix Catarrh Syrup

Description: A liquid containing diphenhydramine (an antihistamine) and menthol for babies and children over the age of 12 months.
Dose: Children aged 6–10 years: 10ml 4 times a day. Children aged 12 months–5 years: 5ml 4 times a day.

COMPLEMENTARY PRODUCTS

HERBAL REMEDIES

WARNING NOTE

• Many herbal remedies are not suitable for children and for pregnant and breast-feeding women. Always check labels.

• Do not exceed stated dose. Several of the products listed below contain lobelia, which can cause nausea and vomiting.

✽ Catarrh Cream

Description: Aromatic herbal decongestant to ease inflamed nasal passages and congestion caused by catarrh. Contains aesculin, barberry, blackthorn, bryonia, camphor, echinacea, eucalyptus, thyme and mercurius sulphuratus.
Dose: Insert a small amount of cream into each nostril, as required. Not suitable for children under 3 years. Do not combine with homoeopathic remedies.

✽ Catarrh-eeze

Description: Traditional herbal remedy for relieving congestion caused by catarrh. Contains horehound, inula and yarrow.
Dose: Adults: 2 tablets 3 times a day. Children aged 5–12 years: 1 tablet 3 times a day.

✽ Ernest Jackson's Catarrh Pastilles

Description: A herbal pastille to treat catarrh. Contains abietis pine oil, creosote, menthol and sylvestris pine oil.
Dose: 1 pastille dissolved in the mouth as required.

✽ Heath & Heather Catarrh Tablets

Description: Herbal remedy to relieve symptoms of cough and catarrh. Contains white horehound and squill.
Dose: 1 tablet 3 times a day. Not suitable for children.

❀ Herbelix

Description: A liquid herbal expectorant to relieve symptoms of catarrh. Contains lobelia, sodium bicarbonate and tolu solution.
Dose: 5ml at bedtime. Children aged 7–14 years: Half adult dose.
Not suitable for children under 7 years.

❀ Potter's Catarrh Mixture

Description: A liquid herbal remedy to relieve nasal and throat catarrh. Contains blue flag, boneset, burdock, capsicum and hyssop.
Dose: Adults: 5ml 3 times a day. Children over 7 years: 5ml twice a day. Not suitable for children under 7 years.

❀ Potter's Chest Mixture

Description: A liquid herbal expectorant to soothe the symptoms of coughs and catarrh. Contains horehound, lobelia, pleurisy root, senega and squill.
Dose: Adults: 5ml every 3 hours. Not suitable for children.

HOMOEOPATHIC REMEDIES

❀ Allium cepa

Description: A homoeopathic remedy for catarrh and colds.
Dose (and manufacturers): Ainsworths 30c, Weleda 6c.

❀ Calcarea phosphorica

Description: A homoeopathic remedy for chronic catarrh.
Dose (and manufacturers): Nelsons 6c, New Era 6x, Weleda 6c and 30c.

❀ Calcarea sulphurica

Description: A homoeopathic remedy for catarrh.
Dose (and manufacturer): New Era 6x.

❀ Kalium bichromicum

Description: A homoeopathic remedy for stringy, persistent catarrh.
Dose (and manufacturers): Ainsworths 30c, Nelsons 6c, Weleda 6c and 30c.

❀ Kalium muriaticum

Description: A homoeopathic remedy for white, sticky catarrh.
Dose (and manufacturer): New Era 6x.

❀ Kalium sulphuricum

Description: A homoeopathic remedy for yellow catarrh.
Dose (and manufacturer): New Era 6x.

❀ New Era Combination Q

Description: A homoeopathic remedy for catarrh and sinus disorders. Contains calc fluor, calc phos, kali phos and mag phos.
Dose: Each dose contains 6x of each of the above ingredients.

❀ Pulsatilla

Description: A homoeopathic remedy for yellow, thick catarrh.
Dose (and manufacturers): Ainsworths 30c, Nelsons 6c, Weleda 6c and 30c.

❀ Thuja

Description: A homoeopathic remedy for catarrh.
Dose (and manufacturers): Nelsons 6c, Weleda 6c and 30c.

COLDS AND FLU

See also Catarrh, page 119, Bronchitis and Coughs, page 102, and Sinusitis, page 141.

There is no cure for the common cold, but a wide range of products give relief from symptoms. They are available in the form of tablets, capsules, liquids, powders, nasal drops and nasal sprays.

These remedies may contain painkillers such as paracetamol, ibuprofen and aspirin, all of which will help to relieve aches and pains and reduce fever and high temperature. Decongestants, such as ephedrine, phenylephrine, phenylpropanolamine and pseudoephedrine, are often included in cold remedies to help relieve stuffiness and congestion. Products containing a decongestant either alone or in combination with a painkiller are useful for nasal congestion and sinusitis.

Nasal drops and nasal sprays for colds and flu also contain decongestants, such as oxymetazoline and xylometazoline. Nasal drops and sprays can cause rebound congestion if used for long periods of time and it is for this reason that they should not be used for longer than 7 days.

Antihistamines, such as brompheniramine, chlorpheniramine, diphenhydramine, diphenylpyraline, pheniramine and triprolidine, may be included and these have a drying effect on mucus and phlegm. Products containing antihistamines are useful for a runny nose. However, antihistamines may cause drowsiness, and if you are affected in this way, you should be careful not to drive or operate any machinery.

Various inhalant oils, rubs and sticks are also available, and these remedies have been popular for a long time. They are safe to use in most people, including children, although you must always check labels for minimum ages.

This section contains a list of products for colds and flu with their main ingredients and how to use them. For specific uses, cautions and warnings, read the product label. For children, check age ranges and doses very carefully. If your child is younger than the age range stated, do not give the product without the advice of a pharmacist or GP.

WARNING NOTE

This applies to all products in this section.

Paracetamol

- Several products listed in this section contain paracetamol. These include painkillers, bronchitis and cough remedies, and colds and flu remedies. Always check the label to see if a product contains paracetamol. If it does, do not take any other product containing paracetamol at the same time.

- If you have a liver or kidney problem, do not take any product containing paracetamol without asking your pharmacist or GP.

Aspirin and ibuprofen

- Do not give products containing aspirin to children under 12 years.

- Do not take products containing aspirin and ibuprofen if you are asthmatic, allergic to aspirin or have stomach problems, for example ulcers.

- Those with blood coagulation problems, including those taking medicines to reduce clotting of the blood, and those with kidney problems and liver problems should not take products containing aspirin or ibuprofen without asking their pharmacist or GP.

- Do not combine aspirin or ibuprofen with other over-the-counter or prescription medications containing aspirin or ibuprofen. This is because you risk overdosing. Always check the labels and if you have any doubts, check with your pharmacist or GP.

Antihistamines

• Remedies containing antihistamines may cause drowsiness.

• Do not combine with other sedative drugs, such as antidepressants and sleeping tablets; or with alcohol, as this will increase the drowsiness. Do not drive or operate machinery if the remedy makes you drowsy.

• Do not use in pregnancy or if you have prostate enlargement, urinary retention, liver disease or glaucoma.

Decongestants

• Over-the-counter remedies containing decongestants should not be used if you are taking Monoamine Oxidase Inhibitor drugs (MAOIs), or for 2 weeks after finishing MAOI therapy, if you are diabetic, have an over-active thyroid, have high blood pressure, or any heart problems or conditions.

Actifed Syrup*

Description: A liquid containing triprolidine (an antihistamine) and pseudo-ephedrine (a decongestant).
Dose: Adults: 10ml every 4–6 hours. Maximum 4 doses in 24 hours. Children 2–12 years: 2.5–10ml, according to age. Check label. Not suitable for children under 2 years.
* Also available in tablet form.

Advil Cold and Sinus Tablets

Description: A tablet containing ibuprofen (a painkiller) and pseudoephedrine (a decongestant).
Dose: 1–2 tablets every 4–6 hours. No more than 6 tablets in 24 hours. Not suitable for children under 12 years.

Afrazine Nasal Spray

Description: A nasal spray containing oxymetazoline (a decongestant).
Dose: Adults and children over 5 years: 2–3 sprays into each nostril morning and night. Do not use continuously or for more than 1 week. Not suitable for children under 5 years. Do not use for more than 7 days.

Beechams All-in-One

Description: A liquid containing paracetamol, phenylephrine (a decongestant) and guaiphenesin (an expectorant).
Dose: 20ml up to 4 times a day. Not suitable for children under 12 years.

Beechams Flu-Plus Caplets

Description: A tablet containing paracetamol, phenylephrine (a decongestant) and caffeine.
Dose: 2 capsules every 4–6 hours as necessary. Maximum of 8 capsules in 24 hours. Not suitable for children under 12 years.

Beechams Flu-Plus Hot Lemon*

Description: A powder in a sachet containing paracetamol, phenylephrine (a decongestant) and vitamin C.
Dose: 1 sachet dose in mug of warm water every 4–6 hours. Maximum of 4 sachets in 24 hours. Not suitable for children under 12 years.
* Also available as Beechams Flu–Plus Hot Berry Fruits.

Beechams Lemon Tablets

Description: A tablet containing aspirin.
Dose: 1–2 tablets every 3–4 hours. Maximum 12 tablets in 24 hours. Not suitable for children under 12 years.

Beechams Powders

Description: A powder in a sachet containing aspirin and caffeine.
Dose: 1 sachet in water every 3–4 hours. Maximum 6 powders in 24 hours. Not suitable for children under 12 years.

Beechams Powders Capsules

Description: A capsule containing paracetamol, phenylephrine (a decongestant) and caffeine.
Dose: Adults: 2 capsules every 3–4 hours if required. Maximum 12 capsules in 24 hours. Children aged 6–12 years: 1 capsule every 3–4 hours if required. Maximum 6 capsules in 24 hours. Not suitable for children under 6 years.

Beechams Warmers Blackcurrant

Description: A powder in a sachet containing paracetamol, phenylephrine (a decongestant) and vitamin C.
Dose: 1 sachet every 4 hours in hot water. Maximum 6 powders in 24 hours. Not suitable for children under 12 years.
* Also available as Beechams Warmers Lemon and Beechams Warmers Lemon and Honey.

Benylin Day and Night Cold Treatment

Description: Yellow daytime tablets containing paracetamol and phenyl-propanolamine (a decongestant). Blue night-time tablet containing paracetamol and diphenhydramine (an antihistamine).
Dose: 1 yellow tablet 3 times a day and 1 blue tablet at night. Not suitable for children under 12 years.

Benylin Four Flu Liquid*

Description: A liquid containing a pseudoephedrine (a decongestant), diphenhydramine (an antihistamine) and paracetamol.
Dose: Adults: 20ml 4 times a day. Children aged 6–12 years: 10ml 4 times a day. Not suitable for children under 6 years.
*Tablet and hot drink versions also available.

Bronalin Decongestant

Description: A liquid containing pseudoephedrine (a decongestant).
Dose: Adults: 10ml 3 times a day. Children aged 6–12 years: 5ml 3 times a day. Children aged 2–5 years: 2.5ml 3 times a day. Not suitable for children under 2 years.

Contac 400

Description: A capsule containing chlorpheniramine (an antihistamine) and phenylpropanolamine (a decongestant).
Dose: 1 capsule in the morning and another at bedtime. Not suitable for children under 12 years.

Day Nurse*

(See also Night Nurse, page 130.)
Description: A liquid containing paracetamol, phenylpropanolamine (a decongestant) and dextromethorphan (a cough suppressant).
Dose: Adults: 20ml every 4 hours. Maximum dose 80ml in 24 hours. Children aged 6–12 years: 10ml every 4 hours. Maximum 40ml in 24 hours. Not suitable for children under 6 years.
* Also available in capsule and hot drink form.

Dimotapp Elixir*

Description: A liquid containing brompheniramine (an antihistamine) and phenylephrine (a decongestant).
Dose: Adults: 5–10ml 3 times a day. Children aged 2–6 years: 5ml 3 times a day. Children aged 2–6 years: 2.5ml 3 times a day. Not suitable for children under 2 years.
* Tablet version and children's version of remedy are also available.

Dolvan Tablets

Description: A tablet containing paracetamol, diphenhydramine (an antihistamine), ephedrine (a decongestant) and caffeine.
Dose: Adults: 1–2 tablets 3 times a day. Elderly: 1 tablet 3 times a day. Not suitable for children under 12 years.

Dristan Decongestant Tablets

Description: A tablet containing aspirin, chlorpheniramine (an antihistamine), phenylephrine (a decongestant) and caffeine.
Dose: 2 tablets 4 times a day. Maximum 8 tablets in 24 hours. Not suitable for children under 12 years.

Dristan Nasal Spray

Description: A nasal spray containing oxymetazoline (a decongestant).
Dose: Adults: 1–2 sprays up each nostril every 8–12 hours. Children aged 6–16 years: 1 spray up each nostril every 8–12 hours. Not suitable for children under 6 years. Do not use for more than 7 days.

Eskornade Capsules*

Description: A capsule containing phenylpropanolamine (a decongestant) and diphenhydramine (an antihistamine).
Dose: 1 capsule every 12 hours. Not suitable for children under 12 years.
* Also available in syrup form.

⚱ Expulin Decongestant for Babies and Children (Linctus)

Description: A sugar-free liquid containing chlorpheniramine (an antihistamine) and ephedrine (a decongestant).
Dose: Children aged 3 months–12 years: 2.5ml–15ml, twice to three times a day according to age. Read dosage instructions on bottle. Not suitable for babies under 3 months.

Fenox Nasal Drops*

Description: Nasal drops containing phenylephrine (a decongestant).
Dose: Adults: 4–5 drops in each nostril night and morning and every 4 hours if required. Children aged 5–12 years: 2 drops in each nostril night and morning and every 4 hours if required. Not suitable for children under 5 years. Do not use for more than 7 days.
* Also available as nasal spray.

Hill's Balsam Extra Strong 2-in-1 Pastilles

Description: A herbal pastille containing ipecacuanha, menthol and peppermint.
Dose: 1 pastille dissolved in mouth, as required. Maximum 10 pastilles in 24 hours. Maximum 7 pastilles in 24 hours for children over 12 years. Not suitable for children under 12 years.

Jackson's Febrifuge

Description: A liquid containing sodium salicylate (an ingredient related to aspirin).
Dose: Adults: 5–10ml in water every 6 hours or 3 times a day. Elderly: Half adult-dose. Not suitable for children under 12 years.

Karvol Decongestant Tablets*

Description: A capsule containing various decongestant oils.
Dose: For babies over 3 months, children, adults and elderly: Squeeze capsule contents onto pillow and sheets so it can be inhaled while sleeping. For adults during the daytime: Squeeze onto a tissue or into a small bowl of hot water and inhale. For young children during the daytime: Squeeze onto handkerchief and safety pin onto child's clothing where they can inhale it but not touch it e.g. pin on to chest area of vest between shirt, blouse or dress. Not suitable for babies under 3 months.
*Also available as decongestant drops.

Lemsip Breathe Easy

Description: A powder in sachets containing paracetamol, phenylephrine (a decongestant) and vitamin C.
Dose: 1 sachet dissolved in hot water every 4 hours, as required. Maximum of 4 sachets in 24 hours. Not suitable for children under 12 years.

Lemsip Combined Relief Capsules

Description: A capsule containing paracetamol, phenylephrine (a decongestant) and caffeine for the relief of cold and flu symptoms.
Dose: 2 capsules every 3–4 hours. Maximum of 8 capsules in 24 hours. Not suitable for children under 12 years.

Lemsip Max Strength

Description: A lemon–flavoured powder in sachets containing paracetamol, phenylephrine (a decongestant) and vitamin C.
Dose: 1 sachet dissolved in hot water every 4–6 hours, as required. Maximum of 4 sachets in 24 hours. Not suitable for children under 12 years.

Lemsip Original*

Description: A lemon-flavoured powder containing paracetamol, phenylephrine (a decongestant) and vitamin C.
Dose: 1 sachet dissolved in hot water every 4 hours, as required. Maximum of 4 sachets in 24 hours. Not suitable for children under 12 years.
* Also available as Lemsip Menthol Extra.

Lemsip Pharmacy Power + Paracetamol

Description: A lemon-flavoured powder in sachets containing paracetamol, pseudoephedrine (a decongestant) and vitamin C.
Dose: 1 sachet dissolved in hot water every 4 hours, as required. Maximum of 4 sachets in 24 hours. Not suitable for children under 12 years.

Lemsip Pharmacy Power Caps

Description: A capsule containing ibuprofen and pseudoephedrine (a decongestant).
Dose: 2 capsules every 4 hours. Maximum 4 capsules in 24 hours. Not suitable for children under 12 years.

Mackenzies Smelling Salts

Description: A liquid containing ammonia with eucalyptus oil.
Dose: Inhale vapour as needed. Not suitable for babies under 3 months.

⚰ Medised*

Description: A suspension containing paracetamol and promethazine (an antihistamine).
Dose: Children aged 12 months–6 years: 10ml up to every 4 hours. Children aged 6–12 years: 20ml up to every 4 hours. Maximum 4 doses in 24 hours. Not suitable for babies under 12 months.
* Also available as Medised Sugar-free, Colour-free suspension.

Mu-Cron

Description: A tablet containing paracetamol and phenylpropanolamine (a decongestant).
Dose: 1 tablet up to 4 times a day. Allow 4 hours between doses. Maximum 4 tablets in 24 hours. Not suitable for children under 12 years.

Night Nurse*

Description: A liquid containing paracetamol, promethazine (an antihistamine) and dextromethorphan (a cough suppressant).
Dose: Adults: 20ml just before bedtime. Children aged 6–12 years: 10ml just before bedtime. Not suitable for children under 6 years.
* Also available in capsule form.

Nurofen Cold and Flu

Description: A tablet containing ibuprofen and pseudoephedrine (a decongestant).
Dose: Take 2 tablets then 1–2 tablets every 4 hours, as necessary. Maximum 6 tablets in 24 hours. Not suitable for children under 12 years.

⚞ Secron

Description: A liquid containing ephedrine (a decongestant) and ipecacuanha (an expectorant).
Dose: Children over 2 years: 2.5–10ml 2–3 times a day, according to age. Read label. Not suitable for children under 2 years.

Sinutab Tablets

Description: A tablet containing paracetamol and phenylpropanolamine (a decongestant).
Dose: Adults: 2 tablets 3 times a day. Maximum 6 tablets in 24 hours. Children aged 6–12 years: 1 tablet 3 times a day. Maximum 3 tablets in 24 hours. Not suitable for children under 6 years.

Sudafed Co Cold and Flu Tablets

Description: A tablet containing paracetamol and pseudoephedrine (a decongestant).
Dose: Adults: 1 tablet every 4–6 hours. Maximum 4 doses in 24 hours. Children aged 6–12 years: Half a tablet every 4–6 hours. Maximum 4 doses in 24 hours. Not suitable for children under 6 years.

Sudafed Nasal Spray

Description: A nasal spray containing oxymetazoline (a decongestant).
Dose: 1–2 sprays into each nostril 2–3 times a day. Not suitable for children under 6 years. Do not use for more than 7 days.

Sudafed Tablets

Description: A tablet containing pseudoephedrine (a decongestant).
Dose: 1 tablet every 4–6 hours. Maximum 4 tablets in 24 hours. Not suitable for children under 12 years.

⚘ Tixylix Inhalant

Description: A capsule containing menthol, eucalyptus oil, camphor and turpentine oil.
Dose: Babies aged 3–12 months: Snip top off capsule, sprinkle contents onto hand-kerchief and tie out of reach. Children aged 12 months and over: At night sprinkle contents on to bed linen, pillow or night clothes or tip the contents of one capsule into a pint of hot water. Ensure that the bowl is out of reach of the child. Do not leave the child alone with the bowl. Not suitable for babies under 3 months.

Vicks Medinite

Description: A liquid containing paracetamol, pseudoephedrine (a decongestant), dextromethorphan (a cough suppressant) and doxylamine (an antihistamine).
Dose: Adults: 30ml at bedtime. Children aged 10–12 years: 15ml at bedtime. Not suitable for children under 10 years.

Vicks Sinex Decongestant Nasal Spray

Description: A nasal spray containing oxymetazoline (a decongestant).
Dose: 1–2 sprays per nostril every 6–8 hours. Not suitable for children under 6 years. Do not use for more than 7 days.

Vicks Vaporub*

Description: Inhalant rub containing camphor, eucalyptus and menthol.
Dose: Rub a small amount onto chest, throat and back at night so it can be inhaled. Alternatively, add 2 teaspoons to bowl of hot water and mix before inhaling vapours. Not suitable for children under 6 months.
* Also available as Vicks Inhaler (not suitable for children under 6 years).

⚘ Woodward's Baby Chest Rub

Description: Inhalant rub containing turpentine, eucalyptus and menthol.
Dose: Rub a small amount onto chest, throat and back at night so it can be inhaled. Not suitable for babies under 3 months.

Wright's Vaporizing Fluid

(To be used with Wright's Vaporizer.)
Description: Inhalant containing chlorocesol.
Dose: Add 10ml to vaporizer block every 8 hours. Not suitable for children under 2 years.

COMPLEMENTARY PRODUCTS

HERBAL REMEDIES

❀ Cold-eeze

Description: A tablet herbal remedy for colds. Contains echinacea and garlic.
Dose: 2 tablets, swallowed whole, 3 times a day. Not suitable for children.

❀ Echinacea and Garlic

Description: A tablet herbal remedy to relieve colds and flu. Contains enchinacea and garlic powder.
Dose: 1–2 tablets 3 times a day. Not suitable for children.

❀ Garlodex

Description: A tablet herbal remedy to treat colds and catarrh. Contains garlic, marshmallow and parsley.
Dose: 1 tablet 3 times a day. Children aged 5–12 years: 1 tablet at bedtime. Not suitable for children under 5 years.

❀ Hofels Garlic and Parsley One-a-Day Tablets*

Description: Tablets containing garlic oil. A herbal remedy to relieve colds, catarrh and hayfever.
Dose: 1 tablet daily with food. Not suitable for children under 7 years.
* Also available: Hofels One-a-Day Garlic Pearles and Hofels Original Garlic Pearles.

❀ Lusty's Garlic Perles

Description: A capsule herbal remedy for colds, runny nose, catarrh and coughs. Contains garlic.
Dose: 1 capsule 3 times a day with meals. Children aged 5–12 years: 1 capsule a day. Not suitable for children under 5 years.

❀ Olbas Inhaler

Description: Inhalant containing eucalyptus, menthol, cajuput and peppermint for relief of colds and flu symptoms including blocked sinuses, catarrh and hayfever.
Dose: Place inhaler in nostril and inhale. Use up to 4 times each hour. Not recommended for children under 7 years.

❀ Olbas Oil

Description: Liquid inhalation to relieve nasal congestion associated with colds, flu, sinusitis, catarrh, hayfever and other infections of the upper respiratory tract. Contains eucalyptus, menthol cajuput, clove, juniper berry, wintergreen and mint.
Dose: Put 2–3 drops onto handkerchief and inhale as required. Can also be added to hot water and used as steam inhalant. For children aged 3 months–2 years: Use 1 drop on a tissue and tie out of reach on clothing or onto bedhead at night. Not suitable for babies under 3 months.

❀ Olbas Pastilles

Description: Pastilles for the relief of colds and flu and their symptoms. Contains peppermint, eucalyptus, menthol, clove, juniper berry and wintergreen.
Dose: 1 pastille dissolved in the mouth as required. Maximum dose 8 pastilles in 24 hours. Not suitable for children under 7 years.

❀ Potter's Eldermint Life Drops

Description: A liquid homoeopathic remedy for colds, flu, fever and sore throat. Contains capsicum, elder flowers and peppermint.
Dose: Adults: 11 drops diluted in warm water every hour. Children over 7 years: 11 drops every 2 hours. Not suitable for children under 7 years. Do not combine with other homoeopathic remedies.

❀ Potter's Garlic Tablets

Description: A tablet herbal remedy for colds and catarrh. Contains garlic.
Dose: Adults: 2 tablets 3 times a day. Children over 8 years: 1 tablet 3–4 times a day.

HOMOEOPATHIC REMEDIES

❀ Aconite

Description: A homoeopathic remedy for the early stages of colds or fever.
Dose (and manufacturers): Ainsworths 30c, Nelsons 6c, Weleda 6c and 30c.

❀ Ferrum phosphoricum

Description: A homoeopathic remedy for the early stages of colds or fever, after using aconite.
Dose (and manufacturers): Ainsworths 30c, Nelsons 6c, New Era 6x, Weleda 6c and 30c.

❀ Silica

Description: A homoeopathic remedy for persistent colds.
Dose (and manufacturers): Ainsworths 30c, Nelsons 6c, New Era 6x, Weleda 6c and 30c.

FEVER

See also **General Pain Relief**, page 78, and **General Pain Relief for Children**, page 89.

COMPLEMENTARY PRODUCTS

The following remedies can be tried to reduce fever in adults. They should not be used as a substitute for proper medical attention.

It is not advisable to use these remedies on children, as fever is often associated with other illnesses. **Always seek your doctor's advice if a child's temperature remains high.**

HOMOEOPATHIC TREATMENT FOR FEVER

❀ Aconite

Description: A homoeopathic remedy for sudden high fevers with intense thirst and dry skin.
Dose (and manufacturers): Nelsons 6c, Weleda 6c and 30c.

❀ Belladonna

Description: A homoeopathic remedy for sudden fevers with flushed face and dilated pupils.
Dose (and manufacturers): Nelsons 6c, Weleda 6c and 30c.

❀ Ferrum phosphoricum

Description: A homoeopathic remedy for early stages of fever before flu or nasal symptoms develop.
Dose (and manufacturers): Nelsons 6c, New Era 6x, Weleda 6c.

❀ Mercurius solubilis

Description: A homoeopathic remedy for feverish head cold with catarrh symptoms.
Dose (and manufacturers): Nelsons 6c, Weleda 6c and 30c.

HAYFEVER

See also Bronchitis and Coughs, page 102, and Colds and Flu, page 122.

A variety of remedies is available for the treatment of hayfever. These include tablets, capsules, liquids, nasal drops and sprays and eye drops. Most over-the-counter remedies for hayfever taken by mouth contain antihistamines. This is because histamine is the main chemical in the body which is responsible for the symptoms of hayfever. Antihistamines, as the name suggests, block the action of histamine, and they are generally all equally effective in controlling the symptoms of hayfever. They work best before histamine is produced, so it is always best to take these products when you expect symptoms of hayfever, rather than when the symptoms have started.

One of the problems with antihistamines is that they can cause drowsiness. However, the antihistamines which have been developed in recent years tend to cause less drowsiness than those antihistamines which have been around for a long time. However, even those which are considered to be 'non-drowsy' may cause drowsiness in some people. So, if you need to drive, for example, always try a product first, and see how it makes you feel. Alcohol will often increase the feeling of drowsiness so it is best to avoid alcohol while taking any antihistamine. Examples of 'non-drowsy' antihistamines include acrivastine, cetirizine and loratadine. Examples of 'drowsy' antihistamines include brompheniramine, chlorpheniramine, promethazine and triprolidine.

In addition to antihistamines, some remedies for hayfever contain decongestants, such as pseudopephedrine and phenylpropanolamine. These ingredients may help to relieve a blocked nose.

Nasal sprays and nasal drops contain a variety of ingredients, including antihistamines, decongestants, corticosteroids (often called steroids) and sodium cromoglycate. Nasal drops and sprays containing decongestants may cause rebound congestion (i.e. they may make the problem worse), so they should not be used for any longer than 7 days.

Corticosteroids included in nasal sprays for hayfever include beclomethasone and flunisolide, and neither one is more effective than the other. Hayfever is an allergic response and these corticosteroids work by suppressing the allergic response. This helps to reduce the symptoms of hayfever. It is best to start using these products before your symptoms start. Once symptoms have appeared, it may be several days before you notice the full benefit of a corticosteroid spray, and you may need to keep using the product throughout the hayfever season.

Sodium cromoglycate is available not only in the form of nasal sprays, but also as eye drops. It appears to work by dampening down the allergic response. Like the steroids, sodium cromoglycate is best used before your symptoms start and continued throughout the hayfever season. Once your symptoms have started, sodium cromoglycate will take several hours to have an effect. It also has a short duration of action and needs to be used several times a day. If you are a hayfever sufferer who experiences red, itchy eyes, you may find sodium cromoglycate eye drops useful, but you should not use them if you suffer from the eye disease glaucoma, or while wearing contact lenses.

This section contains a list of products for hayfever with their main ingredients and how to use them. Products containing an antihistamine can also be used to treat other allergic reactions in addition to hayfever. These include allergic skin rashes and insect bites and stings. For specific uses, cautions and warnings, read the product label. For children, check age ranges and doses very carefully. If your child is younger than the age range stated, do not give the product without the advice of a pharmacist or GP.

WARNING NOTE

Antihistamines
• Remedies containing antihistamines may cause drowsiness.

• Do not combine with other sedative drugs, such as antidepressants and sleeping tablets; or with alcohol, as this will increase the drowsiness. Do not drive or operate machinery if the remedy makes you drowsy.

• Do not use in pregnancy or if you have prostate enlargement, urinary retention, liver disease or glaucoma.

Decongestants
• Over-the-counter remedies containing decongestants should not be used if you are taking Monoamine Oxidase Inhibitor drugs (MAOIs), or for 2 weeks after finishing MAOI therapy, if you are diabetic, have an over-active thyroid, kidney and liver problems, high blood pressure, or any heart problems.

• Nasal sprays containing decongestants should not be used for more than 7 days because of the risk of rebound congestion.

Corticosteroids
• Over-the-counter nasal sprays containing steroids should not be used by children under 12 years or by pregnant and breast-feeding women. They should be avoided if you have infection in the nose or eye.

Sodium cromoglycate
• Do not use eye drops containing this ingredient while wearing contact lenses.

Actifed

Description: A tablet containing triprolidine (an antihistamine) and pseudo-ephedrine (a decongestant).
Dose: 1 tablet up to 4 times a day. Not suitable for children under 12 years.

Actifed syrup.

Description: A liquid containing triprolidine (an antihistamine) and pseudo-ephedrine (a decongestant).
Dose: Adults: 10ml up to 4 times a day. Children aged 6–12 years: 5ml up to 4 times a day. Children aged 2–5 years: 2.5ml up to 4 times a day. Not suitable for children under 2 years.

Afrazine

Description: A nasal spray containing oxymetazoline (a decongestant).
Dose: 2–3 drops in each nostril twice a day. Not suitable for children under 5 years.

Aller-eze Original Formula

Description: A tablet containing clemastine (an antihistamine).
Dose: Adults: 1 tablet at night and in the morning. Children aged 3–12 years: Doses vary depending on age. Read label. Not suitable for children under 3 years.

Aller-eze Plus

Description: A tablet containing clemastine (an antihistamine) and phenyl-propanolamine (a decongestant).
Dose: 1 tablet every 6 hours. Maximum 4 tablets in 24 hours. Not suitable for children under 12 years.

Beconase Allergy

Description: A nasal spray containing beclomethasone (a steroid).
Dose: 2 sprays into each nostril morning and evening. Not suitable for children under 12 years.

Benadryl Allergy Relief

Description: A capsule acrivastine (an antihistamine).
Dose: 1 capsule up to 3 times a day. Not suitable for children under 12 years or the elderly.

Calimal Antihistamine Tablets

Description: A tablet containing chlorpheniramine (an antihistamine).
Dose: Adults: 1 tablet 3–4 times a day. Children aged 6–12 years: Half to 1 tablet 3–4 times a day. Not suitable for children under 6 years.

Clariteyes

Description: Eye drops containing sodium cromoglycate (an anti-inflammatory).
Dose: 1–2 drops into each affected eye up to 4 times a day. Not suitable for children under 5 years.

Clarityn Allergy

Description: A tablet containing loratadine (an antihistamine).
Dose: 1 tablet daily. Not suitable for children under 12 years.

Clarityn Allergy Syrup

Description: A liquid containing loratadine (an antihistamine).
Dose: Adults: 10ml once a day. Children aged 2–5 years: Half adult dose. Not suitable for children under 2 years.

Hay-Crom Hay Fever Eye Drops

Description: Eye drops containing sodium cromoglycate (an anti-inflammatory).
Dose: 1–2 drops into each affected eye up to 4 times a day. Not suitable for children under 5 years.

Haymine

Description: A tablet containing chlorpheniramine (an antihistamine) and ephedrine (a decongestant).
Dose: 1 tablet in the morning. A further tablet may be taken at night, if required. Not suitable for children under 12 years.

Nasobec Hayfever

Description: A nasal spray containing beclomethasone (a corticosteroid).
Dose: 2 sprays twice a day into each nostril. Maximum 8 sprays in 24 hours. Not suitable for children under 12 years.

Opticrom Allergy Eye Drops

Description: Eye drops containing sodium cromoglycate (an anti-inflammatory).
Dose: 1–2 drops into each eye 4 times a day. Not suitable for children under 5 years.

Optrex Hayfever Allergy Eye Drops

Description: Eye drops containing sodium cromoglycate (an anti-inflammatory).
Dose: 1–2 drops in each eye 4 times a day. Not suitable for children under 5 years.

Otrivine-Antistin

Description: Eye drops containing xylometazeline (a decongestant) and antazoline (a topical antihistamine).
Dose: Adults: 1–2 drops into the affected eye(s) 2–3 times a day. Children over 5 years: 1 drop 2–3 times a day. Not suitable for children under 5 years.

Piriton Allergy Tablets

Description: A tablet containing chlorpheniramine (an antihistamine).
Dose: Adults: 1 tablet every 4–6 hours. Maximum 6 tablets in 24 hours. Children aged 6–12 years: half a tablet every 4–6 hours. Maximum 3 tablets in 24 hours. Not suitable for children under 6 years.

Piriton Syrup

Description: A liquid containing chlorpheniramine (an antihistamine).
Dose: Adults: 10ml every 4–6 hours. Children aged 12 months–12 years: 2.5–5ml, depending on age. Not suitable for babies under 12 months.

Rhinolast Hayfever Spray

Description: A nasal spray containing azelastin (an antihistamine).
Dose: 1 spray into each nostril twice a day. Not suitable for children under 12 years.

Rynacrom*

Description: A nasal spray containing sodium cromoglycate (an anti-inflammatory).
Dose: 1 spray into each nostril 2–4 times a day. Not suitable for children under 5 years.
* Also available as Rynacrom Compound, which has a lower strength.

Rynacrom Allergy

Description: A nasal spray containing sodium cromoglycate (an anti-inflammatory) and xylometazoline (a decongestant).
Dose: 1 spray into each nostril 4 times a day. Not suitable for children under 5 years.

Syntaris Hayfever

Description: A nasal spray containing flunisolide (a corticosteroid).
Dose: Adults: 2 sprays into each nostril morning and evening. Maximum 4 sprays per nostril. Children aged 12–16 years: 1 spray into each nostril up to 3 times a day. Maximum 3 sprays per nostril. Not suitable for children under 12 years.

Zirtek

Description: A tablet containing cetirizine (an antihistamine).
Dose: 1 tablet a day. Not suitable for children under 12 years.

COMPLEMENTARY PRODUCTS

HERBAL REMEDIES

❀ Buttercup Pol 'n' Count

Description: A herbal remedy to relieve the symptoms of hayfever. Contains garlic and echinacea.
Dose: 2 tablets 3 times a day. Not suitable for children.

❀ Gencydo*

Description: An ointment to relieve the symptoms of hayfever. Contains boric acid, lemon juice and quince.
Dose: Apply the ointment inside the nostrils several times a day and before retiring.
* Also available as a nasal paint, which can also be diluted with water and used as a nasal spray.

HOMOEOPATHIC PRODUCTS

❀ Allium cepa

Description: A homoeopathic remedy for hayfever.
Dose (and manufacturers): Ainsworths 30c, Weleda 6c.

❀ Natrum muriaticum

Description: A homoeopathic remedy for hayfever.
Dose (and manufacturers): Ainsworths 30c, Nelsons 6c, New Era 6x, Weleda 6c and 30c.

❀ New Era Combination H

Description: A homoeopathic remedy for hayfever and allergic rhinitis. Contains mag phos, nat mur and silica.
Dose: 1 dose contains 6x of each of the above ingredients.

❀ Pollenna

Description: A homoeopathic remedy for hayfever. Contains 6c each of Allium cepa, Euphrasia officinalis and Sabadilla officinarum.
Dose: Adults: 2 tablets every 2 hours for 6 doses, then 2 tablets 3 times a day. Children: Half adult dose. Stop treatment when symptoms cease.

❀ Silica

Description: A homoeopathic remedy for hayfever.
Dose (and manufacturers): Weleda 6c and 30c, Nelsons 6c, New Era 6x, Ainsworths 30c.

❀ Weleda Mixed Pollen

Description: A homoeopathic remedy for hayfever. Contains a wide range of pollens.
Dose: 30c.

SINUSITIS

See also Bronchitis and Coughs, page 102, and Colds and Flu, page 122.

Remedies suitable for sinusitis contain ingredients such as antihistamines, decongestants and painkillers. However, as with all respiratory complaints, there is a great deal of overlap and it is often difficult to distinguish between products, for example between sinusitis remedies and colds and flu remedies.

This section contains a list of products for sinusitis and blocked nose with their main ingredients and how to use them. For specific uses, cautions and warnings, read the product label. For children, check age ranges and doses very carefully. If your child is younger than the age range stated, do not give the product without the advice of a pharmacist or GP.

WARNING NOTE

Paracetamol
- Several products listed in this section contain paracetamol. These include painkillers, bronchitis and cough remedies, and colds and flu remedies. Always check the label to see if a product contains paracetamol. If it does, do not take any other product containing paracetamol at the same time.

- If you have a liver or kidney problem, do not take any product containing paracetamol without asking your pharmacist or GP.

Antihistamines
- Remedies containing antihistamines may cause drowsiness.

- Do not combine with other sedative drugs, such as antidepressants and sleeping tablets; or with alcohol, as this will increase the drowsiness. Do not drive or operate machinery if the remedy makes you drowsy.

- Do not use in pregnancy or if you have prostate enlargement, urinary retention, liver disease or glaucoma.

Decongestants

• Over-the-counter remedies containing decongestants should not be used if you are taking Monoamine Oxidase Inhibitor drugs (MAOIs), or for 2 weeks after finishing MAOI therapy, if you are diabetic, have an over-active thyroid, kidney and liver problems, high blood pressure, or any heart problems.

Afrazine

Description: A nasal spray containing oxymetazoline (a decongestant).
Dose: 2–3 sprays in each nostril twice a day. Not suitable for children under 5 years. Do not use for more than 7 days.

Dristan

Description: A nasal spray containing oxymetazoline (a decongestant).
Dose: Adults: 1–2 sprays in each nostril every 8–12 hours. Children aged 6–12 years: Half adult dose. Not suitable for children under 6 years. Do not use for more than 7 days.

Fenox*

Description: Nasal drops containing phenylephrine (a decongestant).
Dose: Adults: 4–5 drops in each nostril, night and morning, and every 4 hours as necessary. Children aged 5–12 years: 2 drops in each nostril. Not suitable for children under 5 years. Do not use for more than 7 days.
* Also available as a nasal spray.

Galpseud*

Description: A tablet containing pseudopephedrine (a decongestant).
Dose: Adults: 1 tablet 4 times a day. Not suitable for children under 12 years.
* Also available as a liquid.

Mentholair

Description: A liquid used in the bath so aromatic vapour can be inhaled to relieve nasal and sinus congestion. Contains aromatic decongestants.
Dose: 1 measure added to bath-water.

Otrivine*

Description: Nose drops containing xylometazoline (a decongestant).
Dose: Adults: 2–3 drops in each nostril 2–3 times a day. Not suitable for children under 12 years. Do not use for more than 7 days.
* Spray version and a children's version are also available.

Sinutab*

Description: A tablet containing paracetamol and phenylpropanolamine (a decongestant).
Dose: Adults: 2 tablets 3 times a day. Maximum 6 tablets in 24 hours. Children aged 6–12 years: Half adult dose. Maximum 3 tablets in 24 hours. Not suitable for children under 6 years.
* Night-time version also available (this contains an antihistamine).

Vicks Sinex

Description: A nasal spray containing oxymetazoline (a decongestant).
Dose: 1–2 sprays every 6–8 hours. Do not use for more than 7 days. Not suitable for children under 6 years.

COMPLEMENTARY PRODUCTS

HERBAL REMEDIES

❀ Oleum Rhinale

Description: A herbal oil remedy to relieve symptoms of sinus congestion, catarrh and dry rhinitis. Contains eucalyptus, marigold, peppermint and mercurius sulphuratus.
Dose: 2–4 drops into the nostril twice a day. Do not combine with other herbal or homoeopathic remedies.

❀ Sinotar

Description: An antiseptic and decongestant tablet herbal remedy to relieve symptoms of catarrh and sinusitis. Contains echinacea, elderflower and marshmallow.
Dose: 2 tablets 3 times a day before meals. Children aged 5–12 years: Half adult dose. Not suitable for children under 5 years.

HOMOEOPATHIC REMEDIES

❀ New Era Combination Q

Description: A homoeopathic remedy for sinus disorders and catarrh. Contains calc fluor, calc phos, kali phos and mag phos.
Dose: Each dose contains 6x of each of the above ingredients.

SORE THROAT, LARYNGITIS AND TONSILLITIS

See also Colds and Flu, page 122, Catarrh, page 119, **Antiseptics**, page 93, **General Pain Relief**, page 78, and **General Pain Relief for Children**, page 89.

Over-the-counter remedies for sore throats are available in the form of pastilles and lozenges, sprays, gargles and rinses. They contain a variety of soothing ingredients, and those remedies in the form of pastilles and lozenges work mainly by stimulating the production of saliva which helps to keep the area of soreness moist. Many remedies also contain antiseptics, antifungals and antibacterials such as benzalkonium chloride, cetylpyridium and dequalinium, which may contribute to the beneficial effects. Local anaesthetics such as benzocaine are included in throat sprays and these ingredients help to numb the throat and so relieve soreness. Sprays can sometimes be used in children from the age of 6 years, but some are not suitable for children under 12 years. In addition, most children find using mouthwashes difficult and these are best avoided in children under the age of 12 years.

This section contains a list of products for sore throat together with their main ingredients and how to use them. For specific uses, cautions and warnings, read the product label. For children, check age ranges and doses very carefully. If your child is younger than the age range stated, do not give the product without the advice of a pharmacist or GP.

AAA Spray

Description: An aerosol spray containing benzocaine (a local anaesthetic).
Dose: Adults: 2 sprays every 2–3 hours. Maximum 16 sprays in 24 hours. Children over 6 years: Half adult dose. Maximum 8 sprays in 24 hours. Not suitable for children under 6 years.

Bradosol*

Description: A lozenge containing benzalkonium chloride (an antibacterial).
Dose: 1 lozenge sucked as required. Not suitable for children under 5 years.
* Available in cherry menthol and citrus flavours.

Bradasol Plus

Description: A lozenge containing domiphen bromide (an antibacterial) and lignocaine (an anaesthetic).
Dose: 1 lozenge every 2–3 hours. Maximum 8 lozenges every 24 hours. Not suitable for children under 12 years.

De Witt's Throat Lozenges

Description: A lozenge containing cetylpyridium chloride (an antibacterial).
Dose: Adults: 1 lozenge sucked every 3 hours. Maximum 8 lozenges in 24 hours. Children over 6 years: Half adult dose. Maximum 4 lozenges in 24 hours. Not suitable for children under 6 years.

Dequacaine Lozenges

Description: A lozenge containing dequalinium (an antibacterial) and benzocaine (an anaesthetic).
Dose: 1 lozenge sucked every 2 hours, as required. Maximum 8 lozenges in 24 hours. Not suitable for children under 12 years.

Halls Soothers

Description: A medicated sweet. Contains menthol and eucalyptus.
Dose: Suck sweets as required.

Labosept Pastilles

Description: A pastille containing dequalinium (an antibacterial).
Dose: 1 pastille every 3–4 hours. Maximum 8 pastilles in 24 hours. Not suitable for children under 10 years.

Merocaine Lozenges

Description: A lozenge containing cetylpyridium (an antibacterial) and benzocaine (an anaesthetic).
Dose: 1 lozenge every 2 hours. Maximum 8 lozenges in 24 hours. Not suitable for children under 12 years.

Merocets Lozenges*

Description: A lozenge containing cetylpyridium (an antibacterial).
Dose: 1 lozenge every 3 hours, as required. Not suitable for children under 6 years.
* Also available as a mouthwash.

Merothol Lozenges

Description: A lozenge containing cetylpyridium (an antibacterial) with menthol and eucalyptol.
Dose: 1 lozenge every 3 hours, as required. Not suitable for children under 6 years.

Strepsils Direct Action Spray

Description: A spray containing lidocaine (an anaesthetic).
Dose: Spray back of throat 3 times. Repeat every 3 hours, as required. Maximum 6 doses in 24 hours. Not suitable for children under 12 years.

Strepsils Dual Action Lozenges

Description: A lozenge containing lidocaine (an anaesthetic) and amylmetacresol and dichlorobenzyl alcohol (antibacterials).
Dose: 1 lozenge every 2 hours. Maximum 8 tablets in 24 hours. Not suitable for children under 12 years.

Strepsils Original*

Description: A lozenge containing dichlorobenzyl alcohol and amylmetacresol (antibacterials).
Dose: 1 lozenge every 2–3 hours.
* Sugar-free and vitamin C versions also available.

TCP Sore Throat Lozenges

Description: A lozenge containing phenols (antibacterial).
Dose: 1 pastille, as required. Not suitable for children under 6 years.

Tyrozets

Description: A lozenge containing tyrothricin (an antibacterial) and benzocaine (an anaesthetic).
Dose: 1 lozenge every 3 hours. Maximum 8 lozenges in 24 hours. Children aged 3–11 years: 6 lozenges in 24 hours. Not suitable for children under 3 years.

Vicks Ultra Chloraseptic

Description: A throat spray containing benzocaine (an anaesthetic).
Dose: Adults: 3 sprays every 2–3 hours. Children aged 6–12 years: 1 spray every 2–3 hours. Maximum 8 treatments in 24 hours. Not suitable for children under 6 years. Do not use for more than 3 consecutive days.

Vocalzone

Description: A pastille containing soothing ingredients.
Dose: Dissolve 1 pastille in the mouth and inhale deeply. Repeat every 2 hours as necessary. Not suitable for children under 12 years.

COMPLEMENTARY PRODUCTS

HERBAL REMEDIES

❀ Bio-Strath Chamomile Formula

Description: A liquid herbal remedy to ease symptoms of sore throat. Contains camomile, sage and yeast.
Dose: 20 drops diluted in water 3 times a day before meals. Not suitable for children.

HOMOEOPATHIC REMEDIES

❀ Aconite

Description: A homoeopathic remedy for sore and burning throat.
Dose (and manufacturers): Weleda 6c and 30c, Nelsons 6c, Ainsworths 30c.

❀ Allium cepa

Description: A homoeopathic remedy for laryngitis.
Dose (and manufacturers): Weleda 6c, Ainsworths 30c.

❀ Apis mellifica

Description: A homoeopathic remedy for sore and burning throat.
Dose (and manufacturers): Weleda 6c and 30c, Nelsons 6c.

❀ Argentum nitricum

Description: A homoeopathic remedy for hoarseness.
Dose (and manufacturers): Weleda 6c and 30c, Nelsons 6c, Ainsworths 30c.

❀ Drosera

Description: A homoeopathic remedy for sore throat that hurts when swallowing and laryngitis.
Dose (and manufacturers): Weleda 6c and 30c, Nelsons 6c, Ainsworths 30c.

❀ Gelsemium

Description: A homoeopathic remedy for sore throat and difficulty swallowing.
Dose (and manufacturers): Weleda 6c and 30c, Nelsons 6c, Ainsworths 30c.

❊ Ignatia

Description: A homoeopathic remedy for sore throat that feels better if you swallow.
Dose (and manufacturers): Weleda 6c and 30c, Nelsons 6c.

❊ Kalium bichromicum

Description: A homoeopathic remedy for sore throat.
Dose (and manufacturers): Weleda 6c and 30c, Nelsons 6c, Ainsworths 30c.

❊ Kalium muriaticum

Description: A homoeopathic remedy for tonsillitis.
Dose (and manufacturer): New Era 6x.

❊ Kalium phosphoricum

Description: A homoeopathic remedy for hoarseness.
Dose (and manufacturers): Weleda 6c and 30c, Nelsons 6c, New Era 6x.

❊ Lachesis

Description: A homoeopathic remedy for sore throat that extends up to the ear and tonsillitis.
Dose (and manufacturer): Weleda 6c.

❊ Nux vomica

Description: A homoeopathic remedy for a raw, sore throat.
Dose (and manufacturers): Weleda 6c and 30c, Nelsons 6c, Ainsworths 30c.

❊ Phosphorus

Description: A homoeopathic remedy for hoarseness and laryngitis.
Dose (and manufacturers): Weleda 6c and 30c, Nelsons 6c, Ainsworths 30c.

❊ Phytolacca

Description: A homoeopathic remedy for dry sore throat with a burning sensation.
Dose (and manufacturer): Weleda 6c.

DIGESTIVE PROBLEMS

• Constipation • Diarrhoea • Gastritis • Heartburn • Indigestion
• Irritable Bowel Syndrome • Travel Sickness • Nausea • Worms

CONSTIPATION

There are four main types of laxatives in over-the-counter remedies for constipation. These are called bulk forming laxatives, stimulant laxatives, osmotic laxatives and stool softeners.

Bulk forming laxatives such as ispaghula husk, methylcellulose and sterculia work in a similar way to a high fibre diet, that is they increase the bulk of the stools and make them softer and easier to pass. They may take longer to work than some of the other types of laxative, and you may experience wind and flatulence after taking them. Bulk laxatives should always be taken with a large glass of fluid – water, juice, squash, milk, it does not matter which - because there is a risk of causing obstruction in your intestine if you do not have plenty of fluid. They are best taken during the day and not immediately before bedtime.

Stimulant laxatives, including senna and bisacodyl, increase the speed with which the faeces move through the intestine. They normally work within 4–12 hours and for this reason they are best taken at bedtime. They may cause intestinal griping and cramp, and, like all laxatives, are best used for short periods of time (e.g. 2–3 days at most). Osmotic laxatives, such as lactulose, magnesium hydroxide, magnesium sulphate and sodium sulphate, work by drawing water into the bowel and softening the stools. Lactulose is a fairly slow-acting ingredient and you should adjust the dosage if necessary every 48 hours. The only widely used laxative with a stool softening effect is docusate.

This section contains a list of products for constipation with their main ingredients and how to use them. For specific uses, cautions and warnings, read the product label. For children, check age ranges and doses very carefully. If your child is younger than the age range stated, do not give the product without the advice of a pharmacist or GP.

WARNING NOTE

• Those with existing bowel conditions or who suffer vomiting or abdominal pain should first check with their GP or pharmacist before using over-the-counter remedies. This special precaution applies to all the remedies listed in this section, including complementary products.

• If you are pregnant or breast-feeding and are constipated, ask your pharmacist or GP for advice. Never use an over-the-counter remedy, including complementary remedies, without checking first whether it is suitable.

- Constipation remedies are not intended for long-term use. See your GP if constipation does not respond to dietary measures, short-term use of over-the-counter remedies, or if it is chronic.

- Laxatives of any kind should never be used if you suffer from obstruction in your intestine.

- Laxatives containing lactulose should not be used by people with lactose intolerance or the metabolic disorder called galactosaemia.

Califig California Syrup of Figs

Description: A liquid containing senna (a stimulant laxative).
Dose: 7.5–30ml at bedtime, according to age. Read label. Not suitable for babies under 12 months.

Dioctyl*

Description: A capsule containing docusate (a stimulant laxative with some stool softening action).
Dose: Adults: Up to 5 capsules a day, divided into doses. Reduce dosage as condition improves. Not suitable for children under 12 years.
* Also available as a solution and in a lower dose for children.

Dulco-Lax Tablets*

Description: A tablet containing bisacodyl (a stimulant laxative).
Dose: 1–2 tablets at night. Not suitable for children under 10 years.
* Also available as a liquid. Formulations and strengths differ. Children's version available at lower strength.

Dulco-Lax Suppositories*

Description: A suppository containing bisacodyl (a stimulant laxative).
Dose: 1 suppository in the morning. Not suitable for children under 10 years.
* Children's version available at lower strength for children under 10 years.

Duphalac Solution

Description: A liquid containing lactulose (an osmotic laxative).
Dose: Adults: 15ml twice a day. Children aged 5–10 years: 10ml twice a day. Children aged 12 months–5 years: 5ml twice a day. Babies under 12 months: 2.5ml (check with pharmacist).

Ex-Lax Senna

Description: Chocolate tablets containing senna (a stimulant laxative).
Dose: Adults: 1 tablet of chocolate at bedtime. Children over 6 years: Half to one tablet at bedtime. Not suitable for children under 6 years.

Fybogel*

Description: Granules containing ispaghula (a bulking laxative).
Dose: Adults: Dissolve 1 sachet of granules in water and drink after meals twice a day. Children aged 6–12 years: 2.5–5ml of granules twice a day. Not suitable for children under 6 years.
* Also available in orange and lemon flavour.

Fynnon Salts

Description: A powder containing sodium sulphate (an osmotic laxative).
Dose: 5ml 1–2 times a day dissolved in water. Not suitable for children under 12 years.

Isogel

Description: Granules containing ispaghula (a bulking laxative).
Dose: Adults: 10ml 1–2 times a day dissolved in water. Children aged 6–12 years: 5ml 1–2 times a day. Not suitable for children under 6 years.

Juno Junipah Salts*

Description: A powder containing sodium sulphate (an osmotic laxative).
Dose: 20ml 1–2 times a day. Not suitable for children under 12 years.
* Also available in tablet form.

Lactitol

Description: A powder in sachets containing lactitol (an osmotic laxative).
Dose: Adults: 1–2 sachets mixed with a cold drink or sprinkled over food twice a day (total 4 sachets a day). Children aged 6–12 years: Half to 1 sachet a day. Children aged 12 months–6 years: a quarter to half a sachet once a day. Not suitable for babies under 12 months.

Laxoberal

Description: A liquid containing sodium picosulphate (a stimulant laxative).
Dose: 2.5–15ml a night, according to age. Not suitable for children under 2 years.

Manevac

Description: Granules containing fibre and senna (a stimulant laxative).
Dose: Granules should be placed on tongue and swallowed (not chewed) with plenty of water: Adults: 5–10ml 1–2 times a day. Children aged 5–12 years: 5ml once a day. Pregnant women: 5–10ml each morning and evening. Not suitable for children under 5 years.

Mil-Par

Description: A liquid containing magnesium sulphate (an osmotic laxative) and liquid paraffin (a stool softener).
Dose: Adults: 15–30ml a day. Children over 3 years: 5–15ml a day, according to age. Not suitable for children under 3 years.

Milk of Magnesia

Description: A liquid containing magnesium hydroxide (an osmotic laxative).
Dose: Adults: 30–45ml at bedtime. Children over 3 years: 5–10ml at bedtime. Not suitable for children under 3 years.

Nylax

Description: A tablet containing senna (a stimulant laxative).
Dose: Adults: 2 tablets at bedtime. Children aged 5–12 years: 1 tablet at bedtime. Not suitable for children under 5 years.

Regulan*

Description: A powder in sachets containing ispaghula (a bulk forming laxative).
Dose: Adults: 1 sachet dissolved in water 1–3 times a day. Children aged 6–12 years: Half to 1 level teaspoon in water 1–3 times a day. Not suitable for children under 6 years.
* Available in orange and lemon and lime flavours.

Regulose

Description: A liquid containing lactulose (an osmotic laxative).
Dose: Adults and children over 12 years: 15–30ml daily for first 2–3 days, followed by 10–15ml daily as required. Children under 12 years: 10–25ml daily for first 2–3 days followed by 5–15ml daily as required.

Senokot Tablets*

Description: A tablet containing senna (a stimulant laxative).
Dose: 2 tablets at bedtime. Not suitable for children under 12 years.
* Also available as a syrup or as granules.

COMPLEMENTARY PRODUCTS

HERBAL REMEDIES

❀ Clairo Tea

Description: A herbal tea to relieve constipation. Contains senna, a stimulant laxative, aniseed, clove and peppermint.
Dose: Adults: 2.5ml dissolved in boiling water at night. Children over 6 years: Half adult dose taken in the morning. Not suitable for children under 6 years.

❀ Dual-lax*

Description: Tablet herbal remedy to relieve constipation. Contains senna and aloes, stimulant laxatives.
Dose: Adults: 1–2 tablets at night. Children aged 7–14 years: 1 tablet at night. Not suitable for children under 7 years.
* Extra strength version available.

❀ Gladlax

Description: Tablet herbal remedy to relieve constipation. Contains senna and aloes, stimulant laxatives.
Dose: Adults: 1–2 tablets at night. Children aged 7–14 years: 1 tablet at night. Not suitable for children under 7 years.

❀ Herbulax

Description: Tablet herbal remedy to relieve constipation. Contains dandelion and frangula.
Dose: Adults: 1–2 tablets at bedtime. Children aged 5–12 years: Half to 1 tablet at bedtime. Not suitable for children under 5 years.

❀ Lusty's Herbalene

Description: A herbal mixture to relieve constipation. Contains elder, fennel, frangula and senna.
Dose: 2.5–5ml twice a day. Place herb dose on tongue and swallow with water. Not suitable for children under 7 years.

❀ Pilewort Compound

Description: Tablet herbal remedy to relieve constipation, especially when aggravated by piles. Contains cascara, cranesbill, pilewort and senna.
Dose: 1–2 tablets at night. Not suitable for children under 12 years.

❀ Potter's Cleansing Herb

Description: A herbal tablet remedy for occasional or non-persistent constipation. Contains aloes, fennel, holly thistle and valerian.
Dose: 1–2 tablets at bedtime, as required. Do not take during the day as valerian has sedative effect. Not suitable for children under 12 years.

❀ Potter's Cleansing Herb Tablets

Description: A tablet herbal remedy for constipation. Contains aloes, cascara, dandelion, fennel and senna.
Dose: 1–2 tablets at bedtime. Not suitable for children.

❀ Potter's Lion Cleansing Herb Tablets

Description: Tablet herbal remedy to relieve constipation. Contains aloes, cascara, dandelion and fennel.
Dose: 1–2 tablets at bedtime. Not suitable for children.

❀ Potter's Out of Sorts Tablets

Description: Tablet herbal remedy to relieve constipation. Contains aloes, cascara, dandelion, fennel and senna.
Dose: 1–2 tablets at bedtime. Not suitable for children.

❀ Rhuaka Herbal Syrup

Description: A herbal syrup to relieve constipation. Contains cascara, rhubarb and senna.
Dose: Adults: 20ml at bedtime. Children over 7 years: 5ml at bedtime. Not suitable for children under 7 years.

HOMOEOPATHIC REMEDIES

❀ Calcarea carbonica

Description: A homoeopathic remedy to relieve constipation. Contains senna and aloes, stimulant laxatives.
Dose (and manufacturers): Nelsons 6c, Weleda 6c and 30c. Not suitable for children under 7 years.

❀ Causticum

Description: A homoeopathic remedy to relieve constipation when there is ineffectual urging.
Dose (and manufacturer): Weleda 6c.

❀ Graphites

Description: A homoeopathic remedy to relieve constipation.
Dose (and manufacturers): Weleda 6c and 30c, Nelsons 6c.

❀ Ignatia

Description: A homoeopathic remedy to relieve constipation.
Dose (and manufacturers): Weleda 6c and 30c, Nelsons 6c.

❀ Natrum muriaticum

Description: A homoeopathic remedy to relieve constipation.
Dose (and manufacturers): Weleda 6c and 30c, Nelsons 6c, New Era 6x, Ainsworths 30c.

❀ Nux vomica

Description: A homoeopathic remedy to relieve constipation when there is ineffectual urging.
Dose (and manufacturers): Weleda 6c and 30c, Nelsons 6c, Ainsworths 30c.

❀ Silica

Description: A homoeopathic remedy for constipation.
Dose (and manufacturers): Weleda 6c and 30c, Nelsons 6c, New Era 6x, Ainsworths 30c.

DIARRHOEA

The best way to treat diarrhoea is to replace lost water and salts and this can be achieved by oral rehydration therapy. This is particularly important in children and the elderly who can become dehydrated very quickly. There are several over-the-counter oral rehydration products in the form of either sachets or soluble tablets. These contain a mixture of salts and sugar, which when dissolved in water makes an oral rehydration solution. Be careful to follow the directions for making up the solution very precisely.

Other over-the-counter remedies for diarrhoea are best reserved for occasions when diarrhoea is socially inconvenient and if you use one of them, you should still pay attention to fluid and salt replacement. Two basic types of ingredients are included in these remedies. The first type includes codeine, loperamide and morphine. These ingredients work by slowing down the speed at which the stools pass through the intestine. This allows more time for water to be removed from the stools and gives them a firmer consistency. The second type includes kaolin, charcoal and attapulgite, ingredients which work by taking away the toxins produced by bacteria in the intestine. Other ingredients, such as belladonna, may also be found in these products. Belladonna works by slowing down the activity of the intestine, so allowing more time for water to be removed from the stools.

This section contains a list of products for diarrhoea with their main ingredients and how to use them. For specific uses, cautions and warnings, read the product label. For children, check age ranges and doses very carefully. If your child is younger than the age range stated, do not give the product without the advice of a pharmacist or GP.

WARNING NOTE

• If, after the initial phase of the illness, you are vomiting or the diarrhoea fails to improve after 48 hours, you should consult your doctor.

• For severe or repeated bouts of diarrhoea, you will need to replace lost tissue salts in the body. This can easily be achieved by using an oral rehydration product. These products are also listed within this section.

Arret

Description: A capsule containing loperamide.
Dose: 2 capsules followed by 1 at each loose stool movement. Maximum 8 capsules in 24 hours. Not suitable for children under 12 years.

Diasorb

Description: A capsule containing loperamide.
Dose: 2 capsules followed by 1 tablet at each loose stool movement. Maximum 8 capsules in 24 hours. Not suitable for children under 12 years.

Diocalm Dual Action

Description: A tablet containing morphine and attapulgite.
Dose: 2 tablets every 2–4 hours as required. Maximum 12 tablets in 24 hours. Children aged 6–12 years: 1 tablet every 2–4 hours, as required. Maximum of 6 tablets in 24 hours. Not suitable for children under 6 years.

Diocalm Replenish

Description: A powder oral rehydration formula to replace lost water and salts.
Dose: Adults: 1–2 sachets dissolved in measured quantity of water (as per instructions) at start of diarrhoea, repeated after each bowel movement. Children aged 6–12 years: 1 sachet dissolved in water at start of diarrhoea, repeated after each bowel movement. Children under 6 years: 1 sachet after each bowel movement. Maximum 9 sachets in 24 hours. Bottle-fed infants: Use equivalent volume as substitute for bottle feed, gradually reintroducing milk after 24 hours. Consult a pharmacist or GP before giving to babies under 12 months.

Diocalm Ultra

Description: A capsule containing loperamide.
Dose: 2 capsules at start of diarrhoea and 1 capsule at each loose bowel movement. Maximum 8 capsules in 24 hours. Not suitable for children under 12 years.

Dioralyte Natural*

Description: A powder oral rehydration formula to replace lost water and salts.
Dose: Adults: 1–2 sachets dissolved in a measured quantity of water after each loose bowel movement. Children: 1 sachet. Bottle-fed infants should be given a diluted solution instead of feed. See packet for guidelines for feeding infants. Consult a pharmacist or GP before giving to babies under 12 months.
* Also available in blackcurrant and citrus flavours, and in tablet form.

Dioralyte Relief

Description: A powder oral rehydration formula to replace lost water and salts.
Dose: 1 sachet dissolved in a measured quantity of water. Maximum of 5 sachets a day for 3–4 days following a loose bowel motion. Consult a pharmacist or GP before giving to babies under 12 months.

Electrolade*

Description: A rehydration powder to replace lost water, minerals and salts.
Dose: Adults: 1–2 sachets dissolved in a measured quantity of water after every loose bowel motion. Up to 16 sachets in 24 hours. Children: 1 sachet. Maximum 12 sachets in 24 hours. Consult a pharmacist or GP before giving to children under 2 years.
* Available in range of flavours.

Enterosan Tablets

Description: A tablet containing kaolin, morphine and belladonna.
Dose: 4 tablets at onset of diarrhoea followed by 2 tablets every 3–4 hours. Not suitable for children under 12 years.

Entrotabs

Description: A tablet containing kaolin.
Dose: Adults: 4 tablets at onset of diarrhoea followed by 2 tablets every 3–4 hours. Children aged 6–12 years: 1 tablet every 4 hours. Not suitable for children under 6 years.

Imodium Capsules*

Description: A capsule containing loperamide.
Dose: 2 capsules at onset of diarrhoea and 1 capsule after each loose bowel motion. Maximum of 8 capsules every 24 hours. Not suitable for children under 12 years.
* Also available in tablet and liquid forms.

Isogel

Description: Granules containing ispaghula (a bulking agent). Also used to treat constipation.
Dose: Adults: 10ml 3 times a day, dissolved in a measured quantity of water. Children aged 6–12 years: 5ml 3 times a day. Not suitable for children under 6 years.

J Collis Browne's Mixture*

Description: A liquid containing morphine.
Dose: Adults: 10–15ml every 4 hours. Children aged 6–12 years: 5ml every 4 hours. Not suitable for children under 6 years.
* Also available in tablet form.

⚞ Junior Kao-C

Description: A liquid containing kaolin.
Dose: Children: 5–20ml, depending on age, 3 times a day. Read label for specific ages and doses. Not suitable for babies under 12 months.

⚞ KLN

Description: A liquid containing kaolin.
Dose: Children: 5–10ml, depending on age, after each bowel movement for a maximum of 24 hours. Read label for specific ages and doses. Not suitable for babies under 6 months.

Opazimes

Description: A tablet containing kaolin, morphine and belladonna.
Dose: Adults: Chew or suck 2 tablets every 4 hours. Maximum 8 tablets in 24 hours. Children over 6 years: Chew or suck 1 tablet every 4 hours. Maximum 4 tablets in 24 hours. Not suitable for children under 6 years.

Rehidrat

Description: An oral rehydration powder to replace water and salts.
Dose: Dissolve 1 sachet in a measured quantity of fluid and drink after each loose bowel movement. Breast-fed babies should be given dissolved fluid instead of usual feed, if advised by GP. Do not give to infants unless advised by GP.

COMPLEMENTARY PRODUCTS

HERBAL REMEDIES

✿ Cranesbill

Description: A tablet herbal astringent treatment for relief of non-persistent diarrhoea. Contains cranesbill.
Dose: 1–2 tablets as required, up to 3 times a day. Children over 12 years: 1 tablet twice a day. Not suitable for children under 12 years.

✿ Melissa compound

Description: A liquid herbal remedy to relive occasional diarrhoea. Contains alcohol, archangelica, cinnamon, clove, coriander, lemon, lemon balm and nutmeg.
Dose: 10–20 drops in a little water, as required, up to 8 times a day. Children over 8 years: 5–10 drops up to 8 times a day. Not suitable for children under 8 years. Do not combine with other homoeopathic remedies without seeking advice first.

✿ Potter's Spanish Tummy Mixture

Description: A herbal astringent mixture to relieve non-persistent diarrhoea. Contains blackberry root and catechu.
Dose: 5ml every hour, as required. Not suitable for children.

HOMOEOPATHIC REMEDIES

✿ Argentium nitricum

Description: A homoeopathic remedy for nervous diarrhoea.
Dose (and manufacturers): Weleda 6c and 30c, Nelsons 6c, Ainsworths 30c.

✿ Arsenicum album

Description: A homoeopathic remedy for sudden diarrhoea with vomiting.
Dose (and manufacturers): Weleda 6c and 30c, Nelsons 6c, Ainsworths 30c.

❋ Colocynthis

Description: A homoeopathic remedy for diarrhoea, especially with abdominal cramps and spasms.
Dose (and manufacturer): Weleda 6c.

❋ Mercurius solubilis

Description: A homoeopathic remedy for diarrhoea with straining.
Dose (and manufacturers): Weleda 6c and 30c, Nelsons 6c, Ainsworths 30c.

❋ Natrum sulphuricum

Description: A homoeopathic remedy for yellow diarrhoea.
Dose (and manufacturer): New Era 6x.

❋ Sulphur

Description: A homoeopathic remedy for early morning diarrhoea.
Dose (and manufacturers): Nelsons 6c, New Era 6c and 30c, Ainsworths 30c.

INDIGESTION, HEARTBURN AND GASTRITIS

Over-the-counter products for these three ailments are available as tablets, powders and liquids. Liquids often work quicker than tablets, but tablets are obviously easier to carry around and sometimes have a longer lasting effect.

Products basically fall into three main categories – antacids, alginates and histamine H2 antagonists. The most commonly used ingredients are the antacids. Antacid products are usually a mixture of aluminium and magnesium salts, calcium carbonate or sodium bicarbonate. They all work by neutralising the acid in the stomach. Magnesium salts tend to have a laxative effect while aluminium salts can have a constipating effect, so the two are often put together in one product to cancel out these effects. Other ingredients in antacid products include bismuth and dimethicone. Bismuth acts by coating the wall of the stomach, so helping to prevent damage by the stomach acid. Dimethicone is an antiflatulent and helps to release trapped gas in the stomach and so aid belching.

Alginates which are found in several products, often in combination with antacids, work by forming a layer or raft on the top of the stomach contents and form a barrier between the acid in the stomach and the oesophagus (food pipe). Alginates are particularly useful when the symptoms are caused by reflux - that is when the stomach acid moves up into the oesophagus.

Histamine H2 antagonists (e.g. cimetidine, famotidine and ranitidine) work by reducing the production of stomach acid. These are quite powerful products and they work for longer than antacids. There is little to choose between the different H2 antagonists.

Domperidone, a drug which helps to speed up the action of the stomach and intestine in passing food through the gut, can be used for relief of stomach discomfort, such as fullness, nausea, bloating, belching and heartburn which can be experienced after eating.

This section contains a list of products for indigestion, heartburn and related symptoms with their main ingredients and how to use them. For specific uses, cautions and warnings, read the product label. For children, check age ranges and doses very carefully. If your child is younger than the age range stated, do not give the product without the advice of a pharmacist or GP. Few of the remedies are suitable for children because of the nature of the symptoms being treated. Children with indigestion are best taken to the GP.

WARNING NOTE

- If you are pregnant you may be particularly prone to indigestion and heartburn. However, do not use any of these products, including complementary products, without consulting your pharmacist or GP.

- Do not take any of these products for longer than 2 weeks without consulting your pharmacist or GP. This is because symptoms of indigestion, though common, may sometimes be caused by more serious disease.

- Products containing sodium should not be used if you are pregnant, breast-feeding, on a low-sodium diet (for example, if you have heart, liver or kidney disease), or if you have high blood pressure or any heart condition.

- Antacid products may interfere with the absorption of some prescribed drugs such as antibiotics, iron and digoxin. If you are taking any other medication, ask your pharmacist or GP before taking such products.

- Histamine H2 antagonists interact with a number of prescription medicines. They are not suitable if you are pregnant or breast-feeding. It is particularly important to consult your pharmacist or GP before taking these medicines.

- Domperidone should not be taken by children under 16 years nor by pregnant and breast-feeding women. Do not take it if you have any underlying gastrointestinal illness, prolactinoma or liver or kidney problems. Always consult your pharmacist or GP before using this product.

Actal

Description: A tablet containing an antacid.
Dose: 1–2 tablets, as required. Maximum 16 tablets in 24 hours. Not suitable for children under 12 years.

Algicon*

Description: A tablet containing antacids and an alginate. Tablets have a high sugar content. Check with a pharmacist or GP first if you are diabetic.
Dose: 1–2 tablets 4 times a day after meals and at night. Not suitable for children under 12 years.
* Also available in liquid form.

Altacite

Description: A tablet containing an antacid.
Dose: 2 tablets between meals and at bedtime. Children aged 6–12 years: Half adult dose. Not suitable for children under 6 years.

Altacite Plus*

Description: A tablet containing an antacid and dimethicone (an antiflatulent).
Dose: Adults: 2 tablets between meals and at bedtime. Children aged 8–12 years: 1 tablet between meals and at bedtime. Not suitable for children under 8 years.
* Also available as a liquid.

Aludrox*

Description: A tablet containing an antacid.
Dose: Adults: 1–2 tablets 4 times a day and at bedtime. Children aged 6–12 years: 1 tablet 2–3 times a day. Not suitable for children under 6 years.
* Also available as a liquid.

Andrews Antacid*

Description: A tablet containing antacids.
Dose: 1–2 tablets as required. Maximum 12 tablets in 24 hours. Not suitable for children under 12 years. Check with a pharmacist or GP first if taking prescription medication.
* Also available in fruit flavours.

Andrews Original Salts

Description: A powder containing an antacid. Contains sodium.
Dose: Adults: 1 teaspoonful or 1 sachet in water. Maximum 4 doses in 24 hours. Children over 3 years: Half adult dose. Not suitable for children under 3 years.

Asilone Antacid Liquid*

Description: A liquid containing antacids and dimethicone (an antiflatulent).
Dose: 5–10ml after meals and at bedtime or as required. Maximum 40ml in 24 hours. Not suitable for children under 12 years.
* Also available in tablet and suspension form.

Asilone Antacid Tablets*

Description: A tablet containing an antacid.
Dose: 1–2 tablets before meals and at bedtime. Not suitable for children under 12 years.
* Also available in liquid and suspension form.

Birley's Antacid Powder

Description: A powder containing an antacid.
Dose: Adults: 5ml in water after each meal or twice a day. Children: Doses vary, according to age. Check label.

Bismag

Description: A tablet containing an antacid.
Dose: 2–4 tablets after meals. Repeat after 15 minutes if required and at bedtime. Not suitable for children under 12 years.

Bisodol Antacid Powder*

Description: A powder containing an antacid. Contains sodium.
Dose: 5ml of powder diluted with water after meals. Not suitable for children.
* Also available as tablets (2 strengths) and mint flavour.

Carbellon

Description: A tablet containing an antacid.
Dose: Adults: 2–4 tablets 3 times a day. Children over 6 years: 2 tablets 3 times a day. Not suitable for children under 6 years.

Bisodol Heartburn

Description: A tablet containing an antacid. Contains sodium.
Dose: Adults: 1–2 tablets chewed as required. Children aged 6–12 years: 1 tablet after meals and at bedtime. Not suitable for children under 6 years.

De Witt's Antacid Powder*

Description: A powder containing an antacid. Contains sodium.
Dose: 1 teaspoon in water after meals. Not suitable for children under 12 years.
* Also available in tablet form.

Dijex*

Description: A liquid containing an antacid.
Dose: Adults: 5–10ml 4 times a day and at bedtime. Children over 6 years: 5ml 3 times a day. Not suitable for children under 6 years.
* Also available as tablets.

Eno*

Description: A powder containing an antacid. Contains sodium.
Dose: 1 sachet or teaspoon dissolved in water every 2–3 hours as required. Maximum 6 doses in 24 hours. Not suitable for children under 12 years.
* Also available in lemon flavour.

Gastrocote Liquid*

Description: A liquid containing an antacid and an alginate. Contains sodium.
Dose: 5–15ml 4 times a day after meals and at night. Not suitable for children under 6 years.
* Also available as tablets.

Gaviscon 250*

Description: A tablet containing an antacid and alginate. Contains sodium.
Dose: 2 tablets to be chewed as required. Not suitable for children under 12 years.
* Also available in extra strength formula (Gaviscon 500) and liquid formula and as Gaviscon Advance.

Kolanticon

Description: A liquid gel containing an antacid and an antispasmodic.
Dose: 10–20ml every 4 hours. Not suitable for children under 12 years.

Maalox Suspension

Description: A liquid containing an antacid.
Dose: 10–20ml 4 times a day taken 20–60 minutes after meals and just before bedtime, as required. Not suitable for children under 12 years.

Maalox Plus Suspension*

Description: A liquid containing an antacid and simethicone (an antiflatulent).
Dose: 5–10ml 4 times a day taken after meals and just before bedtime, as required. Not suitable for children under 12 years.
* Also available as tablets.

Maclean

Description: A tablet containing an antacid.
Dose: 1–2 tablets sucked or chewed, as required. Maximum 16 tablets in 24 hours. Not suitable for children under 12 years.

Milk of Magnesia*

Description: A liquid containing an antacid.
Dose: Adults: 5–10ml as required. Maximum 60ml in 24 hours. Children aged 3–12 years: Half adult dose. Not suitable for children under 3 years.
* Also available in tablet form.

Moorland

Description: A tablet containing an antacid.
Dose: 2 tablets dissolved in the mouth after meals and at bedtime, as required. Not suitable for children under 6 years.

Motilium 10

Description: A tablet containing domperidone (an ingredient to speed up stomach emptying).
Dose: 1 tablet 3 times a day and at night, as required. Not suitable for children under 16 years.

Nulacin Tablets

Description: A tablet containing an antacid.
Dose: 1 tablet sucked slowly as required. Maximum 8 tablets in 24 hours. Not suitable for children under 12 years.

Opas

Description: A tablet containing an antacid. Contains sodium.
Dose: 1–2 tablets after each meal, as required. Not suitable for children under 12 years.

Pepcid AC

Description: A tablet containing famotidine (a histamine H2 antagonist).
Dose: 1 tablet 1 hour before eating. Maximum 2 tablets in 24 hours. Not suitable for children under 16 years. Do not take for more than 2 weeks.

Pepto-Bismol

Description: A liquid containing bismuth (an ingredient to coat the stomach lining).
Dose: Adults: 30ml every 30 minutes to 1 hour. Children aged 10–14 years: 20ml every 30 minutes to 1 hour. Children aged 6–10 years: 10ml every 30 minutes–1 hour. Children aged 3–6 years: Up to 8 doses in 24 hours. Not suitable for children under 3 years.

Rap-eze

Description: A tablet containing an antacid.
Dose: 2 tablets chewed or sucked as required. Maximum 16 tablets in 24 hours. Not suitable for children under 12 years.

Remegel Original*

Description: A square tablet containing an antacid.
Dose: 1–2 squares to be chewed every hour. Maximum 12 squares in 24 hours. Not suitable for children under 12 years.
*Also available in freshmint and alpine mint with lemon flavours.

Rennie*

Description: A tablet containing an antacid.
Dose: Adults: 2 tablets sucked or chewed as necessary. Maximum 16 tablets in 24 hours. Children aged 6–12 years: 1 tablet, as necessary. Maximum 8 tablets in 24 hours. Not suitable for children under 6 years.
*Also available in aniseed, spearmint and peppermint flavours. Rennie Deflatine also available.

Setlers Antacid Tablets*

Description: A tablet containing an antacid.
Dose: 1–2 tablets sucked or chewed, as required. Maximum 8 tablets in 24 hours. Not suitable for children under 12 years.
* Also available in peppermint, spearmint and fruit flavours. Also available as Setlers Wind-Eze.

Tagamet 100*

Description: A tablet containing cimetidine (a histamine H2 antagonist).
Dose: 2 tablets as symptoms appear. For night-time heartburn, take 1 tablet an hour before bedtime. Maximum 8 tablets in 24 hours. Not suitable for children under 16 years. Do not use for longer than 2 weeks.
* Also available in liquid form.

Topal

Description: A tablet containing an antacid and an alginate.
Dose: 1–3 tablets 4 times a day after meals and at bedtime. Not suitable for children under 12 years.

Tums

Description: A tablet containing an antacid.
Dose: 1–2 tablets, as required. Maximum 16 tablets in 24 hours. Not suitable for children under 12 years.

Unigest

Description: A tablet containing an antacid.
Dose: 1–2 tablets sucked or chewed after meals and at bedtime. Not suitable for children under 12 years.

Zantac 75 Tablets

Description: A tablet containing ranitidine (a histamine H2 antagonist).
Dose: 1 tablet. Repeat if necessary. Maximum 4 tablets in 24 hours. Not suitable for children under 16 years. Do not use for more than 2 weeks.

COMPLEMENTARY PRODUCTS

HERBAL REMEDIES

✿ Bio-Strath Artichoke Formula

Description: A liquid herbal remedy to relieve indigestion after eating fatty foods. Contains artichoke, peppermint, thistle and yeast.
Dose: 20 drops in water 3 times a day before meals. Not suitable for children. Do not combine with other homoeopathic remedies.

❀ Bio-Strath Liquorice formula

Description: A liquid herbal remedy to aid digestion. Contains camomile, gentian, liquorice and yeast.
Dose: 20ml in water 3 times a day. Not suitable for children.

❀ Biobalm Powder

Description: A powder herbal remedy to treat indigestion. Contains camomile, Irish moss, marshmallow and slippery elm.
Dose: 1–2 level teaspoons mixed in fluid up to 4 times a day. Children aged 5–12 years: Half adult dose. Not suitable for children under 5 years.

❀ Digest

Description: A tablet herbal remedy to relieve indigestion and wind. Contains centaury, marshmallow root and parsley.
Dose: 2 tablets 3 times a day before meals. Not suitable for children under 12 years.

❀ Indian Brandee

Description: A liquid for digestive discomfort. Contains capsicum, ginger and rhubarb.
Dose: 5ml in or with water. Repeat 1–2 times, as required. Not suitable for children.

❀ Natraleze

Description: A tablet herbal remedy to treat heartburn, indigestion and wind. Contains liquorice, meadow sweet and slippery elm.
Dose: 2.5–15ml 3 times a day, according to age. Read label. Not suitable for children under 7 years.

❀ New Era Combination C

Description: A homoeopathic remedy for heartburn and indigestion. Contains mag phos, nat phos, nat sulph and silica.
Dose: 1 dose combining 6x each of above ingredients.

❀ Papaya Plus

Description: A tablet herbal remedy to treat heartburn, indigestion and excess wind. Contains charcoal, golden seal, papain and slippery elm.
Dose: 1 tablet before meals 3 times a day. Not suitable for children.

❀ Potter's Indigestion mixture

Description: A liquid herbal remedy to treat heartburn, indigestion and wind. Contains gentian, meadowsweet and wahoo.
Dose: 5ml 3–4 times a day after meals. Not suitable for children.

❀ Potter's Slippery Elm Tablets

Description: A tablet herbal remedy to treat heartburn, indigestion and wind. Contains cinnamon, clove, peppermint and slippery elm.
Dose: 5ml 3–4 times a day after meals. Not suitable for children.

HOMOEOPATHIC REMEDIES

❀ Argentum nitricum

Description: A homoeopathic remedy for heartburn.
Dose (and manufacturers): Weleda 6c and 30c, Nelsons 6c, Ainsworths 30c.

❀ Carbo vegetabilis

Description: A homoeopathic remedy for indigestion with flatulence.
Dose (and manufacturers): Weleda 6c and 30c, Nelsons 6c, Ainsworths 30c.

❀ Kalium muriaticum

Description: A homoeopathic remedy for indigestion caused by fatty foods.
Dose (and manufacturer): New Era 6x.

❀ Natrum phosphoricum

Description: A homoeopathic remedy as an aid to digestion.
Dose (and manufacturer): New Era 6x.

❀ New Era Combination E

Description: A homoeopathic remedy for indigestion. A combination of calc phos, mag phos, nat phos and nat sulph.
Dose: 1 dose of 6x each of the above ingredients.

IRRITABLE BOWEL SYNDROME (IBS)

Over-the-counter treatments for irritable bowel contain ingredients which are thought to help relax the muscle in the intestine. These ingredients include alverine, mebeverine and peppermint oil.

Products containing bulking agents such as ispaghula (see Constipation, page 149) may also be helpful. Bulking agents can help to 'normalise' the consistency of your stools, so they could be helpful if your IBS symptoms include constipation or diarrhoea or both. If you use a bulking agent, take it with a full glass of fluid.

Irritable bowel syndrome is such a variable condition that it is impossible to say which of these ingredients works better than any other. However, before trying any of them, you should get a proper diagnosis of IBS from your GP.

This section contains a list of products for irritable bowel syndrome with their main ingredients and how to use them. For specific uses, cautions and warnings, read the product label. For children, check age ranges and doses very carefully. If your child is younger than the age range stated, do not give the product without the advice of a pharmacist or GP.

WARNING NOTE

- If you suspect irritable bowel syndrome you should get an accurate diagnosis from your GP. Do not use any of the remedies listed below, including the complementary products, without first checking with your GP or pharmacist.

- Do not use any of the following remedies if there is obstruction of the bowel. Pregnant and breast-feeding women should consult their pharmacist or GP before using any of the products listed, including complementary products. Consult your doctor before using any of these remedies if you have abdominal pain or vomiting, change in bowel habits or bleeding from the anus. If you have pain on defecation a bulk forming laxative such as ispaghula may be helpful.

Colofac IBS

Description: A tablet containing mebeverine (an ingredient to help intestinal spasm).
Dose: 1 tablet 3 times a day, preferably 20 minutes before meals. Not suitable for children under 10 years.

Colpermin

Description: A capsule containing peppermint oil (an ingredient to help intestinal spasm).
Dose: 1–2 capsules 3 times a day for up to 2 weeks. Swallow whole to prevent irritation of the oesophagus and throat. Not suitable for children under 15 years.

Equilon

Description: A tablet containing mebeverine (an ingredient to help intestinal spasm).
Dose: 1 tablet up to 3 times a day, preferably 20 minutes before meals. Not suitable for children under 10 years.

Fybogel

Description: Granules containing ispaghula (a bulking agent).
See entry in Constipation, page 151.

Isogel

Description: Granules containing ispaghula (a bulking agent).
See entry in Constipation, page 151.

Mintec

Description: A capsule containing peppermint oil (an ingredient to help intestinal spasm).
Dose: 1 capsule 3 times a day before meals. Swallow whole to prevent irritation of the oesophagus and throat. Not suitable for children under 12 years.

Regulan Lemon and Lime

Description: A powder containing ispaghula husk (a bulking agent).
See entry in Constipation, page 152.

Relaxyl

Description: A capsule containing alverine (an ingredient to help intestinal spasm).
Dose: 1–2 capsules up to 3 times a day. Not suitable for children under 12 years.

COMPLEMENTARY REMEDIES

Not advised without specialist herbalist or homoeopathic advice.

NAUSEA

Very few over-the-counter remedies specifically treat nausea. Consult your pharmacist or GP if symptoms persist.

COMPLEMENTARY PRODUCTS

Although you should always discuss persistent or reccuring nausea with your pharmacist or GP, you may find that the complementary remedies help some of the symptoms associated with this condition. Below you will find a list of remedies which you may wish to consider, but do not use them as an alternative to taking the advice of your doctor if symptoms persist.

HERBAL TREATMENT

❀ Ginger Tablets

Description: A tablet herbal remedy to calm nauseous sensations. Contains ginger.
Dose: 1 tablet 3 times a day. Not suitable for children.

❀ Golden Seal Compound

Description: A tablet herbal remedy to soothe and relieve nausea. Contains cranes-bill, dandelion, golden seal and marshmallow root.
Dose: 2 tablets 3 times a day between meals. Not suitable for children under 12 years.

HOMOEOPATHIC REMEDIES

❀ Ipecacuanha

Description: A homoeopathic remedy for nausea.
Dose (and manufacturers): Weleda 6c and 30c, Nelsons 6c.

TRAVEL SICKNESS

Most of the products for the prevention and treatment of travel sickness contain antihistamines, such as cinnarazine, dimenhydrinate, meclozine, promethazine. All of these antihistamines can cause drowsiness. Promethazine can also cause the skin to be sensitive to sunlight, and this may be a problem if you are travelling in a hot country.

The other main ingredient used in these products is hyoscine. This tends to work quickly, but the effect may not last as long as that of the antihistamines. Side effects are not usually a problem, but there is a possibility of drowsiness, blurred vision, dry mouth and difficulty in passing urine.

This section contains a list of products for the prevention and treatment of travel sickness with their main ingredients and how to use them. For specific uses, cautions and warnings, read the product label. For children, check age ranges and doses very carefully. If your child is younger than the age range stated, do not give the product without the advice of a pharmacist or GP.

WARNING NOTE

• Do not take any of these products, including complementary products, if you are pregnant, breast-feeding, taking other medicines or if you suffer from any medical condition without consulting a pharmacist or GP.

Antihistamines

- Remedies containing antihistamines may cause drowsiness.

- Do not combine with other sedative drugs, such as antidepressants and sleeping tablets; or with alcohol, as this will increase the drowsiness. Do not drive or operate machinery if the remedy makes you drowsy.

- Do not use in pregnancy or if you have prostate enlargement, urinary retention, liver disease or glaucoma.

Hyoscine

- Products containing hyoscine should not be taken by those with glaucoma, kidney and urinary problems, high blood pressure and heart conditions.

Avomine

Description: A tablet containing promethazine (an antihistamine).
Dose: For prevention of travel sickness: Adults and children over 10 years: 1 tablet the night before a long journey or 2 hours before a short journey. Children aged 5–10 years: Half adult dose. Treatment: Adults and children over 10 years: 1 tablet as soon as possible each evening for 2 days. Children aged 5–10 years: Half adult dose. Not suitable for children under 5 years.

Dramamine

Description: A tablet containing an antihistamine.
Dose: Adults: 1–2 tablets 2–3 times a day. First dose should be taken 30 minutes before journey. Children: Quarter to 1 tablet, according to age. Check label. Not suitable for babies under 12 months.

Joy-Rides

Description: A tablet containing hyoscine (an anti-spasmodic ingredient).
Dose: Adults: 2 tablets 20 minutes before journey or at onset of nausea. Repeat dose after 6 hours, if required. Children over 3 years: Half to 2 tablets, according to age. Read label. Maximum of 2 doses in 24 hours. Not suitable for children under 3 years.

Kwells*

Description: A tablet containing hyoscine (an anti-spasmodic ingredient).
Dose: Adults: 1 tablet every 6 hours. Maximum 3 tablets in 24 hours. Children over 10 years: Half adult dose. Not suitable for children under 10 years.
* Also available in children's version (suitable for children over 3 years).

Phenergan*

Description: A tablet containing promethazine (an antihistamine). Available in two strengths (10mg and 25mg).
Dose: Adults and children over 10 years: 1–2 10mg tablets or 1 25mg tablet the night before journey. Repeat dose after 6–8 hours if necessary. Children aged 5–10 years: 1 10mg tablet the night before journey. Repeat after 6–8 hours if necessary. The 25mg tablets are not suitable for children under 10 years (use 10mg strength for children aged 5–10 years). For children aged 2–5 years, use liquid version.
* Also available in liquid form (not suitable for children under 2 years).

Sea-Legs

Description: A tablet containing meclozine (an antihistamine).
Dose: Adults: 2 tablets taken 1 hour before journey or the previous evening. Children over 2 years: Half to 1 tablet, according to age. Read label. Not suitable for children under 2 years.

Sturgeron Tablets

Description: A tablet containing cinnarazine (an antihistamine).
Dose: Adults: 2 tablets 2 hours before the journey, followed by 1 tablet every 8 hours, if required. Children aged 5–12 years: Half adult dose. Not suitable for children under 5 years.

COMPLEMENTARY PRODUCTS

HERBAL REMEDIES

✤ Catassium Herbal Travel Sickness Tablets

Description: A tablet herbal remedy to relieve travel sickness. Contains ginger.
Dose: Adults: 3 tablets 30 minutes before the journey. Children aged 6–12 years: 1–2 tablets. Not suitable for children under 6 years.

HOMOEOPATHIC REMEDIES

✤ Cocculus

Description: A homoeopathic remedy for travel sickness and jetlag.
Dose (and manufacturers): Weleda 6c, Ainsworths 30c.

✤ Ipecacuanha

Description: A homoeopathic remedy for travel sickness.
Dose (and manufacturers): Weleda 6c and 30c, Nelsons 6c.

❀ Nelsons Travella

Description: A tablet homoeopathic remedy for travel sickness.
Dose: Adults: 2 tablets every hour for 2 hours before journey, followed by 2 tablets every hour during the journey. Children: Half adult dose.

WORMS (THREADWORMS, PINWORMS AND ROUNDWORMS)

Over-the-counter remedies for worms contain either mebendazole or piperazine. These ingredients kill worms in the intestine. Look at the instructions very carefully because the dosage can be quite complicated with some products, for example, needing to be taken every day for 7 days while others should be taken as a one-off dose and repeated after 14 days. This is important for ensuring that the worms are killed.

This section contains a list of products for the treatment of worms with their main ingredients and how to use them. For specific uses, cautions and warnings, read the product label. For children, check age ranges and doses very carefully. If your child is younger than the age range stated, do not give the product without the advice of a pharmacist or GP.

WARNING NOTE

• All family members should be treated at the same time.

• Pregnant and breast-feeding women and those on prescription medication or with any medical condition should consult a pharmacist or GP before using.

De Witt's Worm Syrup

Description: A liquid containing piperazine citrate, an anti-worm ingredient.
Dose: Threadworms: Adults: 15ml daily for 7 days. Children: 5–10ml, according to age. Roundworms: Adults: 3 ml (single dose only). Children: 10–25ml, according to age (single dose only). Not suitable for children under 2 years.

Ovex Tablets

Description: A tablet containing mebendazole, an anti-worm ingredient.
Dose: Threadworms: 1 tablet (single dose only). This can be repeated after 2 weeks if infestation is still present. Not suitable for children under 2 years.

Pripsen Mebendazole Tablets

Description: A tablet containing mebendazole, an anti-worm ingredient.
Dose: Threadworms: 1 tablet (single dose only). This can be repeated after 2 weeks if infestation if still present. Not suitable for children under 2 years.

Pripsen Piperazine Citrate Elixir

Description: A liquid containing piperazine citrate, an anti-worm ingredient.
Dose: Threadworms: Adults: 15ml daily for 7 days. Repeat after 7 days if required. Children: 5–10ml, according to age. Children must be treated for 7 days and re-treated for a further 7 days after a 7-day gap.
Roundworms: Adults: 30ml (single dose only). Repeat after 14 days. Children: 10–25ml, according to age (single dose only). Repeat after 14 days. Not suitable for babies under 12 months, unless advised by GP.

Pripsen Piperazine Phosphate Powder

Description: A powder containing piperazine phosphate, an anti-worm ingredient.
Dose: Threadworms and roundworms: Adults and children over 6 years: 1 sachet dissolved in a measured quantity of milk at bedtime (children should take in the morning). Children aged 12 months–6 years: 5ml of sachet's contents in the morning. For threadworms, follow-up dose should be taken 14 days after first dose. For roundworms, additional doses may be taken monthly for up to 3 months to avoid re-infestation. Not suitable for babies aged 3–12 months unless advised by GP.

COMPLEMENTARY PRODUCTS

Not advised.

WOMEN'S PROBLEMS

• Cystitis • Menstrual Problems • Premenstrual Tension
• Menopausal Problems • Vaginal Thrush

CYSTITIS

Over-the-counter remedies for cystitis usually contain sodium or potassium salts. These substances help cystitis by reducing the acidity of the urine. It is the acidity of the urine which causes the symptoms of stinging and burning which you experience during cystitis. Reducing the acidity thus often helps.

This section contains a list of over-the-counter products for cystitis, their main ingredients and how to use them.

WARNING NOTE

• These products are intended for adult women only. Men with symptoms of cystitis should consult a pharmacist or GP.

• Consult your GP if symptoms do not improve after 2 days, or if you feel generally unwell or have a fever or back pain.

• Do not use these products if you are pregnant or breast-feeding.

• Many of these products have a high sodium content. Do not use them if you have heart or kidney disease, high blood pressure or if you are on a low-sodium diet.

• If you are **diabetic**, you should check with your pharmacist or GP before using any of these products.

All these cautions also apply to complementary products.

Cymalon

Description: Granules in sachets containing sodium citrate and sodium bicarbonate.
Dose: 1 sachet of granules dissolved in water 3 times a day for 2 days.

Cystoleve

Description: Granules in sachets containing sodium citrate.
Dose: 1 sachet of granules dissolved in water 3 times a day for 2 days.

Cystopurin

Description: Granules in sachets containing potassium citrate.
Dose: 1 sachet of granules dissolved in water 3 times a day for 2 days.

Effercitrate Tablets

Description: An effervescent tablet containing citric acid and potassium citrate.
Dose: 2 tablets dissolved in water up to 3 times a day after meals.

Effercitrate Sachets

Description: Powder in sachets containing citric acid and potassium bicarbonate.
Dose: 1 sachet dissolved in water 3 times a day after meals.

COMPLEMENTARY PRODUCTS

HERBAL REMEDIES

✤ Potter's Antitis

Description: A tablet herbal remedy to relieve symptoms of cystitis.
Dose: 2 tablets 3 times a day for a maximum of 10 days. Increase fluid intake while taking remedy.

HOMOEOPATHIC REMEDIES
See Homoeopathic Treatment for Women's Problems, page 180.

MENSTRUAL PROBLEMS

See also **General Pain Relief,** page 78.

Three remedies are included in this section and the uses for each are identified because they are somewhat different. Two of the products (Buscopan and Feminax) are basically for period pain, and both contain an antispasmodic for helping stomach cramps. These two products are best avoided if you suffer from glaucoma or if you are pregnant. Feminax also contains paracetamol and the normal cautions and warnings apply to that (see page 79). Aspirin and Ibuprofen (see pages 78 and 79) are also effective in the relief of period pains.

Aqua-Ban

Description: A tablet for premenstrual water retention containing a mild diuretic and caffeine.
Dose: 2 tablets 3 times a day for 4–5 days before period is due. Do not take for more than 5 days in 1 month.

Buscopan Tablets

Description: A tablet for period pain containing an antispasmodic.
Dose: 2 tablets 4 times a day.

Feminax

Description: A tablet for period pain containing an anti-spasmodic, paracetamol, codeine and caffeine.
Dose: 1–2 tablets every 4 hours. Maximum 6 tablets in 24 hours.

COMPLEMENTARY PRODUCTS

HERBAL REMEDIES

✿ Cascade

Description: A tablet herbal remedy to relieve premenstrual water retention. Has a diuretic action. Contains clivers, burdock root and uva ursi.
Dose: 2 tablets 3 times a day before meals.

✿ Heath & Heather Water Relief

Description: A tablet herbal remedy to relieve premenstrual water retention. Has a diuretic action. Contains bladderwrack, burdock root, clivers and ground ivy.
Dose: 1–2 tablets up to 3 times a day for up to 7 days before period is expected.

✿ Potter's Prementaid

Description: A tablet herbal remedy to relieve premenstrual bloating and abdominal discomfort. Contains a diuretic and antispasmodic. Has a mild, sedative effect. Contains motherwort, uva ursi, wild anemone, valerian and vervain.
Dose: 2 tablets 3 times a day when symptoms begin prior to period. Do not use with other sedative medications or alcohol.

✿ Potter's Raspberry Leaf

Description: A tablet herbal remedy to relieve painful menstrual cramps. Has a toning and relaxing effect. Contains raspberry leaf.
Dose: 2 tablets 3 times a day after meals.

HOMOEOPATHIC REMEDIES
See Homoeopathic Treatment for Women's Problems, page 180.

HOMOEOPATHIC TREATMENT FOR WOMEN'S PROBLEMS

Homoeopaths prescribe remedies based on the combination of emotional and physical symptoms. The following remedies are advised for the wide variety of symptoms that may be experienced. Many manufacturers produce homoeopathic remedies and most pharmacies and health food shops will stock them. Always ask your pharmacist or health food shop staff for advice if you are at all confused or concerned.

Do not combine the remedies unless advised to do so by a trained homoeopath or pharmacist.

PREMENSTRUAL TENSION

Apis mellifica	For fluid retention with swollen breasts.
Calcarea carbonica	If feeling tired, with cramping pains during period and if breasts are swollen and painful.
Natrum muriaticum	For mood changes, made worse during a period.
Nux vomica	If feeling argumentative, but feel better for letting feelings show.
Pulsatilla	If feeling emotionally sensitive and wanting to cry. Also for bloating.
Sepia	For exhaustion during a period, which may be late or light.

MENSTRUAL PROBLEMS

Actaea racemosa	If period is heavy, painful and with cramping pains.
Belladonna	If there are cramping pains before period starts.
Pulsatilla	If period is painful, late and scanty. Also if there is abdominal pain, back pain and breast tenderness.
Sepia	For irregular menstrual flow accompanied by back pain.

continues

MENOPAUSAL PROBLEMS	
Belladonna	For hot, throbbing flushes that are sudden in onset and accompanied by headache.
Graphites	If feeling weepy and if usually cold but experiencing hot flushes that come on suddenly.
Sepia	For hot flushes, variable or light periods and mood changes.
CYSTITIS	
Apis mellifica	If there is frequent urge to urinate but little urine is passed. Also if there is a stinging, burning pain.
Belladonna	If there is cystitis with high temperature and sometimes a headache.
Cantharis	If there is a frequent urge to urinate and if there is pain when urinating.
Nux vomica	If there is bladder irritation and an urge to urinate but unable to.
Sepia	If there is a frequent urge to urinate and pain when urinating.

PREMENSTRUAL TENSION

See also Menstrual Problems, page 178, Anxiety and Stress, page 270.

Treatment of premenstrual tension is varied, depending on the underlying causes of the symptoms. Many symptoms can be managed individually but if PMT disrupts your life, you should see your GP for advice and treatment.

COMPLEMENTARY PRODUCTS

Although you should seek medical advice for the treatment of severe PMT, you may find that the complimentary remedies listed in the box on page 180 may help treat some of the symptoms associated with this condition. However, the remedies should not be used as an alternative to taking medical advice of your doctor. Many women find supplements of evening primrose oil help reduce their symptoms.
See page 305 for evening primrose oil products.

MENOPAUSAL PROBLEMS

See also Depression, page 264, Anxiety and Stress, page 270, and Insomnia, page 267.

The following over-the-counter products will help overcome vaginal dryness during sexual intercourse, a very common symptom experienced during and after the menopause. As the menopause has many symptoms, several of them emotional, they can be treated individually. For severe menopausal symptoms that disrupt your life, you should seek the advice of your GP.

KY Jelly*

Description: A lubricating gel to combat vaginal dryness during intercourse.
Dose: Apply a little gel to the vagina.
* Also available as pessaries.

Replens

Description: A gel for post-menopausal women to provide lubrication and ease itchiness and irritation of the vagina.
Dose: Insert 1 dose using applicator into the vagina 3 times a week.

COMPLEMENTARY PRODUCTS

HERBAL REMEDIES

❀ Athera

Description: A traditional tablet herbal remedy for the relief of minor conditions associated with the menopause, such as water retention and constipation. Has a mild tonic effect. Contains vervain, senna leaf, clivers and parsley root.
Dose: 2–3 tablets 3 times a day after meals. Not to be used by pregnant and breast-feeding women.

❀ Potter's Wellwoman

Description: A tablet herbal remedy to promote wellbeing in middle-aged women in perimenopause and menopause. Contains lime flowers, motherwort, scullcap, valerian and yarrow. Has a mild sedative effect.
Dose: 2 tablets 3 times a day. Do not use with other sedative medications. Not suitable for pregnant women.

HOMOEOPATHIC REMEDIES

See Homoeopathic Treatment for Women's Problems, page 180.

THRUSH (VAGINAL)

Most over-the-counter products for vaginal thrush contain drugs known as anti-fungals. These drugs help to stop the growth of the yeast-like organism, Candida albicans – the organism that causes thrush – when it grows out of control. Several antifungals are used to treat thrush and there is little to choose between them. Products are available in the form of creams for external use, vaginal creams and pessaries, and a capsule which is taken by mouth is now also available. Creams for external use need to be used for up to 7 days, while all the other products – for internal use – are usually one dose only. There is little to choose between the internal products, and a pharmacist will advise on which is the most appropriate product for you. External creams are not effective for curing thrush, but are useful if there is itching and irritation in the area around the vagina. Some over-the-counter packs therefore contain both a pessary and a tube of cream.

It can also be useful to treat your partner to prevent reinfection. If an attack of thrush does not clear up after a course of treatment, you should see your doctor for a proper examination and investigation.

TREATING VAGINAL THRUSH

Patients with vaginal thrush should not self-treat if:

- They are a first-time sufferer.
- They have had more than 2 attacks in the last 6 months.
- They are less than 16 years of age or over 60 years of age.
- They have a history of sexually transmitted diseases.
- They experience pain when passing urine.
- They have blood-stained vaginal discharge or irregular bleeding.
- They have abdominal pain, fever, chills, diarrhoea or sickness.
- They are pregnant or breast feeding.

WARNING NOTE

- Treatments for thrush taken by mouth interact with a number of other medicines. If you are taking any other medication, check with a pharmacist or GP.

- Creams and pessaries for thrush may affect rubber contraceptives, such as condoms and diaphragms and reduce the effectiveness of the contraceptive.

Canesten 1 Pessary

Description: A pessary containing clotrimazole 500mg (an antifungal drug). Applicator included in pack.
Dose: Insert the pessary into the vagina at night. This is a single-dose treatment.

Canesten 10% VC Vaginal Cream

Description: A cream containing 10% clotrimazole (an antifungal drug). Applicator included in pack.
Dose: One application of cream into the vagina at night.

Canesten Combi

Description: A cream containing 1% clotrimazole (an antifungal drug) and 1 pessary containing clotrimazole 500mg. Applicator included in pack.
Dose: 1 pessary inserted into the vagina at night. Cream applied twice daily to external area around vagina. Cream also to be applied to the partner's penis.

Diflucan

Description: An oral capsule containing fluconazole 150mg.
Dose: 1 capsule taken orally. This is a single-dose treatment.

Femeron

Description: A cream containing 2% miconazole nitrate.
Dose: Apply to external vaginal area morning and evening.

Femeron Soft Pessary

Description: Pessary containing miconazole nitrate 1200mg.
Dose: 1 pessary inserted into the vagina at night. This is a single-dose treatment.

COMPLEMENTARY PRODUCTS

Not suitable for treatment.

SKIN PROBLEMS

• Abcesses and Boils • Acne and Spots • Athlete's Foot • Bites, Stings and Hives • Bruises • Burns • Corns and Calluses • Cuts and Wounds • Dandruff • Dermatitis and Eczema • Hangnails and Splinters • Lice Infestations • Scars • Sunburn • Warts and Verrucae

WARNING NOTE

• If, when using any of the remedies listed here, you experience an unpleasant sensation or adverse reaction in the texture, colour or appearance of the skin, discontinue using the product and seek advice from a pharmacist or GP.

• When using a remedy, take care to apply it only to the affected area. Do not apply to healthy skin.

• Many of the products listed here contain salicylates, a substance related to aspirin. These should be used with care by those sensitive to aspirin. Asthmatics should avoid these products, unless advised by their GP.

• Those suffering from **diabetes or circulatory problems** should not use foot products or remedies without first checking with their GP.

See also warnings at the beginning of each section.

ABCESSES AND BOILS

See also **Antiseptics**, page 93.

Skin abscesses require medical treatment, but you can support healing by cleaning oozing abscesses with a mild antiseptic and using the following complementary remedies.

Boils may respond to over-the-counter remedies. You can also keep infection from spreading by bathing with a mild antiseptic. However, if you see no improvement to the boil you should see your GP for treatment. If several boils develop in a cluster (carbuncles) do not self-treat. See your GP for treatment.

WARNING NOTE

• Always check first with your GP or pharmacist to ensure that any prescription medication you may be given does not interact adversely with the following homoeopathic remedies.

Magnesium sulphate paste BP

(A non-branded product available from pharmacies.)

Description: A paste used to 'draw out' boils. Contains magnesium sulphate, phenol and glycerol.

Dose: Stir paste and then apply to boil and cover with a clean, dry dressing.

Secaderm

Description: A salve to treat boils and other minor skin infections. Contains an antiseptic and an analgesic.

Dose: Apply to boil 1–2 times a day and cover with a clean, dry dressing.

COMPLEMENTARY PRODUCTS

HERBAL REMEDIES

❀ Weleda Balsamicum Ointment

Description: An ointment herbal remedy to assist in the healing of boils and minor wounds. Contains balsam of Peru, dog's mercury, marigold, metallicum preparatum and stibium.

Dose: Apply to the affected area or apply to a dry dressing and position over boil or wound. Repeat application or dressing several times a day. May cause allergy. Discontinue use if skin reacts.

HOMOEOPATHIC REMEDIES

❀ Calcarea sulphurica

Description: A homoeopathic remedy for helping to heal abscesses after they have begun to emit a discharge.

Dose (and manufacturer): New Era 6x.

❀ Mercurius solubilis

Description: A homoeopathic remedy for abscesses and boils.

Dose (and manufacturers): Weleda 6c and 30c, Nelsons 6c, New Era 6x, Ainsworths 30c.

❀ Silica

Description: A homoeopathic remedy for abscesses and boils.

Dose (and manufacturers): Weleda 6c and 30c, Nelsons 6c, New Era 6x, Ainsworths 30c.

ACNE AND SPOTS

A wide variety of treatments for acne and spots, including creams, gels, ointments, soaps, lotions and face washes, is available over the counter. Over-the-counter treatments contain two main types of ingredients – keratolytics and anti-microbials. All treatment for acne is slow acting, and patience and perseverance are required.

Keratolytics are basically abrasive in nature. They work by opening up blocked skin follicles which allows the sebum (the skin's natural moisturiser) to flow freely. These ingredients are also mild anti-microbials which may contribute to their action. Examples of these ingredients include benzoyl peroxide, resorcinol, salicylic acid and sulphur. Products containing benzoyl peroxide are particularly effective in acne, but they may cause skin irritation and redness or bleach dyed fabrics. It is generally best to start treatment with the lowest available strength. A pharmacist will advise you on this. In addition, they should be used only at night for the first week or so until you are sure that you are not going to experience reddening of the skin. Applying the product at night should at least ensure that any reddening you do experience will have gone down by the following morning.

Ingredients used as anti-microbials include cetrimide, chlorhexidine, povidone iodine and triclosan. A variety of astringent face washes and lotions contain these ingredients and they are thought to help in acne by removing excess sebum from the skin and reducing the number of bacteria on the skin.

A new treatment, nicotinamide, is now also available for acne. Nicotinamide is claimed to help acne by reducing inflammation, but, like benzoyl peroxide, it may cause skin irritation.

This section contains a list of products for acne and/or spots, with their main ingredients and instructions for use. However, there are many more products available for minor spots which are not included here. For specific uses, cautions and warnings for each product, read the product label and leaflet inside the package. This also applies to all complementary products.

WARNING NOTE

- Some of these products may cause skin irritation and redness. Avoid contant with eyes, mouth and lining of the nose, and stop using if irritation occurs.

- Products containing povidone iodine should not be used by pregnant and breast-feeding women, those with thyroid disorders or who are taking lithium drugs.

- Products containing nicotinamide should not be used during pregnancy and breast-feeding without consulting a pharmacist

Acne-Aid

Description: A cleansing bar for acne and greasy skin.
Dose: Use instead of soap. Not suitable for children under 15 years.

Acnidazil

Description: A cream containing benzoyl peroxide and miconazole (an anti-microbial).
Dose: Wash and dry area and apply cream once a day for first week. In second week apply twice a day for the next 4–8 weeks. Not suitable for children under 15 years.

Betadine Skin Cleanser

Description: A liquid facial wash containing povidone iodine (an anti-microbial).
Dose: Apply with a wet sponge, lather and leave on for 3–5 minutes. Rinse with warm water and dry. Apply twice a day. Not suitable for children under 2 years. See also warning for povidone iodine.

Betacept Acne Wash

Description: A liquid face wash containing povidone iodine (an anti-microbial).
Dose: Use twice a day until symptoms clear. Not suitable for children under 15 years. See also warning for povidone iodine.

Brasivol

Description: An abrasive paste. Available in two grades.
Dose: Wet area and rub in paste vigorously. Repeat 1–3 times a day. Use finer grade first, progressing to stronger grade, if necessary. Not suitable for children under 15 years.

Cepton*

Description: A wash containing chlorhexidine (an anti-microbial).
Dose: Apply wash to clean skin and leave for 1 minute, then wash off thoroughly. Not suitable for children under 15 years.
* Also available as a lotion.

Clearasil Max 10

Description: A cream containing benzoyl peroxide.
Dose: Apply once a day for 1 week. After 1 week, if there is no skin irritation, increase applications to twice a day. Not suitable for children under 12 years.

Clearasil Treatment Cream (Regular)

Description: A cream containing triclosan (an anti-microbial) and sulphur.
Dose: Apply twice a day to clean skin. Not suitable for children under 15 years.

Eskamel Cream

Description: A cream containing resorcinol and sulphur.
Dose: Apply once a day. Not suitable for children under 15 years.

Ionax

Description: A facial scrub containing abrasive and antibacterial ingredients.
Dose: Wet face, rub gel in for 1–2 minutes, then rinse. Use 1–2 times a day. Not suitable for children under 12 years.

Nericur

Description: A gel containing benzoyl peroxide (two strengths available).
Dose: Wash and dry affected area, then apply gel once a day. Use lower dose version first, progressing to stronger version if required. Not suitable for children under 15 years.

Oxy 5*

Description: A lotion containing benzoyl peroxide.
Dose: Apply once a day for 1 week. If no irritation occurs, apply twice a day. Use lower dose version first, progressing to stronger version if required. Not suitable for children under 15 years.
*Also available in double-strength as Oxy 10.

Panoxyl Acnegel

Description: A gel containing benzoyl peroxide (two strengths available).
Dose: Apply to clean skin once a day. Use lower dose version first, progressing to stronger version if required. Not suitable for children under 15 years.

Panoxyl Aquagel

Description: A gel containing benzoyl peroxide (three strengths available).
Dose: Apply to clean skin once a day. Use lower dose version first, progressing to stronger versions if required. Not suitable for children under 15 years.

Panoxyl 5 Cream

Description: A cream containing benzoyl peroxide.
Dose: Apply to clean skin once a day. Not suitable for children under 15 years.

Panoxyl Lotion

Description: A lotion containing benzoyl peroxide (two strengths available).
Dose: Apply to clean skin once a day. Use lower dose version first, progressing to stronger version if required. Not suitable for children under 15 years.

Panoxyl Wash

Description: A lotion containing benzoyl peroxide.
Dose: Wet the skin and apply the lotion. Rinse alternately with warm and cold water and then pat dry. Use once a day in the morning. Not suitable for children under 15 years.

Papulex

Description: A gel containing nicotinamide (an anti-inflammatory).
Dose: Apply twice a day after washing. Reduce to once every other day if skin adversely reacts. Not suitable for children under 15 years.

Quinoderm Cream*

Description: An cream containing benzoyl peroxide (two strengths available).
Dose: Massage into the affected area 1–3 times a day. Use lower dose version first, progressing to stronger version if required. Not suitable for children under 15 years.
* Also available as a lotion, gel and antibacterial face wash.

Torbetol

Description: A lotion containing cetrimide and chlorhexidine (anti-microbials).
Dose: Apply to the affected area up to 3 times a day. Not suitable for children under 15 years.

COMPLEMENTARY PRODUCTS

HERBAL REMEDIES

❀ Potter's Skin Clear Ointment

Description: An astringent and mild antiseptic ointment to ease the symptoms of mild acne and eczema. Contains sulphur, tea tree oil and zinc oxide.
Dose: Apply twice a day. Not suitable for children under 5 years.

❋ Potter's Skin Clear Tablets

Description: A tablet herbal remedy to relieve and help prevent minor skin blemishes and acne. Contains echinacea.
Dose: 2 tablets 3 times a day. Not suitable for children or for pregnant and breastfeeding women.

HOMOEOPATHIC REMEDIES

❋ Belladonna

Description: A homoeopathic remedy for acne.
Dose (and manufacturers): Weleda 6c and 30c, Nelsons 6c, Ainsworths 30c.

❋ Calcarea phosphorica

Description: A homoeopathic remedy for acne.
Dose (and manufacturers): Weleda 6c and 30c, Nelsons 6c, New Era 6x.

❋ Calcarea sulphurica

Description: A homoeopathic remedy for acne.
Dose (and manufacturer): New Era 6x.

❋ Sulphur

Description: A homoeopathic remedy for acne.
Dose (and manufacturers): Weleda 6c and 30c, Nelsons 6c, Ainsworths 30c.

ATHLETE'S FOOT

Products for athlete's foot are available in the form of creams, ointments, sprays and powders. Powders are useful for dusting into socks, tights and shoes and they can be used in addition to a cream or ointment or on their own to help prevent athlete's foot from reoccurring. Good foot hygiene is vital and you should always wash and dry your feet before applying any of these products. Always apply them well beyond the area of the foot which is infected, and use them regularly and for the recommended time of treatment on the product package. Do not stop using the product just because the infection looks better. Treatment should be continued for two weeks after the symptoms have disappeared to make sure that the problem has been completely cured.

Athlete's foot products usually contain an antifungal such as clotrimazole, miconazole, tolnaftate or undecenoic acid. This is because athlete's foot is a fungal infection. Other ingredients include anti-microbials as well as benzoyl peroxide (see page 187) and salicylic acid. The last two each have an abrasive action, which helps the skin to shed.

This section contains a list of products for athlete's foot, with their main ingredients and instructions for use. For specific uses, cautions and warnings for each product, read the product label and leaflet inside the package. This also applies to all complementary products.

WARNING NOTE

• All these products are suitable for use by all children except the very young, who do not usually suffer from athlete's foot. If you suspect athlete's foot in a very young child, see your GP for diagnosis and treatment.

Canesten AF Cream

Description: A cream containing clotrimazole (an antifungal).
Dose: Apply thinly 2–3 times a day, rubbing in gently. Use for 4 weeks.

Canesten AF Powder

Description: A powder containing clotrimazole (an antifungal).
Dose: Sprinkle powder onto affected part 2–3 times a day. Also dust inside of footwear and socks each day. Use for 4 weeks.

Canesten Hydrocortisone

Description: A cream containing clotrimazole (an antifungal) and a steroid.
Dose: Apply thinly to affected area and rub in gently. Do not use for more than 7 days.

Canesten AF Spray

Description: A spray containing clotrimazole (an antifungal).
Dose: Wash and dry feet, especially between toes, and then spray thinly over affected area 2–3 times a day for at least 1 month.

Daktarin Dual Action Cream

Description: A cream containing miconazole (an antifungal).
Dose: Apply cream to area twice a day. Continue treatment for a further 10 days after infection has cleared.

Daktarin Dual Action Powder*

Description: A powder in spray form containing miconazole (an antifungal).
Dose: Apply to the affected area twice a day. Continue treatment for a further 10 days after infection has cleared.
*Also available in spray form.

Ecostatin

Description: A cream containing econazole (an antifungal).
Dose: Apply to affected area twice a day.

Healthy Feet

Description: A cream containing undecylenic acid (an antifungal).
Dose: Apply to affected area as required.

Masnoderm

Description: A cream containing clotrimazole (an antifungal).
Dose: Apply to affected area twice a day for 4 weeks.

Monphytol Paint

Description: A liquid treatment containing a mixture of antifungals.
Dose: Apply liquid to affected area twice a day. Repeat treatment each day until infection has cleared.

Mycil Athlete's Foot Spray

Description: A powder spray containing tolnaftate (an antifungal).
Dose: Use in morning and evening until symptoms disappear and then continue treatment for a further 7 days.

Mycil Gold Clotrimazole

Description: A cream containing clotrimazole (an antifungal).
Dose: Apply thinly to clean, dry feet 2–3 times a day for up to 1 month.

Mycil Ointment

Description: An ointment containing tolnaftate (an antifungal).
Dose: Apply to affected area morning and evening. Continue treatment for a further 7 days after infection has cleared.

Mycil Powder

Description: A powder containing tolnaftate (an antifungal).
Dose: Sprinkle over affected area morning and evening. Continue treatment for a further 7 days after infection cleared.

Mycota Cream

Description: A cream containing undecenoic acid (an antifungal).
Dose: Apply to clean and dry skin. Continue treatment for a further 7 days after infection has cleared.

Mycota Powder*

Description: A powder containing undecenoic acid and zinc undecenoate (antifungals).
Dose: Sprinkle over affected area morning and evening. Continue treatment for a further 7 days after infection has cleared.
* Also available as a spray.

Pervaryl*

Description: A cream containing econazole (an antifungal).
Dose: Apply twice a day.
* Also available as a lotion and a powder.

Quinoped Cream

Description: A cream containing benzoyl peroxide.
Dose: Massage cream into affected area twice a day.

Scholl Athlete's Foot Cream*

Description: A cream containing tolnaftate (an antifungal).
Dose: Apply to affected area twice a day. Continue treatment for a further 2 weeks after infection has disappeared.
* Also available as a powder and a foot spray.

Tinaderm Cream

Description: A cream containing tolnaftate (an antifungal).
Dose: Apply morning and evening to affected area.

Tinaderm Powder Plus*

Description: A powder containing tolnaftate (an antifungal).
Dose: Sprinkle over affected area twice a day. Also sprinkle into socks and footwear.
* Also available as a spray.

Toepedo

Description: A cream containing keratolytics (see page 187).
Dose: Apply sparingly to affected area twice daily. Continue treatment until infection has cleared.

Trosyl Dermal Cream

Description: A cream containing tioconazole (an antifungal).
Dose: Apply to the affected area 1–2 times a day.

COMPLEMENTARY PRODUCTS

HERBAL REMEDIES

✽ Nelsons candida

Description: A homoeopathic tablet remedy for athlete's foot. Contains Candida albicans 6c.
Dose: Adults: 2 tablets every hour for 6 doses. Then reduce dose to 2 tablets 3 times a day. Children: Half adult dose.

HOMOEOPATHIC REMEDIES

✽ Silica

Description: A homoeopathic remedy for athlete's foot.
Dose (and manufacturers): Weleda 6c and 30c, Nelsons 6c, New Era 6x, Ainsworths 30c.

BITES, STINGS AND HIVES

See also **Antiseptics**, page 93, and **General Pain Relief**, page 78.

The main ingredients in products for bites, stings and hives are antihistamines. This is because the main ingredient in insect stings is histamine. Antihistamines therefore help to reduce the pain, itching and inflammation associated with bites and stings. In addition to the products in this section, antihistamines taken by mouth in tablet and liquid form can be helpful (see Hayfever, page 135).

Other ingredients included in these products are local anaesthetics to help numb the pain and also astringents such as witch hazel. One product contains a steroid. It is possible to experience a skin reaction when using any of these products and you should stop using them immediately if this occurs. In addition, they are not generally appropriate for use on broken skin.

This section contains a list of products for bites, stings and hives with their main ingredients and instructions for use. Many of these products are also suitable for other allergic skin reactions. For specific uses, cautions and warnings, read the product labels and the information leaflets inside the package. This also applies to all complementary products.

WARNING NOTE

- It is possible to experience an acute allergic reaction (an anaphylactic shock) after being bitten by insects. This is characterised by swelling of the lips and tongue, difficulty in breathing, tightness in the chest and collapse. If this is the case, urgent medical attention is required from the accident and emergency department of the nearest hospital.

- Any of these products may cause skin rash. If this occurs, stop using the product.

- These products are not generally suitable for use on broken skin.

- Many of these products are not suitable for children under 3 years (check labels).

- For cautions and warnings for steroids, see page 211.

After Bite

Description: A pen containing ammonia.
Dose: Apply as required. Not suitable for children under 2 years.

Aller-eze Cream

See entry in Hayfever, page 137.

Anethaine

Description: A cream containing a mild anaesthetic.
Dose: Apply 2–3 times a day. Not suitable for children under 3 years.

Anthisan Cream

Description: A cream containing an antihistamine.
Dose: Apply cream to affected area 2–3 times a day for up to 3 days. Not suitable for children under 3 years.

Anthisan Plus Sting Relief Spray

Description: A metered–dose spray containing an antihistamine and a mild anaesthetic.
Dose: Press the nozzle head to deliver a single dose: do this 2–3 times to the affected part. Use 2–3 times a day for up to 3 days. Not suitable for children under 3 years.

Caladryl Cream*

Description: A cream containing an antihistamine.
Dose: Apply cream to affected area 2–3 times a day.
* Also available as a lotion.

Dayleve

See entry in Dermatitis and Eczema, page 211.

Dermacort

See entry in Dermatitis and Eczema, page 211.

Dermidex Cream

Description: A cream containing an anaesthetic and antiseptic.
Dose: Apply every 3 hours. Not suitable for children under 4 years.

Eurax Cream (and Lotion)

See entry in Dermatitis and Eczema, page 213.

Eurax HC Cream

See entry in Dermatitis and Eczema, page 213.

HC45 Hydrocortisone Cream

See entry in Dermatitis and Eczema, page 213.

Jungle Formula Bite and Sting Relief Cream

Description: A cream containing a steroid.
Dose: Apply sparingly to affected area 1–2 times a day. Do not use for more than 7 days. Not suitable for children under 10 years.

Lanacane Creme

Description: A cream containing a local anaesthetic.
Dose: Apply to affected area 3 times a day.

Lanacort Creme (and Ointment)

See entry in Dermatitis and Eczema, page 214.

Solarcaine Cream*

Description: A cream containing a mild anaesthetic.
Dose: Apply to the affected area 3–4 times a day. Not suitable for children under 3 years.
* Also available as a lotion and spray.

Stingose

Description: A pump spray containing aluminium sulphate (a soothing ingredient).
Dose: Apply liberally to the affected area. Respray as required. Not suitable for children under 3 years.

Swarm

Description: A cream containing witch hazel and an anti-microbial.
Dose: Apply to the affected area as required.

Wasp-Eze Ointment*

Description: An ointment containing an antihistamine.
Dose: Apply to affected area immediately. Repeat every hour as necessary for up to 24 hours. Not suitable for babies under 12 months.
* Also available as a spray.

Witch Doctor Gel*

Description: An astringent gel containing witch hazel.
Dose: Apply to the affected area as required.
* Also available in stick form.

COMPLEMENTARY PRODUCTS

HERBAL REMEDIES

❈ Nelsons Pyrethrum*

Description: A liquid herbal remedy for insect bites and stings, and hives. Contains arnica, calendula, echinacea, hypericum, ledum palustre, pyrethrum and rumex crispus.
Dose: Apply to affected area as soon as possible after sting or bite occurs.
* Also available as a spray.

HOMOEOPATHIC REMEDIES

❈ Apis mellifica

Description: A homoeopathic remedy for burning and stinging pains, and bites and stings that are red and swollen. Made from honey bee venom.
Dose (and manufacturers): Weleda 6c and 30c, Nelsons 6c, Ainsworths 30c.

❈ Ledum

Description: A homoeopathic remedy for insect bites, bee stings and puncture wounds.
Dose (and manufacturers): Weleda 6c, Ainsworths 30c.

BRUISES

The following remedies are for minor bruises only. Bruising over large areas of the body require medical investigation, as such widespread injury may also involve other injuries such as broken bones and internal damage. Most minor bruises will subside, given time. Most preparations for bruises contain heparinoid, an ingredient that helps to resolve bruising.

This section contains a list of products suitable for bruises with their main ingredients and instructions for use. For specific uses, cautions and warnings, read the product label and information leaflet inside the package. This also applies to all complementary remedies.

WARNING NOTE

• These products should not be used on broken or sensitive skin.

• Discontinue using the product if you experience an allergic reaction.

• These products should not be used during pregnancy without checking with a pharmacist.

Hirudoid Cream*

Description: A cream containing heparinoid (an ingredient that helps to resolve bruising).
Dose: Apply to bruise up to 4 times a day. Not suitable for children under 5 years.
* Also available as a gel.

Lasonil

Description: An ointment containing heparinoid (an ingredient that helps to resolve bruising).
Dose: Apply to affected area 2–3 times a day.

Witch Doctor Gel

See entry in Bites, Stings and Hives, page 198.

COMPLEMENTARY PRODUCTS

HERBAL REMEDIES

❀ Nelsons Arnica Cream

Description: A cream herbal remedy to treat bruises. Contains arnica.
Dose: Apply to bruise as required.

❀ Potter's Comfrey Ointment

See entry in Joints and Muscles, page 237.

❀ Weleda Arnica Ointment

See entry in Joints and Muscles, page 238.

HOMOEOPATHIC REMEDIES

❀ Arnica

Description: A homoeopathic remedy for bruising.
Dose (and manufacturers): Weleda 6c and 30c, Nelsons 6c, Ainsworths 30c.

❀ Hamamelis

Description: A homoeopathic remedy for sore bruising.
Dose (and manufacturers): Weleda 6c and 30c, Nelsons 6c.

❀ Phosphorus

Description: A homoeopathic remedy for those who tend to bruise easily.
Dose (and manufacturers): Weleda 6c and 30c, Nelsons 6c, Ainsworths 30c.

BURNS AND SCALDS

See also **General Pain Relief**, page 78, and **Antiseptics**, page 93.

Products for minor burns and scalds mainly contain antiseptics, which help to heal the burn and reduce the risk of it becoming infected. After cleaning, protect the burn from damage or infection with a suitable dressing.

This section contains a list of products suitable for minor burns and scalds with their main ingredients and instructions for use. However, most of these products can also be used for basic first aid in cuts and grazes, and many of the antiseptics (see page 93) could also be used for burns and scalds. For specific uses, cautions and warnings read the product labels and the information leaflets inside the package. This also applies to all complementary remedies.

WARNING NOTE

- Only provide self-treatment for minor, simple and small burns or scalds. **Always** seek emergency medical treatment for burns or scalds that are serious, that affect large areas of skin or that affect important areas such as the eyes.

- Minor burns or scalds that do not respond to self-treatment should be seen by your GP.

- Products containing povidone iodine should not be used by those who are pregnant, breast-feeding, have thyroid problems or are taking lithium without first checking with a pharmacist or GP.

Acriflex Cream

Description: A cream containing chlorhexidine (an antiseptic).
Dose: Smooth onto the affected area. Repeat after 15 minutes, if required.

Betadine Spray

Description: A dry powder spray containing povidone iodine (an anti-microbial).
Dose: Spray onto the affected area 1–2 times a day, as required. Cover with a clean dressing after spraying. Not suitable for children under 2 years.

Burneze

Description: A spray containing benzocaine (an anaesthetic).
Dose: Spray onto the affected area. Repeat after 15 minutes, if required.

Cetavlex

Description: A cream containing cetrimide (an antiseptic).
Dose: Apply to the affected area, as required.

Inadine

Description: A non-stick dressing containing povidone iodine (an anti-microbial).
Dose: Apply to the affected area, as required.

Jelonet

Description: A sterile gauze dressing impregnated with soft paraffin (to prevent dressing fibres from sticking to the burn).
Dose: Apply to the affected area, as required.

Solarcaine Cream (and Lotion and Spray)

See entry in Bites, Stings and Hives, page 198.

Witch Doctor Gel

See entry in Bites, Stings and Hives, page 198.

COMPLEMENTARY PRODUCTS

HERBAL REMEDIES

❀ Nelsons Burns Ointment

Description: An ointment herbal remedy to ease minor burns. Contains calendula, echinacea, hypericum and urtica urens.
Dose: Apply as required to the affected area and cover with a dry dressing.

❀ Weleda Combudoron Lotion*

Description: A lotion herbal remedy to ease minor burns and scalds. Contains arnica and small nettle.
Dose: Add 5ml of lotion to a cup of boiled water that has been left to cool. Moisten a pad and apply as a compress. Keep moist.
* Also available as an ointment.

❀ Weleda WCS Dusting Powder

Description: A powder herbal remedy to treat minor burns. Contains arnica, echinacea, marigold, silica, stibium and metallicum praep.
Dose: Apply the powder to the affected area and cover with a dry dressing. Change dressing twice a day.

HOMOEOPATHIC REMEDIES

❀ Cantharis

Description: A homoeopathic remedy for minor burns after receiving first aid treatment.
Dose (and manufacturers): Weleda 6c and 30c, Nelsons 6c, Ainsworths 30c.

❀ Causticum

Description: A homoeopathic remedy for minor burns after receiving first aid treatment.
Dose (and manufacturer): Weleda 6c.

❀ Sulphur

Description: A homoeopathic remedy for old burns that refuse to heal.
Dose (and manufacturers): New Era 6c and 30c, Nelsons 6c, Ainsworths 30c.

❀ Urtica Urens

Description: A homoeopathic remedy for minor burns without blistering.
Dose (and manufacturer): Weleda 6c.

CORNS AND CALLUSES

Treatments for corns and calluses usually contain salicylic acid. This helps to soften the hard skin so that it can then be removed by gentle scraping. These products should be carefully applied to the corn or callus and not the surrounding healthy skin. This is because salicylic acid can burn.

This section contains a list of products for corns and calluses with their main ingredients and instructions for use. Some of them are also appropriate for the treatment of warts and verrucae (see page 222). For specific uses, cautions and warnings, read the product label and information leaflet inside the package. This also applies to complementary products.

WARNING NOTE

• Those suffering from **diabetes** or who have **circulatory problems** should not use any foot products or remedies without first checking with their GP.

• Many of these remedies contain salicylic acid, a substance related to aspirin. They should be used with care by those sensitive to aspirin, including asthmatics. Check with a pharmacist.

• Take care to apply the remedy only to the corn or callus. Avoid touching healthy skin with the preparation.

Bazuka Gel*

Description: A gel treatment with applicator and emery board containing salicylic acid. The gel dries to form a water-resistant barrier.
Dose: Apply 1–2 drops each night. Rub down once a week with the emery board. Not suitable for children under 6 years.
* Also available as Bazuka Extra Strength.

Carnation Callus Caps

Description: A medicated plaster containing salicylic acid.
Dose: Apply plaster to affected area and change after 3 days. Remove callus after 6 days. Not suitable for children under 16 years.

Carnation Corn Caps

Description: A medicated plaster containing salicylic acid.
Dose: Apply and change every 2 days. Remove corn after 6 days. Not suitable for children under 15 years, unless advised by a GP. Do not use for more than 10 days or use more than 5 caps in that period of time.

Cuplex

Description: A gel containing salicylic acid.
Dose: Apply gel at night to affected part – when dried it provides a protective film. Remove film in morning. May take 6–12 weeks to be effective. Not suitable for young children.

Noxacorn

Description: A liquid containing salicylic acid.
Dose: Apply liquid every night to affected area. Use for 3–6 nights. Not suitable for children under 6 years.

Pickle's Ointment

Description: An ointment containing salicylic acid.
Dose: Apply to area at night for 4 nights. Allow treated skin to fall off before reapplying.

Salactol Wart Paint

Description: A paint containing salicylic acid.
Dose: Apply to affected area daily, followed by rubbing down with an emery board.

Scholl Corn and Callous Removal Liquid

Description: A liquid containing salicylic acid.
Dose: Apply liquid to affected area twice a day. Do not use for more than 2 weeks. Not suitable for children under 16 years.

Scholl Corn Removal Pads*

Description: A medicated pad containing salicylic acid.
Dose: Apply fresh medicated pad to affected area until corn can be removed. Not suitable for children under 16 years.
*Also available as Scholl Soft Corn Removal Pads.

Scholl Corn Removal Plasters*

Description: A medicated plaster containing salicylic acid.
Dose: Apply fresh medicated plaster to affected area until corn can be removed. Not suitable for children under 16 years.
* Waterproof plasters also available.

Scholl Polymer Gel Corn Removers

Description: A gel treatment containing salicylic acid.
Dose: Apply new plaster each day to the affected area until corn can be removed. Not suitable for children under 16 years.

COMPLEMENTARY PRODUCTS

Not suitable for complementary treatment.

CUTS AND WOUNDS (MINOR)

Most minor cuts and wounds can be treated using antiseptics to clean the area and help overcome the potential for infection. After cleaning, cover the cut or wound with either a plaster or dry dressing to protect the area from further damage while it is healing.

More serious or larger cuts and wounds require emergency first aid treatment from your nearest hospital's Accident and Emergency Department.

This section contains a list of products for cuts and wounds with their main ingredients and instructions for use. They are also suitable for treating burns. For specific uses, cautions and warnings, read the product label and information leaflet inside the package. This also applies to complementary products.

WARNING NOTE

• Cuts or wounds that fail to heal within a week or which develop an infection should be seen by your GP.

Acriflex Cream

See entry in Burns, page 201.

Betadine Spray

See entry in Burns, page 201.

Cetavlex

See entry in Burns, page 201.

Germolene New Skin

Description: A liquid that forms a waterproof and germ-proof barrier to protect minor cuts and wounds.
Dose: Apply to cut or wound and allow to dry.

COMPLEMENTARY PRODUCTS

HERBAL REMEDIES

❀ Nelsons Hypercal

Description: A cream and tincture herbal remedy to soothe surface cuts and sores. Contains hypericum and calendula.
Dose: Apply cream to affected skin. Apply tincture neat to minor wounds or dilute with 1 part tincture to 10 parts water for larger wounds. Cover if required.

❀ Weleda Balsamicum Ointment

See entry in Abscesses and Boils, page 186.

❀ Weleda Calendolon Ointment

Description: An ointment herbal remedy that acts as an antiseptic and anti-inflammatory to treat cuts and minor wounds and skin abrasions. Contains marigold.
Dose: Apply to the affected area 2–3 times a day. Cover with a clean dressing, if required. Do not apply to infected wounds. Pregnant women should consult a pharmacist or GP before using.

❋ Weleda Calendula Lotion

Description: A lotion herbal remedy to treat cuts, minor wounds and skin abrasions. Contains marigold.
Dose: Add 5ml of liquid to boiled water and allow to cool. Use to clean wounds or moisten a clean pad and apply as a dressing. Do not apply to infected wounds. Pregnant women should consult a pharmacist or GP before using.

HOMOEOPATHIC REMEDIES

❋ Calcarea sulphurica

Description: A homoeopathic remedy for wounds that are taking a while to heal.
Dose (and manufacturer): New Era 6x.

❋ Hepar sulphuris

Description: A homoeopathic remedy for wounds that ooze.
Dose (and manufacturers): Weleda 6c and 30c, Nelsons 6c, Ainsworths 30c.

❋ Hypericum

Description: A homoeopathic remedy for wounds affecting nerve endings.
Dose (and manufacturers): Weleda 6c and 30c, Nelsons 6c.

❋ Ledum

Description: A homoeopathic remedy for puncture wounds.
Dose (and manufacturers): Weleda 6c, Ainsworths 30c.

DANDRUFF

Dandruff is best treated by regular twice-weekly use of an ordinary dandruff shampoo – and there are a great number on the market. However, the products listed in this section contain additional ingredients which may be helpful if the dandruff does not improve with dandruff shampoos. Ingredients in the products listed below include zinc pyrithione and selenium sulphide, both of which reduce the speed with which the top layer of skin is shed from the scalp. Another ingredient is ketoconazole, an antifungal, which interferes with the production of skin cells on the surface of the scalp and which therefore helps to clear dandruff. Other ingredients include various anti-microbials such as povidone iodine, coal tar and salicylic acid.

WARNING NOTE

• Some of these products can cause irritation of the scalp. Stop using them if this occurs.

- Some of these products contain peanut oil. Check labels very carefully. If you are allergic to peanuts, do not use these products.

- Try to avoid getting these products in your eyes. If this happens, rinse your eyes well.

- If you are pregnant, check with a pharmacist before using any of these products.

- Products containing selenium sulphide should not be used for children under 5 years.

- Products containing selenium sulphide should not be used within 48 hours of using hair colouring or perming products.

- Products containing povidone iodine should not be used by those with thyroid conditions or those taking lithium. They are not suitable for pregnant and breast-feeding women.

Alphosyl Shampoo 2-in-1

Description: A medicated shampoo containing coal tar with a hair conditioner.
Dose: Use as a shampoo every 2–3 days.

Betadine Shampoo

Description: A medicated shampoo containing povidone iodine (an anti-microbial).
Dose: Use as a shampoo twice a week. Adults: 2–3 capfuls. Children aged 2–12 years: 1–2 capfuls. Not suitable for children under 2 years.

Capasal Therapeutic Shampoo

Description: A medicated shampoo containing coal tar, salicylic acid and coconut oil.
Dose: Use as a shampoo when required.

Ceanel Concentrate

Description: A medicated shampoo containing various anti-microbials.
Dose: Use as a shampoo 3 times a week for 1 week, then twice a week as required.

Clinitar

Description: A medicated shampoo containing coal tar.
Dose: Apply up to 3 times a week.

Cocois Scalp Ointment

Description: An ointment containing coal tar.
Dose: Apply to scalp once a week as necessary. For severe conditions, apply daily for 3–7 days. Shampoo after 1 hour. Not suitable for children under 6 years.

Denorex Anti-Dandruff Shampoo*

Description: A medicated shampoo containing coal tar.
Dose: Use as a shampoo on alternate days for 10 days; then use 2–3 times a week, if required.
* Also available as a shampoo with conditioner.

Gelcotar Liquid

Description: A liquid containing coal tar.
Dose: Use as a shampoo twice a week.

Ionil T

Description: A medicated shampoo containing coal tar and an antiseptic.
Dose: Use as a shampoo 1–2 times a week.

Lenium

Description: A medicated shampoo containing selenium sulphide.
Dose: Shampoo twice a week until dandruff clears, then use as required. Not suitable for children under 5 years.

Meted Shampoo

Description: A medicated shampoo containing salicylic acid.
Dose: Use as a shampoo at least twice a week.

Nizoral Dandruff Shampoo

Description: A medicated shampoo containing ketoconazole.
Dose: Use as a shampoo, leave in for 2–3 minutes and then rinse. Use twice a week for 2–4 weeks, reducing to once every 1–2 weeks to prevent dandruff returning.

Pentrax

Description: A medicated shampoo containing coal tar.
Dose: Use as a shampoo at least twice a week.

Polytar AF

Description: A liquid containing zinc pyrithione and coal tar. Also contains peanut oil.
Dose: Massage into hair and scalp and leave for 2–3 minutes before rinsing. Use 2–3 times a week.

Polytar Liquid

Description: A liquid containing coal tar. Also contains peanut oil.
Dose: Wet hair and massage lotion into hair and scalp. Rinse and repeat. Use 1–2 times a week.

Polytar Plus

Description: A liquid containing coal tar and a hair conditioner. Also contains peanut oil.
Dose: Wet hair and massage lotion into hair and scalp. Rinse and repeat. Use 1–2 times a week.

Selsun

Description: A liquid containing selenium sulphide.
Dose: Shampoo twice a week for 2 weeks, then once a week for 2 weeks until dandruff clears. Not suitable for children under 5 years.

T-Gel

Description: A medicated shampoo containing coal tar.
Dose: Wet hair and massage lotion into hair and scalp. Rinse and repeat. Use 1–2 times a week.

COMPLEMENTARY PRODUCTS

HERBAL REMEDIES

❊ Potter's Adiantine

Description: A herbal remedy to treat dandruff and improve hair condition. Contains bay oil, rosemary, southernwood and witch hazel.
Dose: Massage into scalp morning and evening. Not suitable for children.

❀ Potter's Extract of Rosemary

Description: A liquid herbal remedy to improve hair condition. Can be used for mild cases of dandruff. Contains bay oil, rosemary, rosegeranium and methyl sali-cylate.
Dose: Massage into scalp twice a day until symptoms clear. Not suitable for children.

DERMATITIS AND ECZEMA

With dermatitis and eczema the principal problems are excessive dryness of the skin and itching, and so the most useful treatments are emollient (moisturising) oils. These oils are available in the form of creams, ointments, sprays and liquids for the bath. All these products should be used liberally, and it is beneficial to use an oil in the bath and an oil or a cream during the rest of the day, applying it 3 or 4 times a day.

Some of the products in this section contain hydrocortisone, which is a steroid. These products can be used to treat flare-ups of dermatitis and eczema, and they help to reduce the inflammation and itching. They are also suitable for use on insect bites and stings. However, unlike the emollient oils, steroid creams should be used in small amounts and no more than twice a day. In addition, they should be used for no longer than 7 days without checking with your GP. Over-the-counter steroid creams are not licensed by the authorities for use on the eyes and face, so if you have eczema on the face you should ask the advice of your GP.

This section contains a list of products suitable for eczema, dermatitis and similar dry skin conditions. Products containing a steroid are also suitable for insect bites and stings. For specific uses, cautions and warnings, read the product labels and the leaflets inside the package. This also applies to all complementary remedies.

WARNING NOTE

- Some of the products in this section contain peanut oil or lanolin. If you are allergic to these ingredients, do not use these products. Always check the full list of ingredients.
- Many of the products listed here contain steroids (hydrocortisone). These should not be used near the eyes, on the face or on broken or infected skin. They should not be used for more than 7 days without consulting your GP.
- Products containing steroids should not be used by children under 10 years or by pregnant women and breast-feeding women. Ask the advice of your GP.

Alpka Keri Bath Oil

Description: An emollient bath additive containing various oils. Contains lanolin oil.
Dose: Add to bathwater.

Balneum

Description: An emollient bath additive containing oil.
Dose: Add to bathwater or use in shower.

Balneum Plus

Description: An emollient bath additive containing oil with soothing ingredients.
Dose: Add to bathwater or use in shower.

Clinitar

Description: A cream containing coal tar.
Dose: Apply 1–2 times a day.

Cream E45

Description: An emollient cream containing a mixture of oils. Also contains lanolin (which has been treated to make it hypoallergenic).
Dose: Apply 2–3 times a day to affected area.

Dayleve

Description: A cream containing hydrocortisone (a steroid).
Dose: Apply thinly to affected area twice a day. Not suitable for children under 10 years.

Dermacort Cream

Description: A cream containing hydrocortisone (a steroid).
Dose: Apply to affected area 1–2 times a day. Not suitable for children under 10 years.

Dermamist

Description: An emollient spray containing a mixture of oils.
Dose: Spray on affected area after bath or shower.

Dermidex Cream

See entry in Bites, Stings and Hives, page 197.

Diprobase

Description: An emollient cream containing a mixture of oils.
Dose: Apply as required.

Diprobath

Description: An emollient bath additive containing oil.
Dose: Add liquid to bathwater.

Emulsiderm Emollient

Description: An emollient bath additive containing various oils and an antiseptic.
Dose: Add liquid to bathwater or apply directly to skin.

Eurax Cream*

Description: A cream containing crotamiton (an ingredient to help itching).
Dose: Apply as required.
* Also available as a lotion.

Eurax HC Cream

Description: A cream containing crotamiton and hydrocortisone (a steroid).
Dose: Apply sparingly to affected area twice a day. Not suitable for children under 10 years.

HC45 Hydrocortisone Cream

Description: A cream containing hydrocortisone (a steroid).
Dose: Apply sparingly 1–2 times a day. Not suitable for children under 10 years.

Hydromol Cream

Description: An emollient cream containing a mixture of oils. Also contains peanut oil.
Dose: Apply liberally and use as often as required.

Hydromol Emollient

Description: An emollient bath additive containing various oils.
Dose: 1–3 capfuls added to a shallow (20cm) bath.

Imuderm Therapeutic Oil

Description: An emollient bath additive containing various oils.
Dose: Use directly on the skin after a bath or add 15–30ml to bathwater.

Lanacort Creme*

Description: A cream containing hydrocortisone (a steroid).
Dose: Apply sparingly 1–2 times a day. Not suitable for children under 10 years.
* Also available as an ointment.

Morhulin Ointment

Description: An emollient ointment containing oil.
Dose: Apply thinly to affected area.

Oilatum Emollient*

Description: An emollient liquid containing various oils.
Dose: Add to bathwater, or apply to skin and then rinse off.
* Also available as a shower gel, gel for hands, and bath additive.

Oliatum Plus

Description: An emollient liquid containing various oils and antiseptics.
Dose: Add to bathwater.

⚰ Oilatum Junior Flare up*

Description: An emollient liquid containing various oils and antiseptics (for children).
Dose: Add to bathwater.
, * Also available as Oilatum Junior.

Polytar Emollient

Description: A medicated liquid containing coal tar. Also contains peanut oil.
Dose: Add 2–4 capfuls to a shallow (20cm) bath.

Psorigel

Description: A gel containing coal tar.
Dose: Rub into the affected area and allow to dry. Use 1–2 times a day.

Ultrabase

Description: An emollient cream containing various oils.
Dose: Apply as required.

Unguentum Merck

Description: An emollient cream containing various oils.
Dose: Apply as required.

COMPLEMENTARY PRODUCTS

HERBAL REMEDIES

❀ Blue Flag Root Compound

Description: A tablet herbal remedy with antiseptic, anti-inflammatory and anti-itch properties to treat the symptoms of eczema and other minor skin conditions. Contains blue flag root, burdock and sarsaparilla.
Dose: 1 tablet 3 times a day after meals. Not suitable for children under 12 years. Pregnant women should consult a pharmacist or GP before using this product.

❀ Dermatodoron Ointment

Description: An ointment herbal remedy to relieve eczema symptoms. Contains loosestrife and woody nightshade.
Dose: Apply ointment 3–4 times a day.

❀ Heath & Heather Skin Tablets

Description: A tablet herbal remedy to relieve symptoms of skin blemishes and dry eczema. Contains burdock root and wild pansy.
Dose: 2 tablets 3 times a day. Not suitable for children. Pregnant women should consult a pharmacist or GP before using this product.

❀ Herbheal Ointment

Description: An ointment herbal remedy with anti-itch properties to relieve skin conditions where itching and irritation occur. Contains chickweed, colophony, lanolin, marshmallow, sulphur and zinc oxide.
Dose: Apply twice a day. Not suitable for children under 5 years.

❀ Kleer Tablets

Description: A tablet herbal remedy for minor skin conditions and eczema. Contains burdock root, echinacea and stinging nettle.
Dose: Adults: 2 tablets 3 times a day before meals. Children aged 5–12 years: 1 tablet 3 times a day before meals. Not suitable for children under 5 years or for pregnant or breast-feeding women.

❀ Potter's Eczema Ointment

Description: An ointment herbal remedy to relieve symptoms of eczema. Contains benzoic acid, chickweed, lanolin, salicylic acid and zinc oxide.
Dose: Apply twice a day. Not suitable for children under 5 years.

❀ Potter's Skin Clear Ointment

See entry in Acne, page 190.

❀ Potter's Eruptions Mixture

Description: A herbal remedy mixture to treat symptoms of mild eczema. Contains blue flag, buchu, burdock root, cascara, sarsaparilla and yellow dock.
Dose: Adults: 5ml 3 times a day. Children over 8 years: 5ml every 12 hours. Not suitable for children under 8 years. Pregnant and breast-feeding women should consult a pharmacist or GP before using this product.

HOMOEOPATHIC REMEDIES

❀ Calcarea carbonica

Description: A homoeopathic remedy for cracked and itching skin.
Dose (and manufacturers): Weleda 6c and 30c, Nelsons 6c.

❀ Graphites

Description: A homoeopathic remedy for eczema with weepy and cracked skin.
Dose (and manufacturers): Weleda 6c and 30c, Nelsons 6c.

❀ Hepar sulphuris

Description: A homoeopathic remedy for eczema.
Dose (and manufacturers): Weleda 6c and 30c, Nelsons 6c, Ainsworths 30c.

❀ Natrum muriaticum

Description: A homoeopathic remedy for eczema.
Dose (and manufacturers): Weleda 6c and 30c, Nelsons 6c, New Era 6x, Ainsworths 30c.

❀ Nelsons Graphites Cream

Description: A homoeopathic remedy for dermatitis. Contains graphites 6x.
Dose: Apply when required.

❀ Rhus toxicodendron

Description: A homoeopathic remedy for eczema.
Dose (and manufacturers): Weleda 6c and 30c, Nelsons 6c, Ainsworths 30c.

❀ Sulphur

Description: A homoeopathic remedy for eczema.
Dose (and manufacturers): Weleda 6c and 30c, Nelsons 6c.

HANGNAILS AND SPLINTERS

See **Antiseptics**, page 93, to treat or prevent any infection.

WARNING NOTE

- Those with diabetes should see their GP for investigation and treatment if an infection develops.

LICE INFESTATIONS

Several types of products are available for the treatment of lice and scabies, including lotions and shampoos. Lotions are generally more effective than shampoos, but they also have to be left on the head for a lot longer, preferably for 12 hours. Some of the lotions contain alcohol and these should not be used by young children or those with asthma because there is a risk of causing an asthmatic attack. Ingredients in lice products are known as insecticides and includ malathion, permethrin and phenothrin.

The active ingredients in these preparations are anti-infestation chemicals. Until recently, your local health authority may have had a policy of recommending the various ingredients in rotation, but this recommendation is now considered to be outdated. What is now recommended is that one product should be tried, and then if that fails to work, a product with a different ingredient should be tried the next time.

There is a misconception that using these products all the time instead of ordinary shampoo will keep the family clear of lice. However, this only encourages resistance, and the products may eventually become ineffective. In addition, there is also the idea that all the family should be treated if one member gets lice. Again, this could encourage resistance and there is no point in using these products until lice have actually been seen on the person's head. If one member of the family has lice, it is important to keep checking everyone else, using a nit comb (a special comb with very fine teeth) on wet hair. If lice are found, start treatment immediately.

Treatment for lice usually requires that the product is applied twice, the second application being 7 days after the first. Always follow the instructions on the package carefully. People sometimes complain that lice treatments fail to work and a common reason for this is that the instructions may not have been properly followed.

Piperonal aldehyde is used to prevent reinfestation after the lice have been treated with an insecticide and is available in spray form. It is not intended for routine use to prevent or get rid of lice.

In treating scabies the whole body from the neck downwards should be coated in lotion for 24 hours. Irritation will be slow to clear as the scabies mites are still in the skin. This does not mean that the treatment has not worked; do not apply a second coat. Crotamiton (see Eurax on page 213), which has anti-itch properties, may help with the irritation.

This section contains a list of over-the-counter treatments for lice, both head and pubic lice, with their main ingredients and instructions for use. For specific uses, warnings and cautions, read the product labels and information leaflets inside the package.

WARNING NOTE

- Asthmatics and those with eczema may react to alcohol-based lotions. Products containing alcohol are identified in this section.

- Avoid the face area and take great care not to get the product in eyes, particularly with babies and young children. If this occurs, rinse eyes with copious amounts of cold water.

- Permed, bleached or coloured hair may be affected by these products. Check with a pharmacist.

Derbac M Liquid

Description: A liquid containing malathion.
Dose: For head lice, apply to affected area, leave to dry naturally and then wash out after 12 hours. Comb hair while still wet. For pubic lice, leave on for 1–12 hours – the longer, the better. For scabies, apply to whole body and wash off after 24 hours. Not suitable for babies under 6 months.

Full Marks Lotion

Description: A lotion containing phenothrin. Also contains alcohol.
Dose: Rub into dry hair and leave on for at least 2 hours, or overnight. Wash out. Comb hair while still wet. Not suitable for babies under 6 months.

Full Marks Liquid

Description: A liquid containing phenothrin.
Dose: Rub into scalp and allow to dry naturally. Leave on for at least 12 hours and then wash off. Comb hair while still wet. Not suitable for babies under 6 months.

Lyclear Creme Rinse

Description: A lotion containing permethrin.
Dose: Shampoo hair and then apply lotion to hair and scalp. Leave for 10 minutes and then wash out. Comb hair while still wet. Not suitable for babies under 6 months.

Prioderm Cream Shampoo

Description: A shampoo containing malathion.
Dose: Shampoo hair and leave for 5 minutes. Rinse and repeat. Repeat twice more at 3-day intervals. Not suitable for babies under 6 months. May be used for pubic lice.

Prioderm Lotion

Description: A lotion containing malathion. Also contains alcohol.
Dose: For head or pubic lice, apply to affected area and leave to dry naturally for at least 2 hours, preferably for 12 hours. Wash off. Comb hair while still wet. For scabies, apply to whole body and wash off after 24 hours. Not suitable for babies under 6 months.

Quellada-M Cream Shampoo

Description: A shampoo containing malathion.
Dose: Apply to dry hair and skin of scalp, and/or to pubic area. Leave for 4 minutes and then lather and rinse. Not suitable for babies under 6 months.

Quellada-M Lotion

Description: A lotion containing malathion. Also contains alcohol.
Dose: For head or pubic lice, apply to affected area and leave to dry naturally for at least 2 hours, preferably for 12 hours. Wash off. Comb hair while still wet. For scabies, apply to whole body and wash off after 24 hours. Not suitable for babies under 6 months.

Suleo M Lotion

Description: A lotion containing malathion. Also contains alcohol.
Dose: Apply lotion to dry hair and rub well into hair and scalp. Allow hair to dry naturally (do not use a hairdryer) and wash out after 12 hours. Comb hair while still wet. Not suitable for babies under 6 months unless advised by a GP.

COMPLEMENTARY PRODUCTS

Not suitable for complementary treatment.

SCARS

See also Burns, page 200, Acne, page 187, Cuts and Wounds, page 205.

Scarring can be minimised by taking vitamin C and zinc supplements to promote skin healing. (See Vitamin and Mineral Supplements, pages 286-88.)

COMPLEMENTARY PRODUCTS

Complementary products may help in treating scars.

HERBAL REMEDIES

❀ Nelsons Hypercal

Description: A cream and tincture herbal remedy to soothe skin and promote healing. Contains hypericum and calendula.
Dose: Apply cream to affected skin. Apply tincture neat to affected area or dilute with 1 part tincture to 10 parts water for larger areas. Cover if required.

❀ Weleda Calendolon Ointment

Description: An ointment herbal remedy that acts as an antiseptic and anti-inflammatory to treat skin problems. Contains calendula.
Dose: Apply to the affected area 2–3 times a day. Do not apply to infected wounds. Pregnant women should consult a pharmacist or GP before using this product.

❀ Weleda Calendula Lotion

Description: A lotion herbal remedy to treat cuts, minor wounds and skin abrasions. Contains calendula.
Dose: Add 5ml of liquid to boiled water, allow to cool and apply to affected area. Do not apply to infected wounds. Pregnant women should consult a pharmacist or GP before using this product.

HOMOEOPATHIC REMEDIES

❀ New Era Elasto

Description: A homoeopathic remedy to promote the formation of elastic, responsible for the repair and health of tissues in the body. Contains 6x each of calc fluor, calc phos, ferr phos and mag phos.
Dose: 1 tablet provides 6x of each of the above ingredients.

❀ Calcarea fluorica

Description: A homoeopathic remedy to promote tissue elasticity and promote scar and adhesion healing.
Dose (and manufacturers): Weleda 6c and 30c, Nelsons 6c, New Era 6x.

❀ Calcarea sulphurica

Description: A homoeopathic remedy for wounds that are slow to heal and to aid skin healing.
Dose (and manufacturer): New Era 6x.

❀ Hepar sulphuris

Description: A homoeopathic remedy that encourages suppuration of wounds to rid area of foreign bodies and so assist healing.
Dose (and manufacturers): Weleda 6c and 30c, Nelsons 6c, Ainsworths 30c.

SUNBURN

Any soothing, emollient cream will help ease sunburn. Any product containing calomine lotion will also help. In addition, the following remedies will help reduce pain caused by the sunburn.

For specific uses, warnings and cautions, read the product labels and information leaflets inside the package.

WARNING NOTE

- Sunburn in children and severe sunburn in adults, especially if it is accompanied by fever, requires urgent medical attention.

Caladryl Cream

See entry in Bites, Stings and Hives, page 197.

Drapolene Cream

See entry in Nappy Rash, page 278.

E45 Cream

Description: An emollient cream containing petroleum jelly, liquid paraffin and lanolin.
Dose: Apply to affected area as required.

Eurax Cream (and Lotion)

See entry in Dermatitis and Eczema, page 213.

Lacto-Calamine Lotion

Description: A lotion containing calamine and zinc oxide.
Dose: Apply to affected area as required.

Lanacane Creme

See entry in Bites, Stings and Hives, page 197.

Solarcaine Cream (and Lotion and Spray)

See entry in Bites, Stings and Hives, page 198.

Witch Doctor Gel

See entry in Bites, Stings and Hives, page 198.

WARTS AND VERRUCAE

Treatments for both verrucae and warts contain the same ingredients because they are caused by the same virus. The only real difference between warts and verrucae is their location: verrucae are found in the feet, while warts usually appear on the hands, fingers, and, more rarely, on the elbows.

Ingredients in the products for these ailments include salicylic acid, lactic acid, formaldehyde and glutaraldehyde. They all work by gradually softening the wart or verruca and slowly dissolving it. Treatment can take a very long time, so do not expect results overnight. The process can be speeded up by gently rubbing the wart or verruca with a pumice stone or emery board, but never try cutting with a knife or razor blade. Always avoid putting the product on healthy skin. Place it only on the wart or verruca.

This section contains a list of products for warts and verrucae with their main ingredients and instructions for use. For specific uses, warnings and cautions, read the product label and the information leaflet inside the package.

WARNING NOTE

• Only apply remedy to affected area. Avoid healthy skin. Do not apply remedy to broken, inflamed or irritated skin. Do not apply to moles or other skin blemishes.

- Never use any of the preparations on warts on the face, or in the anal or genital areas unless advised by a GP.

- Always ask for advice from a pharmacist or GP when treating warts and verrucae in children and be particularly careful when using the products on children.

- Diabetics, those with circulatory problems, and pregnant or breast-feeding women should not use any of these products without first checking with their GP that it is safe for them to do so.

Avoca Wart & Verruca Set

Description: A kit containing a caustic pencil, emery file, dressings and protector pads.
Dose: Apply pencil to wart or verruca for 1–2 minutes. Repeat after 24 hours if necessary. Protect with dressings and protector pad. Maximum 3 treatments for warts, 6 treatments for verrucae.

Bazuka Gel*

Description: A gel treatment with applicator and emery board containing salicylic acid. The gel dries to form a water-resistant barrier.
Dose: Apply 1–2 drops each night. Rub down once a week with the emery board. Not suitable for children under 6 years.
* Also available as Bazuka Extra Strength.

Carnation Verruca Care

Description: A medicated pad containing salicylic acid.
Dose: Apply pad, changing every 2 days, for up to 10 days. Treatment may be repeated after 28 days. Check with pharmacist for children under 6 years.

Compound W

Description: A liquid containing salicylic acid.
Dose: Apply to affected area daily. Use for up to 12 weeks. Check with pharmacist for children under 6 years.

Cuplex

Description: A gel containing salicylic acid.
Dose: Apply gel at night to affected part – when dried it provides a protective film. Remove film in morning. May take 6–12 weeks to be effective. Not suitable for young children.

Duofilm

Description: A liquid containing salicylic acid and lactic acid.
Dose: Apply 1–2 times a day. Allow 6–12 weeks to take effect. Consult a pharmacist or GP for children under 6 years before using this product.

Glutarol

Description: A liquid containing glutaraldehyde.
Dose: Apply to the wart twice a day after soaking.

Occlusal

Description: A liquid containing salicylic acid.
Dose: Apply to affected area and allow to dry. Repeat treatment daily. Consult a pharmacist or GP for children under 6 years before using this product.

Salactol Wart Paint

Description: A paint containing salicylic acid.
Dose: Apply to affected area daily, followed by rubbing down with an emery board.

Scholl Seal and Heal Verruca Removal Gel

Description: A liquid containing salicylic acid.
Dose: Apply 1–2 drops to the affected area once a day and allow to dry. Repeat treatment daily until verruca can be removed. Not suitable for children under 12 years.

Scholl Verruca Removal System

Description: A medicated plaster containing salicylic acid.
Dose: Apply the correct size of plaster to verruca or wart. Leave in position for 48 hours and repeat treatment. Continue for up to 12 weeks, if required. Consult a pharmacist or GP for children under 6 years before using this product.

Veracur

Description: A gel containing formaldehyde.
Dose: Apply twice a day.

Verrugon

Description: An ointment containing salicylic acid.
Dose: Place felt ring on verruca, apply ointment and cover with plaster. Repeat daily. Consult a pharmacist or GP for children under 6 years before using this product.

Wartex Ointment

Description: An ointment containing salicylic acid.
Dose: Apply to wart daily until wart can be removed. Consult a pharmacist or GP for children under 6 years before using this product.

COMPLEMENTARY PRODUCTS

HOMOEOPATHIC REMEDIES

❀ Thuja

Description: A homoeopathic remedy for warts.
Dose (and manufacturers): Weleda 6c and 30c, Nelsons 6c.

JOINTS AND MUSCLES

- Arthritis (Osteoarthritis and Rheumatoid Arthritis)
- Back Pain • Bunions and Bursitis • Cramp • Frozen Shoulder
- Gout • Muscular Aches and Pains • Sciatica • Sprains
- Stiffness • Tendinitis • Tennis Elbow

Muscular aches and pains, rheumatic and back pain, sciatica, sprains and stiffness, frozen shoulder, gout and tennis elbow can be treated with analgesics taken orally (see **General Pain Relief**, page 78). However, analgesic creams, ointments, gels and sprays are also available, and these can be applied directly to the affected part of the body.

There are two main types of ingredients in analgesic products for external use. These are rubefacients, sometimes known as counter irritants, and non-steroidal anti-inflammatories (NSAIDs).

Rubefacients include substances such as salicylates, nicotinates, camphor, menthol and capsicum. They work by increasing blood flow in the area of the skin where they are applied and rubbing the remedy in gently helps this process considerably. Salicylates are substances related to aspirin and products that contain them are best avoided by asthmatics and those sensitive to aspirin.

NSAIDs used externally include benzydamine, felbinac, ibuprofen, ketoprofen and piroxicam. They reduce pain and inflammation by reducing the body's inflammatory response.

WARNING NOTE

- Avoid eyes, lips and mucous membranes when using these products.

- Some preparations may cause skin irritation. Discontinue use if skin is affected.

- Do not use these products on broken, irritated, sensitive or damaged skin. Use oral painkillers instead (see **General Pain Relief**, page 78).

- Do not use products containing a salicylate if you are asthmatic or sensitive to aspirin.

- Do not use remedies containing non-steroidal anti-inflammatory (NSAID) ingredients if you are already taking other NSAID medication. Asthmatics and those allergic to aspirin should avoid products containing NSAIDs.

- Do not take NSAIDs with any other prescription or over-the-counter remedy without checking with your pharmacist or GP.

- Check with a pharmacist or GP if you are pregnant or breast-feeding before using these products.

- Avoid excessive exposure to sunlight of the treated area in case of photo-sensitivity (an eczema-like skin reaction).

- These warnings also apply to all complementary remedies featured in this section.

BUNIONS AND BURSITIS

See **General Pain Relief**, page 78.

Scholl Antiseptic Foot Balm

Description: An antiseptic foot balm containing methyl salicylate and menthol.
Dose: Apply to the affected area morning and evening.

CRAMP

Crampex

Description: A tablet remedy containing nicotinic acid (an ingredient to improve circulation).
Dose: 1–2 tablets before bedtime. Not suitable for children.

COMPLEMENTARY PRODUCTS

HERBAL REMEDIES

❀ Weleda Massage Balm with Arnica

Description: A balm herbal remedy to ease symptoms of rheumatic pain, muscular aches and pains, stiffness, backache, fibrositis and muscle cramps. Contains arnica, lavender, rosemary and silver birch.
Dose: Massage into the affected area 3–4 times a day.

HOMOEOPATHIC REMEDIES

❀ Colocynthis

Description: A homoeopathic remedy for cramps and spasms, particularly cramp in the calves.
Dose (and manufacturer): Weleda 6c.

❄ Magnesia phosphorica

Description: A homoeopathic remedy for cramp.
Dose (and manufacturer): New Era 6x.

FROZEN SHOULDER

See **General Pain Relief**, page 78.

GENERAL JOINT AND MUSCLE PRODUCTS

See also **General Pain Relief**, page 78.

All the following remedies are suitable for the relief of:
• Arthritis (osteoarthritis and rheumatoid arthritis) • Back pain • Gout
• Muscular aches and pains • Sciatica   • Sprains • Stiffness • Tendinitis
• Tennis elbow

Algesal

Description: A cream rub containing a rubefacient. Contains a salicylate (an aspirin derivative).
Dose: Massage into the affected area 3 times a day. Not suitable for children under 6 years.

Algipan Rub

Description: A cream rub containing rubefacients. Contains a salicylate (an aspirin derivative).
Dose: Massage into the affected area 2–3 times a day. Not suitable for children under 6 years.

Balmosa Cream

Description: A cream rub containing rubefacients. Contains a salicylate (an aspirin derivative).
Dose: Massage into the affected area as required. Not suitable for children under 6 years.

BN Liniment

Description: A liniment containing rubefacients. Contains a salicylate (an aspirin derivative).
Dose: Adults: Massage into the affected area 2–3 times a day. Children over 6 years: Dilute liniment with equal amounts of olive oil before applying. Not suitable for children under 6 years.

Cremalgin

Description: A cream rub containing rubefacients. Contains a salicylate (an aspirin derivative).
Dose: Massage into the affected area 2–3 times a day. Not suitable for children under 6 years.

Cuprofen Ibutop Gel

Description: A gel containing ibuprofen, a non-steroidal anti-inflammatory (NSAID).
Dose: Apply the gel to the affected area. Allow at least 4 hours between applications. Do not use more than 4 times in 24 hours. Not suitable for children under 12 years.

Deep Freeze

Description: A spray containing a cooling ingredient.
Dose: Spray onto the affected area. Do not use more than 3 times in 24 hours. Not suitable for children under 6 years.

Deep Freeze Cold Gel

Description: A gel containing a cooling ingredient.
Dose: Rub into affected muscles 3–4 times a day. Not suitable for children under 5 years.

Deep Heat Massage Liniment

Description: A liniment containing rubefacients. Contains a salicylate (an aspirin derivative).
Dose: Rub into the affected area 3–4 times a day. Not suitable for children under 5 years.

Deep Heat Maximum Strength

Description: A cream rub containing a rubefacient. Contains a salicylate (an aspirin derivative).
Dose: Massage into the affected area 2–3 times a day. Not suitable for children under 5 years.

Deep Heat Rub

Description: A cream rub containing rubefacients. Contains a salicylate (an aspirin derivative).
Dose: Massage into the affected area 2–3 times a day. Not suitable for children under 6 years.

Deep Heat Spray

Description: A spray containing rubefacients. Contains a salicylate (an aspirin derivative).
Dose: Spray 2–3 short bursts of aerosol on to the affected area. Not suitable for children under 6 years.

Deep Relief

Description: A gel containing ibuprofen, a non-steroidal anti-inflammatory (NSAID).
Dose: Massage into the affected area up to 3 times a day. Not suitable for children under 12 years.

Difflam

Description: A cream containing benzydamine, a non-steroidal anti-inflammatory (NSAID).
Dose: Massage into the affected area 3 times a day. Not suitable for children under 6 years.

Dubam Spray

Description: A spray containing rubefacients. Contains a salicylate (an aspirin derivative).
Dose: Spray onto the affected area for 2 seconds up to 4 times a day. Not suitable for children under 6 years. Asthmatics and those allergic to aspirin may adversely react to this product.

Elliman's Universal Embrocation

Description: An embrocation containing a rubefacient.
Dose: Apply every 3 hours on first day, then use twice a day until pain eases. Not suitable for children under 12 years.

Feldene P Gel

Description: A gel containing piroxicam, a non-steroidal anti-inflammatory (NSAID).
Dose: Apply to affected area up to 4 times a day. Not suitable for children under 12 years.

Fenbid Gel*

Description: A gel containing ibuprofen, a non-steroidal anti-inflammatory (NSAID).

Dose: Massage into the affected area no more than every 4 hours. Do not use more than 4 times in 24 hours. Not suitable for children under 14 years.
★ Also available as a cream (which also contains a salicylate, an aspirin derivative) and an ointment.

Fiery Jack

Description: A cream rub containing a rubefacient.
Dose: Apply to affected area twice a day. Not suitable for children under 6 years.

Goddard's Embrocation

Description: An embrocation containing a rubefacient.
Dose: Apply to the affected area 1–2 times a day. Not suitable for children under 6 years.

Ibuleve Gel*

Description: A gel containing ibuprofen, a non-steroidal anti-inflammatory (NSAID).
Dose: Massage into the affected area up to 3 times a day. Not suitable for children under 12 years.
★ Also available in spray and mousse form.

Ibuleve Sports

Description: A gel containing ibuprofen, a non-steroidal anti-inflammatory (NSAID).
Dose: Massage into the affected area up to 3 times a day. Not suitable for children under 12 years.

Ibuspray

Description: A spray containing ibuprofen, a non-steroidal anti-inflammatory.
Dose: Spray on to the affected part and massage 3–4 times a day. Not suitable for children under 12 years.

Ralgex Ibutop Gel

Description: A gel containing ibuprofen, a non-steroidal anti-inflammatory (NSAID).
Dose: Apply to the affected area 3–4 times a day. Allow at least 4 hours between applications. Do not use more than 4 times in 24 hours. Not suitable for children under 12 years.

Intralgin

Description: A gel containing a rubefacient and a local anaesthetic.
Dose: Massage gently into affected area as required.

Lloyd's Cream

Description: A cream rub containing a rubefacient. Contains a salicylate (an aspirin derivative).
Dose: Apply to the affected area up to 3 times a day. Not suitable for children under 6 years.

Mentholatum

Description: An ointment containing rubefacients. Contains a salicylate (an aspirin derivative).
Dose: Apply lightly to the affected area 2–3 times a day. Not suitable for babies under 12 months.

Movelat Relief Cream*

Description: A cream containing salicylic acid (an aspirin derivative) and an ingredient to reduce swelling.
Dose: Apply to the affected area up to 4 times a day. Not suitable for children under 12 years.
* Also available as a gel.

Nasciodine

Description: A cream containing rubefacients. Contains a salicylate (an aspirin derivative).
Dose: Massage into the affected area 2–3 times a day. Not suitable for children under 6 years.

Oruvail

Description: A gel containing ketoprofen, a non-steroidal anti-inflammatory (NSAID).
Dose: Massage gel into the affected area 3 times a day. Not suitable for children under 12 years.

PR Freeze Spray

Description: A spray containing cooling ingredients.
Dose: Apply to the affected area up to 3 times a day. Not suitable for children under 6 years.

PR Heat Spray

Description: A spray containing rubefacients. Contains a salicylate (an aspirin derivative).
Dose: Apply to the affected area up to twice a day. Not suitable for children under 5 years.

Proflex Pain Relief

Description: A cream containing ibuprofen, a non-steroidal anti-inflammatory (NSAID).
Dose: Massage into the affected area 3–4 times a day. Not suitable for children under 12 years.

Radian-B Heat Spray*

Description: A spray containing rubefacients. Contains a salicylate (an aspirin derivative).
Dose: Spray onto the affected area. Follow with a second application 10–15 minutes later and massage into the area. Repeat up to 3 times a day, reducing applications as symptoms subside. Not suitable for children under 6 years.
*Also available as a muscle lotion and as a muscle rub.

Radian-B Ibuprofen Gel

Description: A gel containing ibuprofen, a non-steroidal anti-inflammatory (NSAID).
Dose: Apply to the affected area until absorbed. Use every 4 hours as required. Maximum 4 applications in 24 hours. Not suitable for children under 14 years.

Ralgex Cream

Description: A cream containing rubefacients. Contains a salicylate (an aspirin derivative).
Dose: Apply to the affected area up to 4 times a day. Not recommended for children under 12 years.

Ralgex Freeze Spray

Description: A spray containing cooling ingredients. Contains a salicylate (an aspirin derivative).
Dose: Apply to affected area up to 4 times a day. Not suitable for children under 5 years.

Ralgex Heat Spray

Description: A spray containing rubefacients. Contains a salicylate (an aspirin derivative).
Dose: Spray 2–3 short bursts on the painful area every 2 hours. Do not use more than 4 times a day. Not suitable for children under 5 years.

Ralgex Stick

Description: An embrocation stick containing rubefacients. Contains a salicylate (an aspirin derivative).
Dose: Apply to the affected area. Do not massage or rub in. Not suitable for children.

Salonair

Description: A spray containing rubefacients. Contains a salicylate (an aspirin derivative).
Dose: Spray on to the affected area 1–2 times a day. Not suitable for children under 6 years.

Salonpas Plasters

Description: A plaster containing rubefacients. Contains a salicylate (an aspirin derivative).
Dose: Apply plaster to the affected area. Renew plaster up to 3 times a day. Not suitable for children under 12 years. Do not use for more than 7 days.

Solpaflex Gel

Description: A gel containing ketoprofen, a non-steroidal anti-inflammatory (NSAID).
Dose: Massage the gel into the affected area 2–4 times a day. Not suitable for children under 15 years.

Tiger Balm Red (Regular and Extra Strength)

Description: An ointment containing rubefacients.
Dose: Rub gently into the affected area 2–3 times a day. Not suitable for children under 2 years.

Transvasin Heat Rub

Description: A cream containing rubefacients. Contains a salicylate (an aspirin derivative).

Dose: Apply to the affected area up to 3 times a day. Not suitable for children under 6 years.

Transvasin Heat Spray

Description: A spray containing rubefacients. Contains a salicylate (an aspirin derivative).
Dose: Spray onto the affected area up to 3 times a day. Not suitable for children under 5 years.

Traxam Pain Relief Gel

Description: A gel containing felbinac, a non-steroidal anti-inflammatory (NSAID).
Dose: Rub gel onto the affected area 2–4 times a day. Not suitable for children under 12 years.

COMPLEMENTARY PRODUCTS

HERBAL REMEDIES

❀ Belladonna Plaster

Description: An adhesive plaster impregnated with a rubefacient to relieve muscular and rheumatic pain, strains, stiffness and lumbago. Contains belladonna alkaloids.
Dose: Apply plaster to the affected area and leave for 2–3 days. Not suitable for children under 10 years.

❀ Bio-Strath Willow Formula

Description: A liquid herbal remedy to relieve muscular pain, backache, lumbago, sciatica and fibrosis. Contains primula, willow bark and yeast.
Dose: 1.5ml diluted in water 3 times a day before meals. Not suitable for children.

❀ Dragon Balm Ointment

Description: An ointment herbal remedy to relieve rheumatism and other joint conditions. Contains balsam of Peru, camphor, cassia, eucalyptus, guaiacum, nutmeg, turpentine and thymol.
Dose: Apply to the affected area as required. Not suitable for children under 6 years.

❀ Gerard House Celery Tablets

Description: A tablet herbal remedy for symptoms of rheumatic pain. Contains celery.
Dose: Use as directed on label, depending on symptoms. Not suitable for children.

❀ Gerard House Ligvites

Description: A tablet herbal remedy to relieve rheumatic pain, stiffness, backache and lumbago. Contains black cohosh, guaiacum, poplar bark, sarsaparilla and white willow bark. See warning on aspirin, page 78.
Dose: 2 tablets twice a day with food. Not suitable for children under 12 years.

❀ Gonne Balm

Description: A herbal remedy to relieve muscular aches and pains including stiffness, backache, sciatica and lumbago. Contains camphor, eucalyptus oil, levo-menthol, methyl salicylate (an aspirin derivative) and turpentine.
Dose: Massage into the affected area 2–3 times a day. Repeat once at night if required. Not suitable for children under 12 years.

❀ Heath & Heather Celery Tablets

Description: A tablet herbal remedy for symptoms of rheumatic pain. Contains celery.
Dose: Use as directed on label, depending on symptoms. Not suitable for children.

❀ Heath & Heather Rheumatic Pain Tablets

Description: A tablet herbal remedy to relieve symptoms of backache, lumbago, fibrositis and rheumatic pain. Contains bogbean, celery and guaiacum.
Dose: 1 tablet 3 times a day. Not suitable for children.

❀ Olbas Oil

Description: An oil to treat muscular pain and stiffness. Contains oils of cajuput, clove, eucalyptus, juniper berry, menthol, mint and wintergreen. Acts as an analgesic and rubefacient.
Dose: Massage into the affected area 3 times a day. Not suitable for children.

❀ Nelsons Ointment for Strains

Description: An ointment herbal remedy for strains and sprains. Contains ruta graveolens.
Dose: Apply to affected area as required.

❀ Nelsons Rhus Tox Cream

Description: A cream herbal remedy for rheumatic pains and strains. Contains rhus toxicondendron.
Dose: Massage cream into the affected area as required.

❀ Potter's Backache Tablets

Description: A tablet herbal remedy to relieve pain caused by backache. Contains buchu, gravel root, hydrangea and uva ursi.
Dose: 2 tablets 3 times a day. Not suitable for children.

❀ Potter's Comfrey Ointment

Description: An ointment herbal remedy to relieve sprains and bruises. Contains comfrey.
Dose: Apply the ointment to the affected area twice a day after bathing. Do not use for more than 10 days.

❀ Potter's Nine Rubbing Oils

Description: A 9-oil mix rubefacient herbal remedy for easing the symptoms of muscular pain and stiffness including backache, sciatica, lumbago, fibrositis, strains and rheumatic pains. Contains amber, arachis, clove, eucalyptus, mustard, menthyl salicylate (an aspirin derivative), linseed, peppermint and turpentine.
Dose: Rub oil into the affected area as required. Do not combine with other homoeopathic remedies.

❀ Potter's Rheumatic Pain tablets

Description: A tablet herbal remedy to relieve rheumatic aches and pains. Contains bogbean, burdock, guaiacum, nutmeg and yarrow.
Dose: 2 tablets 3 times a day. Not suitable for children. Do not use if suffering from diarrhoea.

❀ Potter's Sciargo*

Description: A tablet herbal remedy with anti-inflammatory properties to relieve sciatica and lumbago. Contains clivers, juniper berry, shepherd's purse, uva ursi and wild carrot.
Dose: 2 tablets 3 times a day. Not suitable for children.
* Also available as teabags to make a herbal tea.

❀ Potter's Tabritis

Description: A tablet herbal remedy with analgesic and anti-inflammatory properties to relieve symptoms of rheumatism and stiffness. Contains clivers, burdock, elderflowers, prickly ash bark, poplar bark, uva ursi and yarrow.
Dose: 2 tablets 3 times a day. Not suitable for children.

❀ Reumalex

Description: A tablet herbal remedy to relieve rheumatic aches and pains. Contains black cohosh, guaiacum, poplar bark, sarsaparilla and white willow bark. See warning on aspirin, page 78.
Dose: 2 tablets twice a day. Not suitable for children.

❀ Rheumasol

Description: A tablet herbal remedy for joint and muscle pain and stiffness. Contains guaiacum resin and prickly ash bark.
Dose: 1 tablet 3 times a day with meals. Not suitable for children.

❀ Vegetex

Description: A tablet herbal remedy to relieve rheumatic pain, fibrositis and lumbago. Contains black cohosh, buckbean and celery.
Dose: 3 tablets 3 times a day with meals. Not suitable for children.

❀ Weleda Arnica Ointment*

Description: An ointment herbal remedy to relieve muscular pains, stiffness, strains and bruises. Contains arnica.
Dose: Apply the ointment to the affected area 3–4 times a day, massaging in gently.
★ Also available as a lotion.

❀ Weleda Copper Ointment

Description: An ointment herbal remedy to relieve muscular rheumatic pain. Contains cuprum metallicum praep.
Dose: Apply the ointment to the affected area 1–2 times a day.

❀ Weleda Massage Balm with Arnica

See entry in Cramp, page 227.

❁ Weleda Rheumadoron 102A Drops

Description: A liquid herbal remedy to ease muscular rheumatic pain. Contains arnica, aconite, birch and mandragora root.
Dose: 5–10 drops 3–4 times a day.

❁ Weleda Rheumadoron Ointment

Description: An ointment herbal remedy to ease muscular rheumatic pain. Contains arnica, birch, mandrake, rosemary and wolfbane.
Dose: Massage into the affected area twice a day.

❁ Weleda Rhus Tox Ointment

Description: An ointment herbal remedy to relieve rheumatic pain. Contains rhus toxicodendron.
Dose: Apply to the affected area or smear some ointment on a clean dressing and wrap over the area.

❁ Weleda Ruta Ointment

Description: An ointment herbal remedy to ease and assist healing of strains and sprains. Contains rue tincture.
Dose: Apply to the affected area or smear some ointment onto a clean dressing and wrap over the area.

HOMOEOPATHIC REMEDIES

❁ Actaea racemosa

Description: A homoeopathic remedy for stiff neck, rheumatic pains in the back and neck, and muscle ache after exercise.
Dose (and manufacturers): Weleda 6c and 30c, Nelsons 6c.

❁ Apis mellifica

Description: A homoeopathic remedy for arthritis with red and swollen joints and hot, red swellings in the body.
Dose (and manufacturers): Weleda 6c and 30c, Nelsons 6c, Ainsworths 30c.

❁ Arnica

Description: A homoeopathic remedy for sprains, aching and bruised muscles.
Dose (and manufacturers): Weleda 6x, 6c and 30c, Nelsons 6c, Ainsworths 30c.

❀ Bryonia

Description: A homoeopathic remedy for arthritis and sharp pains.
Dose (and manufacturers): Weleda 6c and 30c, Nelsons 6c, Ainsworths 30c.

❀ Calcarea fluorica

Description: A homoeopathic remedy for arthritis that responds to warmth and movement.
Dose (and manufacturers): Weleda 6c and 30c, Nelsons 6c, New Era 6x.

❀ Ferrum phosphoricum

Description: A homoeopathic remedy for rheumatism.
Dose (and manufacturers): Weleda 6c and 30c, Nelsons 6c, New Era 6x, Ainsworths 30c.

❀ Kalium muriaticum

Description: A homoeopathic remedy for rheumatic swelling.
Dose (and manufacturer): New Era 6x.

❀ Kalium sulphuricum

Description: A homoeopathic remedy for rheumatism that moves from joint to joint.
Dose (and manufacturer): New Era 6x.

❀ Ledum

Description: A homoeopathic remedy for rheumatic and arthritic conditions starting in the lower limbs but which move up the body.
Dose (and manufacturers): Weleda 6c, Ainsworths 30c.

❀ Magnesia phosphorica

Description: A homoeopathic remedy for sciatica and muscular spasms.
Dose (and manufacturer): New Era 6x.

❀ Natrum phosphoricum

Description: A homoeopathic remedy to assist removal of excess lactic acid in the body to help rheumatic conditions.
Dose (and manufacturer): New Era 6x.

❀ Nelsons Rheumatica

Description: A homoeopathic remedy for rheumatic pains. Contains rhus toxico-dendron 6c.
Dose: Adults: 2 tablets every hour for 6 doses, followed by 2 tablets 3 times a day. Children: Half adult dose.

❀ New Era Combination A

Description: A homoeopathic remedy for sciatica. Contains ferr phos, kali phos and mag phos.
Dose: Contains 6x of each of the above ingredients.

❀ New Era Combination G

Description: A homoeopathic remedy for backache and lumbar pain. Contains calc fluor, calc phos, kali phos and nat mur.
Dose: Contains 6x of each of the above ingredients.

❀ New Era Combination I

Description: A homoeopathic remedy for muscular pain and fibrositis. Contains ferr phos, kali sulph and mag phos.
Dose: Contains 6x of each of the above ingredients.

❀ New Era Combination P

Description: A homoeopathic remedy for aching legs and feet. Contains calc fluor, calc phos, kali phos and mag phos.
Dose: Contains 6x of each of the above ingredients.

❀ Phytolacca

Description: A homoeopathic remedy for rheumatism and shooting pains in the body.
Dose (and manufacturer): Weleda 6c.

❀ Pulsatilla

Description: A homoeopathic remedy for arthritis.
Dose (and manufacturer): Weleda 6c and 30c, Nelsons 6c, Ainsworths 30c.

❀ Rhus toxicodendron

Description: A homoeopathic remedy for muscular strains, sprains, joint stiffness, rheumatism, arthritis and sciatica.
Dose (and manufacturers): Weleda 6c and 30c, Nelsons 6c, Ainsworths 30c.

❀ Ruta graveolens

Description: A homoeopathic remedy for muscular strains, sprains, rheumatism, tennis elbow, tendon injuries and aching limbs when rhus toxicodendron is ineffective.
Dose (and manufacturers): Weleda 6c and 30c, Nelsons 6c, Ainsworths 30c.

❀ Symphytum

Description: A homoeopathic remedy for cartilage injuries and painful old injuries.
Dose (and manufacturer): Weleda 6c.

EAR, EYE AND MOUTH PROBLEMS

• Earache • Earwax • Conjunctivitis • Mouth Problems
• Cold Sores • Mouth Ulcers • Toothache • Oral Thrush

See also **General Pain Relief**, page 78, and **General Pain Relief for Children**, page 89.

EAR PROBLEMS

EARACHE

In adults, earache may be associated with colds and flu. Provided the pain is not severe, it can be treated with oral painkillers (see **General Pain Relief**, pages 78). Earache in children can cause a lot of distress and painkillers will make them more comfortable and calmer. You should seek advice from a GP that day or the following morning. **Never attempt to treat earache yourself.**

COMPLEMENTARY PRODUCTS

HOMOEOPATHIC REMEDIES

❀ Aconite

Description: A homoeopathic remedy for earache after exposure to cold dry wind.
Dose (and manufacturers): Weleda 6c and 30c, Nelsons 6c, Ainsworths 30c.

❀ Argentum nitricum

Description: A homoeopathic remedy for earache causing buzzing in the ears.
Dose (and manufacturers): Weleda 6c and 30c, Nelsons 6c, Ainsworths 30c.

❀ Belladonna

Description: A homoeopathic remedy for throbbing earache.
Dose (and manufacturers): Weleda 6c and 30c, Nelsons 6c, Ainsworths 30c.

❀ Chamomilla

Description: A homoeopathic remedy for children with earache.
Dose (and manufacturers): Weleda 3x and 30c, Ainsworths 30c.

❀ Hepar sulphuris

Description: A homoeopathic remedy for earache.
Dose (and manufacturers): Weleda 6c, Nelsons 6c, Ainsworths 30c.

❀ Lalium Muriaticum

Description: A homoeopathic remedy for relieving earache caused by blocked Eustachian tubes.
Dose (and manufacturer): New Era 6c.

❀ Mercurius solubilis

Description: A homoeopathic remedy for earache.
Dose (and manufacturers): Weleda 6c, Nelsons 6c, Ainsworths 30c.

EAR WAX

Wax in the ears is the only ear problem which it is safe to treat yourself, and even then it is best to get your ears looked at by a GP or nurse to make sure your ear problem really is wax and not some other ear infection or conditions.

Ear drops for removal of wax contain various ingredients such as oils, docusate, glycerol, hydrogen peroxide and paradichlorobenzene. There is little to choose between these different ingredients.

Ear drops should be used as follows: warm the drops by holding the bottle in your hands for a few minutes. Put your head on a flat surface with the affected ear uppermost and put the required number of drops (according to the product label) in your ear. If possible, get someone else to put them in for you. Keep your head down for at least 5 minutes and then plug your ear with cotton wool that has been moistened with a few more drops of the remedy.

This section contains a list of products for ear wax with their main ingredients and instructions for use. For specific uses, cautions and warnings, read product labels and information leaflets inside the packages.

WARNING NOTE

- Always try to get ear wax diagnosed by a GP or nurse before using any of these products.
- Do not use one of these products for an ear problem where you do not know the cause.
- These products are not suitable for children. Always get ear problems in children diagnosed by a GP.

- Do not use one of these products if you have a perforated ear drum.
- Some of these products contain peanut oil. Do not use if you are allergic to peanuts.

Audax Ear Drops

Description: Ear drops containing a mild analgesic and ingredient to soften wax.
Dose: To soften wax, fill ear with liquid and plug with cotton wool. Use twice a day for 4 days. Not suitable for babies under 12 months.

Cerumol Ear Drops

Description: Ear drops containing a mild analgesic and ingredient to soften wax. Also contains peanut oil.
Dose: Put 5 drops into the ear and leave for 20 minutes. Repeat 2–3 times a day for 3 days.

Earex Ear Drops

Description: Ear drops containing various oils to soften wax. Also contains peanut oil.
Dose: Use applicator to drop 4 drops of liquid into outer ear and apply cotton wool plug. Repeat morning and night for 4 days until wax clears.

Earex Plus Ear Drops

Description: Ear drops containing a mild analgesic and an ingredient to soften wax.
Dose: To soften wax, fill ear with liquid and plug with cotton wool. Use twice a day for 4 days. Not suitable for babies under 12 months.

Exterol Ear Drops

Description: Ear drops containing ingredients for softening wax.
Dose: Put up to 5 drops into the ear, once or twice a day. Use for 3–4 days.

Molcer Ear Drops

Description: Ear drops containing ingredients for softening wax.
Dose: Fill ear with drops and plug with cotton wool until the next treatment. Do this for 2 nights and then clear out ear.

Otex Ear Drops

Description: Ear drops containing ingredients for softening wax.
Dose: Put 5 drops in each ear once or twice a day for 3–4 days until wax loosens.

Wax Wane Ear Drops

Description: Ear drops containing ingredients for softening wax.
Dose: Put 4–5 drops in the ear and then plug with cotton wool. Repeat 2–3 times daily for a few days until the wax is sufficiently soft.

Waxsol Ear Drops

Description: Ear drops containing ingredients for softening wax.
Dose: Fill the ear with the drops on not more than 2 consecutive nights before having ears syringed.

EYE PROBLEMS

CONJUNCTIVITIS

The products listed in this section are for conjunctivitis and similar minor eye infections. Both eye drops and eye ointments are available. Conjunctivitis is a potentially serious problem, so you should never use any of these products without asking a pharmacist for advice, and you should never use any of them for more than 2 days without asking your GP.

These products contain a mild anti-microbial – either propamidine or dibromo-propamidine. Eye drops contain the former ingredient and eye ointments the latter. Both types of product can cause stinging in the eye when you first apply them. Eye drops need to be used four times a day, simply because their effect does not last very long. Eye ointments stay longer on the surface of the eye and only need to be used twice a day, but because they are sticky they can cause blurred vision. It is often useful to use drops during the day and ointment at night.

This section contains a list of products for conjunctivitis with their main ingredients and instructions for use. For specific uses, cautions and warnings, read the product labels and information leaflets in the packages.

WARNING NOTE

- Do not use any of these products for more than 2 days without asking your GP.
- These products are suitable for children but always ask the advice of a pharmacist before treating eye problems in children.
- Throw away all eye drops within 4 weeks of opening.
- Do not wear contact lenses while using these products.

Brolene Eye Drops

Description: Eye drops containing propamidine (an anti-microbial).
Dose: 1–2 drops up to 4 times a day.

Brolene Eye Ointment

Description: Eye ointment containing dibromopropamidine (an anti-microbial).
Dose: With clean hands or using a cotton bud, apply ointment to affected eye twice a day.

Golden Eye Ointment

Description: Eye ointment containing dibromopropamidine (an anti-microbial).
Dose: With clean hands or a cotton bud, apply to affected eye 1–2 times a day.

COMPLEMENTARY PRODUCTS

HOMOEOPATHIC REMEDIES

❀ Euphrasia

Description: A homoeopathic remedy for conjunctivitis with tears.
Dose (and manufacturers): Nelsons 6c, Weleda 6c and 30c.

STYES

A stye may be treated by bathing it with warm water. However, there are over-the counter eye ointments which may also help. These contain an antibacterial and should be applied to the affected area once or twice daily. Eye drops are not suitable for the treatment of styes.

Brolene Eye Ointment

See entry under Conjunctivitis, above.

Golden Eye Ointment

See entry under Conjunctivitis, above.

COMPLEMENTARY PRODUCTS

HOMOEOPATHIC REMEDIES

❀ Graphites

Description: A homoeopathic remedy for styes.
Dose (and manufacturers): Weleda 6c and 30c, Nelsons 6c.

MOUTH PROBLEMS

ABSCESSES (TOOTH)

See also **General Pain Relief**, page 78, and **Antiseptics**, page 93.

Abscesses usually need to be treated by a dentist. You may need antibiotics, but general painkillers are suitable for use until you can see a dentist. The complementary products listed below may provide relief from the symptoms.

COMPLEMENTARY PRODUCTS

HOMOEOPATHIC REMEDIES

❀ Calcarea sulphurica

Description: A homoeopathic remedy to help heal abscesses after they have begun to emit a discharge.
Dose (and manufacturer): New Era 6x.

❀ Mercurius solubilis

Description: A homoeopathic remedy for abscesses.
Dose (and manufacturers): Weleda 6c and 30c, Nelsons 6c.

❀ Silica

Description: A homoeopathic remedy for abscesses.
Dose (and manufacturers): Weleda 6c and 30c, Nelsons 6c, New Era 6x, Ainsworths 30c.

BAD BREATH AND GINGIVITIS (SORE GUMS)

See also **Antiseptics**, page 93.

A wide range of products is available over the counter for the treatment of bad breath (halitosis) and sore gums (gingivitis). Most of them come in the form of gels and mouthwashes and they contain anti-microbial agents which help to fight bacteria in the mouth. Many antiseptic products are suitable to use as mouthwashes (see **Antiseptics**, page 93).

Gels are suitable for sore gums, while mouthwashes are suitable for both sore gums and bad breath. Some mouthwashes are available in a variety of different flavours, and you may find that you prefer one more than another. Always follow the instructions carefully when using mouthwashes. This is because some need to be diluted before use while others can be used in undiluted form.

This section contains a list of products for bad breath and sore gums with their main ingredients and instructions for use. For specific uses, cautions and warnings for each product, read the product label and information leaflet inside the package.

WARNING NOTE

- Do not swallow any of these products.

- Most gels and liquids in this section are not suitable for teething pains in infants. Always check the pack.

Bansor

Description: A liquid containing cetrimide (an anti-microbial).
Dose: For sore gums, apply a few drops to the affected area.

Bocasan

Description: Mouthwash in powder form for dissolving in water containing sodium perborate (an anti-microbial and cleanser).
Dose: Dissolve 1 sachet of granules in water and use as a mouthwash 3 times a day after meals. Treat for a maximum of 7 days. Not suitable for children under 5 years. Supervise use in children aged 5–12 years.

Corsodyl

Description: A mouthwash containing chlorhexidine (an anti-microbial).
Dose: Rinse with 10ml of mouthwash for 1 minute. Use for 1 month.

Eludril Mouthwash*

Description: A mouthwash containing chlorhexidine (an anti-microbial).
Dose: Rinse mouth with 10–15ml of wash diluted in water. 2–3 times a day. Not recommended for children.
*Also available as Eludril Spray

Medijel

Description: A gel containing lignocaine (a local anaesthetic).
Dose: For sore gums, apply the gel every 20 minutes, as necessary.

Oraldene

Description: A mouthwash containing hexetidine (an anti-microbial).
Dose: Rinse or gargle with 15ml of liquid 2–3 times a day. Do not dilute. Not suitable for children under 5 years.

COMPLEMENTARY PRODUCTS

HOMOEOPATHIC REMEDIES

✤ Mercurius solubilis

Description: A homoeopathic remedy for bad breath.
Dose (and manufacturers): Weleda 6c and 30c, Nelsons 6c.

COLD SORES

Cold sores are very difficult to treat, but various over-the-counter products are available. The main ingredients in them are aciclovir, and also various anti-microbials, including povidone iodine, astringents and anaesthetics.

Cold sores are caused by a virus infection, and aciclovir is an antiviral agent. If it is used at the stage when the cold sore first starts to tingle, it can prevent the progress of the cold sore, stop it altogether or reduce the severity of the attack. It must be applied five times a day at four-hourly intervals, and treatment must continue for 5 days. If the cold sore has not gone by this time, treatment can be continued for a further 5 days. At the end of 10 days, if it is still not better, ask a pharmacist or GP for advice. When you apply a cream containing aciclovir, you may experience stinging and burning. Avoid getting the product inside your mouth or eyes. Aciclovir is safe for use in children, but it is best always to check with a pharmacist before treating cold sores in young children.

This section contains a list of products for cold sores with their main ingredients and instructions for use. For specific uses, cautions and warnings read the product label and information leaflet inside the package.

WARNING NOTE

• If you suffer from recurrent cold sores, you should see your GP for investigation and treatment.

• If cold sore does not clear after 10 days, seek medical advice.

• Patients on corticosteroid treatments should consult a pharmacist or GP before using one of these products.

• Any of these products could cause irritation. If this happens, stop using the product.

• Povidone iodine: products containing this ingredient should **not** be used by pregnant and breast-feeding women, those with thyroid disorders and those taking lithium.

Blisteze

Description: A cream containing ammonia (a soothing ingredient).
Dose: Apply hourly, as required.

Bonjela

Description: A gel containing choline salicylate (an aspirin derivative) and cetalkonium (an antiseptic).
Dose: Apply a small quantity of gel every 3 hours. Maximum 6 applications in 24 hours.

Brush Off Cold Sore Lotion

Description: A solution containing povidone iodine (an antiseptic).
Dose: Apply twice a day.

Colsor*

Description: A cream containing tannic acid, phenol (both astringents) and menthol (a soothing ingredient).
Dose: Apply cream when required.
* Also available in lotion form.

Cymex

Description: A cream containing cetrimide (an antiseptic) and urea (a soothing agent).
Dose: Apply sparingly every hour.

Herpetad Cold Sore Cream

Description: A cream containing aciclovir (an antiviral).
Dose: Use as soon as tingling from developing cold sore is felt. Cover sore and surrounding skin every 4 hours, 5 times a day for 5 days.

Lypsyl Cold Sore Gel

Description: A gel containing lignocaine (a local anaesthetic), cetrimide (an antiseptic) and zinc sulphate (an astringent).
Dose: Apply to sore 3–4 times a day.

Soothelip

Description: A cream containing aciclovir (an antiviral).
Dose: Use as soon as tingling from developing cold sore is felt. Apply to sore every 4 hours, 5 times a day for 5 days. If cold sore does not go, continue applying for a further 5 days.

Virasorb

Description: A cream containing aciclovir (an antiviral).
Dose: Use as soon as tingling from cold sore is felt. Apply every 4 hours, 5 times a day for 5 days. If healing does not occur, use for a further 5 days.

Zovirax Cold Sore Cream

Description: A cream containing aciclovir (an antiviral).
Dose: Use as soon as tingling from developing cold sore is felt. Apply to sore every 4 hours, 5 times a day for up to 10 days.

COMPLEMENTARY PRODUCTS

HOMOEOPATHIC REMEDIES

✿ Natrum muriaticum

Description: A homoeopathic remedy suited to viral skin conditions.
Dose (and manufacturers): Weleda 6c, New Era 6x, Nelsons 6c, Ainsworths 30c.

✿ Rhus toxicodendron

Description: A homoeopathic remedy suited to viral skin conditions.
Dose (and manufacturers): Weleda 6c and 30c, Nelsons 6c, Ainsworths 30c.

MOUTH ULCERS

See also **Antiseptics**, page 93.

A wide variety of products is available to treat mouth ulcers. The most effective treatments seem to be those which contain an anti–inflammatory agent, such as a corticosteroid, although other ingredients such as carbenoxolone and benzydamine also have ulcer–healing activity. Local anaesthetics, astringents and antiseptics are included in some products. Note too that the gels and mouthwashes listed in Bad Breath and Gingivitis (page 248) are also suitable for mouth ulcers.

This section contains a list of products for mouth ulcers with their main ingredients and instructions for use. For specific uses, cautions and warnings, read the product labels and information leaflets inside the packaging.

WARNING NOTE

• If you suffer from recurrent mouth ulcers, see your GP.

• If you suffer from a mouth ulcer which is painless, see your GP immediately.

• If mouth ulcers do not clear after 10 days, see your GP.

• Any of these products could cause irritation. If this happens, stop using the product.

Adcortyl in Orabase

Description: A paste containing triamcinolone (a corticosteroid).
Dose: Apply paste (do not rub) to the affected area up to 3 times a day after meals and once at night. Use for up to 5 days.

Anbesol

Description: A liquid containing lidocaine (an anaesthetic) and chlorocresol and cetylpyridium (antiseptics).
Dose: Up to 2 applications to the affected area, as required. Allow at least 30 minutes between applications. Maximum 8 applications in 24 hours.

Anbesol Adult Strength Gel

Description: A gel containing lidocaine (an anaesthetic), chlorocresol and cetylpyridium (antiseptics).
Dose: Apply gel up to 4 times a day for 7 days. Not suitable for young children.

Bioral

Description: A gel containing carbenoxolone (an ulcer-healing drug).
Dose: Rub gel on after meals and at bedtime. Leave the gel in contact with the ulcer for as long as possible. Not suitable for children.

Bonjela*

Description: A gel containing choline salicylate (an analgesic) and cetalkonium (an antiseptic).
Dose: Use every 3 hours. Maximum 6 applications in 24 hours.
* Also available as Bonjela Pastilles.

Corlan

Description: A tablet containing hydrocortisone (a corticosteroid).
Dose: Dissolve 1 pellet near the site of the ulcer 4 times a day. Not suitable for children under 12 years unless advised by GP.

Corsodyl Dental Gel*

Description: A gel containing chlorhexidine (an antiseptic).
Dose: Apply gel directly onto affected area 1–2 times a day for 1 minute.
* Also available as Corsodyl Mouthwash and Corsodyl Spray.

Frador

Description: A liquid containing antiseptic and astringent ingredients.
Dose: Apply to ulcer with applicator supplied 4 times a day after meals and before bedtime. Not suitable for children.

Medijel

See entry under Bad Breath and Gingivitis, page 249.

Pyralvex

Description: A liquid containing salicylic acid (an analgesic).
Dose: Apply with the brush supplied to the affected area 3–4 times a day. Not suitable for children under 12 years.

Rinstead Adult Gel*

Description: A gel containing benzocaine (an anaesthetic) and chloroxylenol (an antiseptic).
Dose: Apply to affected area up to 6 times a day. Not suitable for young children.
* Also available as Rinstead Pastilles.

TOOTHACHE

See also **General Pain Relief**, page 78, and **General Pain Relief for Children**, page 89.

Toothache should always be investigated by your dentist. The earlier you receive treatment, the sooner the pain will stop. While you are waiting for your appointment you can take painkillers (see **General Pain Relief**, page 78). The products listed below may also help.

For toothache in young children, see **General Pain Relief for Children**, page 89, and also Teething Problems, page 280.

Complementary remedies should not be used as a substitute for receiving dental treatment.

Dentogen

Description: A gel to ease toothache. Contains clove oil.
Dose: Apply gel to affected tooth.

COMPLEMENTARY PRODUCTS

HERBAL REMEDIES

❀ Pickle's Soothake Gel

Description: A gel to relieve toothache. Contains clove oil and an antiseptic.
Dose: Apply to the tooth as required and then seek dental treatment. Not suitable for children.

❀ Pickle's Soothake Toothache Tincture

Description: A tincture used for treating toothache. Contains a mild local anaesthetic.
Dose: Apply to the tooth to ease pain as required.

HOMOEOPATHIC REMEDIES

❀ Chamomilla

Description: A homoeopathic remedy for treating toothache that is worse when taking warm drinks.
Dose (and manufacturers): Weleda 30c and 3x, Ainsworths 30c.

❀ Coffea

Description: A homoeopathic remedy for treating toothache with shooting pains.
Dose (and manufacturer): Weleda 6c.

❀ Thuja

Description: A homoeopathic remedy for tooth decay at roots.
Dose (and manufacturers): Weleda 6c and 30c, Nelsons 6c.

THRUSH (ORAL)

Oral thrush is best treated by a GP. However, a couple of products are included in this section. Both contain anti-microbial ingredients, which may help to reduce the infection. If the symptoms persist for more than about 5 days, you should see your GP.

Corsodyl Dental Gel*

Description: A gel containing chlorhexidine (an antibacterial).
Dose: Apply gel to affected area for 1 minute, 1–2 times a day. Continue treatment for 2 days after infection has cleared.
*Also available as Corsodyl Mouthwash (see page 249).

Daktarin Oral Gel

Description: A gel containing miconazole (an antifungal).
Dose: Adults: Apply a small amount of gel 4 times a day. Hold in mouth for as long as possible and then spit out. Children: Doses vary according to age. Check label to ensure correct dosage. Continue for 2 further days after thrush symptoms have gone.

Eludril Mouthwash

See entry under Bad Breath and Gingivitis, page 249.

Oraldene

See entry under Bad Breath and Gingivitis, page 249.

COMPLEMENTARY PRODUCTS

HOMOEOPATHIC TREATMENT

❀ Nelsons Candida

Description: A treatment for Candida albicans infections, including oral thrush.
Dose: Adults: 2 6c tablets every hour for 6 doses, followed by 2 tablets 3 times a day. Children: Half the adult dose.

BLOOD AND CIRCULATORY PROBLEMS

• Anaemia • Chilblains • Piles • Varicose Veins

ANAEMIA

Over-the-counter remedies are not appropriate. Anaemia requires investigation and treatment from your GP.

COMPLEMENTARY PRODUCTS

Although you should always seek medical advice for the treatment of anaemia, you may find that the complementary remedies help some of the symptoms associated with this condition. Below you will find a remedy which you may wish to consider, but do not use it as an alternative to taking the advice of your doctor.

HOMOEOPATHIC REMEDIES

❀ Ferrum phosphoricum

Description: A homoeopathic remedy for anaemia.
Dose (and manufacturers): Weleda 6c and 30c, New Era 6x, Nelsons 6c. If anaemia persists, consult your doctor.

CHILBLAINS

With the widespread use of central heating, chilblains are now a very rare occurrence. However, for those who do tend to suffer from them, keeping warm at home and wrapping up well whenever you go out will help prevent them. If the skin becomes cracked, the chilblains can be treated with antiseptics (see **Antiseptics**, page 93) to reduce risk of infection.

Vitathone

Description: An ointment for relieving itchiness experienced with chilblains. Contains menthyl nicotinate, to stimulate the circulation.
Dose: Apply every 2–3 hours as needed. Not suitable for children.

COMPLEMENTARY PRODUCTS

HERBAL REMEDIES

❀ Pickle's Chilblain Cream

Description: A herbal cream for treating chilblains. Contains a rubifacient (an ingredient that helps create warmth on the skin).
Dose: Apply sparingly morning and night and more frequently if required. Not suitable for pregnant or breast-feeding women.

❀ Pickle's Snowfire

Description: A herbal ointment for treating chilblains. Contains benzoin, citronella and oils of thyme, clove and cade.
Dose: Apply as required.

❀ Weleda Frost Cream

Description: A cream homoeopathic remedy to relieve symptoms of chilblains. Contains balsam of Peru, rosemary oil and stibium metallicum.
Dose: Apply cream to affected area several times a day. May cause allergy. Carry out skin patch test first.

HOMOEOPATHIC REMEDIES

❀ Hamamelis

Description: A homoeopathic remedy for chilblains with a blue tinge.
Dose (and manufacturers): Weleda 6c and 30c, Nelsons 6c. Not suitable for children.

❀ Nelsons Ointment for Chilblains

Description: A homoeopathic ointment for treating unbroken chilblains. Contains tamus communis 6x.
Dose: Apply as required.

PILES

Remedies for piles usually contain local anaesthetics or astringents or both. Anaesthetics include cinchocaine, lidocaine and lignocaine and these ingredients help to numb the discomfort and itching. Astringents include allantoin, bismuth salts, peru balsam and zinc oxide, and these ingredients help to reduce swelling. One product in this section contains hydrocortisone (a steroid) which reduces inflammation, rather than just numbing the discomfort.

This section contains a list of products for piles with their main ingredients and instructions for use. For specific uses, warnings and cautions read product labels and information leaflets inside the package.

WARNING NOTE

• None of these products is suitable for children under 12 years. Children should always be seen by a GP if piles is suspected.

• All the products listed have the potential to increase irritation in the anus. If this happens, stop using the product immediately. Particularly, products containing local anaesthetics may cause anal irritation.

• Products containing hydrocortisone and local anaesthetics should not be used for longer than 7 days.

• Pregnant women and those less than 18 years should not use products containing hydrocortisone.

Anacal Rectal Ointment

Description: An ointment containing mucopolysaccharide (an ingredient thought to strengthen tissue in the anus).
Dose: Apply ointment to the affected area 1–4 times a day. Not suitable for children under 12 years.

Anacal Suppositories

Description: A suppository containing mucopolysaccharide (an ingredient thought to strengthen tissue in the anus).
Dose: 1 suppository to be inserted 1–2 times a day. Not suitable for children under 12 years.

Anodesyn Ointment

Description: An ointment containing benzocaine (a mild local anaesthetic) and allantoin (an astringent).
Dose: Use twice a day and after each bowel movement. Not suitable for children under 12 years. Do not use for more than 1 week unless recommended by your GP.

Anodesyn Suppositories

Description: A suppository containing lignocaine (a mild local anaesthetic) and allantoin (an astringent).
Dose: 1 suppository to be inserted morning and evening and after each bowel movement. Not suitable for children under 12 years. Do not use for more than 2 weeks unless recommended by your GP.

Anusol Ointment and Cream

Description: A cream or ointment, both containing bismuth, balsam Peru and zinc oxide (astringents).
Dose: Apply night and morning and after each bowel movement. Not suitable for children under 12 years.

Anusol Suppositories

Description: A suppository containing bismuth, balsam Peru and zinc oxide (astringents).
Dose: 1 suppository to be inserted morning and evening and after each bowel movement. Not suitable for children under 12 years.

Anusol Plus HC Ointment*

Description: An ointment containing similar ingredients to Anusol, plus hydro-cortisone (a steroid).
Dose: Apply sparingly to affected area at night in the morning and after each bowel movement. Not suitable for children under 18 years. Do not use for more than 7 days.
* Also available as Anusol Plus HC suppositories.

Germoloids Cream*

Description: A cream containing lidocaine (a mild local anaesthetic) and zinc oxide (an astringent).
Dose: Apply twice a day and after each bowel movement. Applications not to exceed 4 per day. Not suitable for children under 12 years.
* Also available as Germoloids Ointment and Suppositories.

Hemocane Cream

Description: A cream containing lignocaine (a mild local anaesthetic) and zinc oxide (an astringent) with other ingredients.
Dose: Adults: Apply morning and evening and after each bowel movement. Not suitable for children under 12 years.

Nupercainal

Description: An ointment containing cinchocaine (a mild local anaesthetic).
Dose: Apply ointment sparingly to affected area up to 3 times a day. Not suitable for children under 12 years.

Preparation H Ointment*

Description: An ointment containing shark oil (a skin protectant).
Dose: Apply morning and evening and after each bowel movement. Not suitable for children under 12 years.
* Also available as Preparation H Suppositories.

COMPLEMENTARY PRODUCTS

HERBAL REMEDIES

❀ Lanes Heemex

Description: An astringent ointment to soothe the discomfort of piles. Contains witch-hazel.
Dose: Apply morning and evening and after each bowel movement. Can cause allergy. Not suitable for children.

❀ Nelsons Haemorrhoid Cream

Description: A cream used as a herbal remedy to soothe and treat symptoms of piles. Contains witch-hazel, horse chestnut, calendula and paeonia officinalis.
Dose: Apply as needed. Not suitable for children.

❀ Potter's Pile Tabs

Description: A tablet herbal remedy to relieve the symptoms of piles. Has an astringent and laxative effect. Contains pilewort, agrimony, cascara and stone root.
Dose: 2 tablets 3 times a day. Elderly should take 2 tablets twice a day. Not suitable for children or pregnant women.

❀ Potter's Pilewort Ointment

Description: An ointment used as a herbal remedy to relieve the symptoms of piles. Contains pilewort and lanolin.
Dose: Apply twice a day. Not suitable for children. Do not use if sensitive to lanolin.

HOMOEOPATHIC REMEDIES

❀ Calcarea fluorica

Description: A homoeopathic remedy for piles that promotes tissue elasticity.
Dose (and manufacturers): Weleda 6c and 30c, Nelsons 6c, New Era 6x. Not suitable for children.

❀ Hamamelis

Description: A homoeopathic remedy for piles.
Dose (and manufacturers): Weleda 6c and 30c, Nelsons 6c. Not suitable for children.

❀ Nux vomica

Description: A homoeopathic remedy for itchy piles.
Dose (and manufacturers): Weleda 6c and 30c, Nelsons 6c, Ainsworths 30c. Not suitable for children.

VARICOSE VEINS

Over-the-counter remedies are not appropriate. Treatment is required from your GP.

COMPLEMENTARY PRODUCTS

Although you should always seek medical advice for the treatment of varicose veins, you may find that the complementary remedies help some of the symptoms associated with this condition. Below you will find a list of remedies which you may wish to consider, but do not use them as an alternative to taking the advice of your doctor.

HERBAL REMEDIES

❀ Potter's Varicose Ointment

Description: An ointment herbal remedy for varicose veins. Contains cade oil, witch hazel and zinc oxide.
Dose: Apply twice a day. Do not apply on broken skin.

HOMOEOPATHIC REMEDIES

❀ Calcarea fluorica

Description: A homoeopathic remedy for varicose veins that promotes tissue elasticity.
Dose (and manufacturers): Weleda 6c and 30c, Nelsons 6c, New Era 6x.

❁ Hamamelis

Description: A homoeopathic remedy for varicose veins.
Dose (and manufacturers): Weleda 6c and 30c, Nelsons 6c. Not suitable for children.

❁ New Era Combination L

Description: A homoeopathic remedy for varicose veins. Contains calc fluor, ferr phos and nat mur.
Dose: The prepared remedy contains 6x each of the above ingredients.

❁ Pulsatilla

Description: A homoeopathic remedy for varicose veins associated with poor circulation.
Dose (and manufacturers): Weleda 6c and 30c, Nelsons 6c, Ainsworths 30c.

MENTAL AND EMOTIONAL WELLBEING

• Depression • Fatigue • Insomnia • Anxiety and Stress

DEPRESSION (MILD)

Over-the-counter remedies are not appropriate. Orthodox treatment required by GP.

COMPLEMENTARY PRODUCTS

Although you should always seek medical advice for the treatment of depression you may find that the complementary remedies help some of the symptoms associated with this condition. Below you will find a list of remedies which you may wish to consider, but do not use them as an alternative to taking the advice of your doctor.

WARNING NOTE

• The following complementary remedies are for mild and temporary depression only. See your GP if depression continues, or is severe.

See also Anxiety and Stress, page 270.

HOMOEOPATHIC REMEDIES

❋ Actaea racemosa

Description: A homoeopathic remedy for depression.
Dose (and manufacturers): Weleda 6c, Nelsons 6c.

❋ Hypericum

Description: A herbal remedy for mild depression. Made from the St John's wort plant.
Dose (and manufacturers): Weleda 6c and 30c, Nelsons 6c, Ainsworths 30c.

❋ Kalium phosphoricum

Description: A homoeopathic remedy for treating mild depression.
Dose (and manufacturers): Weleda 6c and 30c, Nelsons 6c, New Era 6x.

❀ Natrum muriaticum

Description: A homoeopathic remedy for mild depression.
Dose (and manufacturers): Weleda 6c and 30c, New Era 6x, Nelsons 6c, Ainsworths 30c.

❀ Sepia

Description: A homoeopathic remedy for mild depression.
Dose (and manufacturers): Weleda 6c and 30c, Nelsons 6c, Ainsworths 30c.

FATIGUE

See also Iron, page 287.

WARNING NOTE

- Fatigue may be a symptom of a wide range of disorders. If the condition persists, consult your GP. This section contains a list of over-the-counter tonics which may, in the short term, help those who feel tired or run down. They contain mixtures of vitamins and mild stimulants such as caffeine.

Effico Tonic

Description: A liquid containing caffeine, vitamin B1 and nicotinamide.
Dose: Adults: 10ml 3 times a day after food. Children: 2.5–5ml, depending on age, 3 times a day after food.

Labiton

Description: A liquid containing alcohol, caffeine, vitamin B1 and kola nut dried extract.
Dose: 10–20ml twice a day. Not suitable for children under 12 years.

Metatone

Description: A liquid containing calcium, potassium, sodium, manganese and vitamin B1.
Dose: Adults: 5–10ml 2–3 times a day. Children aged 6–12 years: 5ml 2–3 times a day. Not suitable for children under 6 years.

Minadex Tonic

Description: A liquid containing vitamins A and D3, calcium, copper, iron, manganese and potassium.
Dose: Adults: 10ml 3 times a day. Children aged 3–12 years: 5ml 3 times a day. Children aged 6 months–3 years: 5ml twice a day. Not suitable for babies under 6 months.

Yestamin Plus Tablets

Description: A tablet containing caffeine, yeast and glucose.
Dose: 2 tablets 3 times a day. Not suitable for children.

Yeast-Vite

Description: A tablet containing caffeine, vitamin B1 and nicotinamide.
Dose: 2 tablets every 3–4 hours as required. Maximum 12 tablets in 24 hours. Not suitable for children.

COMPLEMENTARY PRODUCTS

HERBAL REMEDIES

❀ Bio-Strath Elixir

Description: A herbal elixir containing yeast to help fatigue and tiredness.
Dose: 5ml 3 times a day before meals. Not suitable for children under 12 years.

❀ Curzon

Description: A herbal stimulant in tablet form to relieve nervous strain. Contains damiana.
Dose: 2 tablets at night and 2 in the morning. Not suitable for children under 12 years. Can cause side-effects – read labels.

❀ Potter's Chlorophyll

Description: A herbal stimulant in tablet form to relieve temporary tiredness. Contains kola nut and chlorophyll.
Dose: 1–2 tablets 3 times a day.

❀ Potter's Elixir of Damiana and Saw Palmetto

Description: An elixir to take as a restorative. Contains damiana, saw palmetto and cornsilk.
Dose: 10ml 3 times a day for 7 days, reducing dose by half for following days. Not suitable for children under 12 years. Can cause side-effects – read labels.

❀ Potter's Strength Tablets

Description: A herbal tablet stimulant for fatigue after illness. Contains damiana, kola and saw palmetto.
Dose: 2 tablets 3 times a day. Not suitable for children. Can cause side-effects – read labels.

HOMOEOPATHIC REMEDIES

❋ Calcarea phosphorica

Description: A homoeopathic remedy for fatigue in adolescents.
Dose (and manufacturers): Weleda 6c, Nelsons 6c, New Era 6x.

❋ Gelsemium

Description: A homoeopathic remedy for fatigue.
Dose (and manufacturers): Weleda 6c, Nelsons 6c, Ainsworths 30c.

❋ Kalium phosphoricum

Description: A homoeopathic remedy for nervous exhaustion.
Dose (and manufacturers): Weleda 6c, Nelsons 6c, New Era 6x.

❋ New Era Combination B

Description: A homoeopathic remedy for general debility. Contains calc phos, kali phos and ferr phos.
Dose: 1 tablet contains 6x of each of the above ingredients.

❋ Sepia

Description: A homoeopathic remedy for tiredness.
Dose (and manufacturers): Weleda 6c and 30c, Nelsons 6c, Ainsworths 30c.

INSOMNIA

Over-the-counter medicines for sleeplessness contain antihistamines. Antihistamines are found in many over-the-counter remedies, including those for colds and flu, coughs, hayfever and travel sickness. One of the main side-effects of antihistamines is drowsiness. Hence they are used in over-the-counter medicines to help promote sleep. However, their effects can last into the next day, and you may feel less alert the following morning. If this is the case, be very careful about driving or operating machinery. Alcohol adds to the sedative effects of antihistamines and so is best avoided while taking these products (see also Warning Note, below).

These medicines should not be used for long periods of time (e.g. more than 3–4 days). They are intended for temporary use only. Indeed, if you are having trouble sleeping it is best to try simple lifestyle changes first, as outlined in the Insomnia entry (page 53) of the **Ailments** chapter.

WARNING NOTE

Antihistamines

• Remedies containing antihistamines may cause drowsiness (for products in this section, this is a deliberately used action).

- Do not combine with other sedative drugs, such as antidepressants and sleeping tablets, or with alcohol, as this will increase the drowsiness. Do not drive or operate machinery if the remedy makes you drowsy.

- Do not use if pregnant or if you have prostate enlargement, urinary retention, liver disease or glaucoma.

- These cautions also apply to all complementary remedies listed in this section.

Nytol*

Description: Tablet containing diphenhydramine (an antihistamine).
Dose: 2 tablets taken 20 minutes before bedtime. Not suitable for children under 16 years.
* Also available as Nytol One-a-Night.

Paxidorm Tablets*

Description: A tablet containing diphenhydramine (an antihistamine).
Dose: 1–2 tablets just before bedtime Not suitable for children under 16 years.
* Also available as Paxidorm Syrup.

Phenergan Nightime

Description: A tablet containing promethazine (an antihistamine).
Dose: 2 tablets at night. Not suitable for children under 16 years.

Sominex

Description: A tablet containing promethazine (an antihistamine).
Dose: 1 tablet at bedtime. Not suitable for children under 16 years.

COMPLEMENTARY PRODUCTS

HERBAL REMEDIES

❀ Heath & Heather Quiet Night Tablets

Description: Tablet remedy to aid sleep. Contains hops, passionflower and valerian.
Dose: 2 tablets 1 hour before bedtime. Not suitable for children.

❀ Natrasleep

Description: A herbal tablet remedy to promote natural sleep. Contains hops and valerian.
Dose: 1–3 tablets 30 minutes before bedtime. Not suitable for children.

❀ Naturest

Description: A tablet herbal remedy for temporary insomnia due to stress. Contains passiflora.
Dose: 2 tablets 3 times a day and 1–3 tablets at bedtime. Not suitable for children.

❀ Noctura

Description: A tablet remedy for insomnia. Contains kali brom, coffea, passiflora, avena sativa, alfalfa and valeriana.
Dose: 2 tablets 4 hours before bedtime and 2 tablets immediately before bedtime. 2 further tablets can be taken during the night, if required. 1 tablet contains 6c of each of the ingredients above. Not suitable for children.

❀ Nytol Herbal

Description: A tablet remedy to relieve temporary insomnia. Contains hops, Jamaican dogwood, passiflora, pulsatilla and wild lettuce.
Dose: 2 tablets before bedtime. Not suitable for children.

❀ Potter's Nodoff Passiflora Tablets

Description: A tablet herbal remedy to promote sleep. Also suitable for diabetics. Contains passiflora.
Dose: 2 tablets in early evening and 2 tablets before bedtime. Not suitable for children.

❀ Somnus

Description: A tablet herbal remedy to encourage natural sleep. Contains hops, valerian and wild lettuce.
Dose: 2 tablets 1 hour before bedtime. Not suitable for children.

❀ Valerian Compound

Description: A tablet herbal remedy to encourage natural sleep. Contains hops, Jamaican dogwood, passionflower, valerian and wild lettuce.
Dose: 2 tablets in early evening and 2 just before bedtime. Not suitable for children.

HOMOEOPATHIC REMEDIES

❀ Arsenicum album

Description: A homoeopathic remedy for insomnia caused by an overactive mind.
Dose (and manufacturers): Weleda 6c and 30c, Nelsons 6c, Ainsworths 30c.

❀ Calcarea carbonica

Description: A homoeopathic remedy for insomnia.
Dose (and manufacturers): Nelsons 6c, Weleda 6c and 30c.

❀ Chamomilla

Description: A homoeopathic remedy for insomnia caused by pain or anger. Also available in drops.
Dose (and manufacturers): Ainsworths 30c, Weleda 3x and 30c.

❀ Coffea

Description: A homoeopathic remedy for insomnia caused by an overactive mind.
Dose (and manufacturer): Weleda 6c.

❀ Sulphur

Description: A homoeopathic remedy for unrefreshing sleep.
Dose (and manufacturers): Ainsworths 30c, Nelsons 6c, New Era 6c and 30c.

ANXIETY AND STRESS

Over-the-counter remedies are not appropriate. Orthodox treatment is required via your GP.

See also Insomnia, page 267.

COMPLEMENTARY PRODUCTS

Although you should always seek medical advice for the treatment of anxiety and stress, you may find that the complementary remedies help some of the symptoms associated with this condition. Below you will find a list of remedies which you may wish to consider, but do not use them as an alternative to taking the advice of your doctor.

WARNING NOTE

These warnings apply to all products:

• Do not use if taking other sedative medicines. Not suitable for pregnant and breast-feeding women.

• Those on prescription medication should not take before checking with a pharmacist or GP. Those with clinical depression should not use. Avoid alcohol.

❈ Avena Sativa Comp

Description: A liquid herbal remedy with a sedative and analgesic effect to treat irritability, tension, tension-induced aches and pains and sleep problems. Contains coffea, oats, passionflower and valerian.
Dose: Adults: 10–20 drops in water 30 minutes before bedtime. Children aged 2–12 years: 5–10 drops. Not suitable for children under 2 years.

❈ Biophyllin

Description: A tablet herbal remedy to treat tension, restlessness and irritability. Also helps promote sleep. Contains black cohosh, Jamaican dogwood, scullcap and valerian.
Dose: 2 tablets after meals 3 times a day. Not suitable for children.

❈ Bio-Strath Valerian Formula

Description: A liquid herbal remedy to relieve tension, irritability, stress and emotional strain. Encourages natural sleep. Contains passionflower, peppermint, valerian and yeast.
Dose: 20 drops in water 3 times a day before meals. Not suitable for children. Do not combine with other homoeopathic remedies.

❈ Fragador

Description: A tablet remedy to relieve temporary irritability and emotional unrest caused by common emotional stresses and strains. Contains aniseed, conchae, lovage, sage, scurvy grass, stinging nettle, wheatgerm, wild strawberry, glycogen 10x, ferrum phosphoricum 4x, natrum carbonicum 1x and radix mel 1x.
Dose: 2 tablets 3 times a day. Not suitable for children. Do not combine with other homoeopathic remedies.

❈ Heath & Heather Becalm

Description: A tablet remedy to aid relaxation caused by stress. Also has a sedative effect. Contains hops, passionflower and valerian.
Dose: 1 tablet 3 times a day. Not suitable for children.

❈ Kalms Tablets

Description: A tablet herbal remedy to relieve symptoms of anxiety, irritability and stress. Encourages natural sleep. Contains gentian, hops and valerian.
Dose: 2 tablets 3 times a day after meals. Not suitable for children.

❋ Motherwort Compound

Description: A tablet remedy to treat symptoms of emotional stress and strain. Also has sedative effect. Contains limeflower, motherwort and passionflower.
Dose: 2 tablets 3 times a day after meals. Not suitable for children.

❋ Natracalm

Description: A tablet remedy to relieve stress, strain and nervous tension. Contains passionflower.
Dose: 1 tablet 3 times a day. Not suitable for children.

❋ Potter's Ana-sed

Description: A sedative herbal remedy that also treats irritability and tension. Contains hops, Jamaican dogwood, passionflower, pulsatilla and wild lettuce.
Dose: 1–2 tablets 3 times a day and 2 at bedtime. Not suitable for children.

❋ Potter's Newrelax

Description: A tablet remedy to relieve symptoms of irritability, emotional tension and stress, and tension–induced aches and pains. Also has a sedative and analgesic action. Contains hops, scullcap, valerian and vervain.
Dose: 2 tablets 3 times a day. Not suitable for children.

❋ Quiet Life

Description: A tablet remedy for irritability, nervousness, tension and sleeplessness. Also has a mild sedative action. Contains hops, motherwort, passionflower, valerian, wild lettuce and vitamins B1, B2 and B3.
Dose: 2 tablets twice a day and 2–3 tablets before bedtime. Not suitable for children.

❋ Serenity

Description: A tablet remedy to relieve emotional stress, strain and irritability. Contains hops, passionflower and valerian.
Dose: 2 tablets 3 times a day after food. Not suitable for children.

❋ Sunerven

Description: A tablet remedy to relieve anxiety, irritability, emotional stress, fatigue and insomnia. Contains motherwort, passionflower, valerian and vervain.
Dose: 2 tablets 3 times a day after meals and 2 tablets before bedtime. Not suitable for children.

❀ Valerina Day Tablets*

Description: A tablet to relieve tension and irritability and promote sleep. Contains lemon balm and valerian.
Dose: 2 tablets 3 times a day. Not suitable for children.
* Also available as Valerina Night Tablets, which also promotes sleep.

HOMOEOPATHIC PRODUCTS

❀ Argentum nitricum

Description: A homoeopathic remedy for anxiety caused by nervousness or anticipatory fear.
Dose (and manufacturers): Nelsons 6c, Weleda 6c and 30c.

❀ Arsenicum album

Description: A homoeopathic remedy for anxiety with fear.
Dose (and manufacturers): Nelsons 6c, Weleda 6c and 30c.

CHILDHOOD COMPLAINTS

• Chickenpox • Colic and Wind • Cradle Cap • Measles
• Mumps • Nappy Rash • Teething Problems

CHICKENPOX

See Paracetamol or Ibuprofen remedies in **General Pain Relief for Children**, page 89, to relieve pain and reduce temperature.

Soothe skin by applying aqueous calamine cream, available in generic form from your pharmacist. Request at the counter.

WARNING NOTE

• Do not give aspirin to children under 12 years.

COMPLEMENTARY PRODUCTS

Not suitable.

COLIC AND WIND

Over-the-counter colic mixtures usually contain sodium bicarbonate, which acts as antacid to reduce stomach acidity, or dimethicone, an ingredient which helps to get rid of excess gas in the stomach and hence the wind. Various other ingredients such as caraway and dill oil are included and these help to settle the stomach.

This section contains a list of products for colic and wind in babies with their main ingredients and instructions for use. For specific uses, cautions and warnings, read the product label and information leaflet inside the package. This also applies to all complementary remedies.

WARNING NOTE

• If, in addition to symptoms of colic, your baby is unwell, vomiting or suffering a fever, seek the advice of your GP immediately.

⚔ Atkinson and Barker's Infant Gripe Mixture

Description: A liquid containing sodium bicarbonate (an antacid) with dill and caraway oils.
Dose: 2.5–10ml every 4 hours, depending on age. Read label. Not suitable for babies under 1 month.

⚐ Dentinox Infant Colic Drops

Description: A liquid containing dimethicone (an anti-wind ingredient).
Dose: 2.5ml with or after each feed. Maximum 6 doses a day. Can be used from birth onwards.

⚐ Infacol

Description: A liquid containing simethicone (an anti-wind ingredient). Measuring dropper supplied in pack.
Dose: 1 dropper dose (0.5ml) before each feed. Can be used from birth onwards.

⚐ Neo Baby Mixture

Description: A liquid containing sodium bicarbonate (an antacid), dill oil and ginger.
Dose: 2.5–15ml 3 times a day, according to age. Read label.

⚐ Nurse Harvey's Gripe Mixture

Description: A liquid containing sodium bicarbonate (an antacid) with dill oil and caraway oil.
Dose: 5–10ml, depending on age, after or during feeds. Maximum 6 doses in 24 hours. Not suitable for babies under 1 month.

⚐ Woodward's Colic Drops

Description: A liquid containing dimethicone (an anti-wind ingredient). Measuring dropper supplied in pack.
Dose: Children under 2 years: 1 dropper dose (3ml) before each feed.

⚐ Woodward's Gripe Water

Description: A liquid containing sodium bicarbonate (an antacid) and dill oil.
Dose: 5–10ml, depending on age, after or during feeds. Maximum 6 doses in 24 hours. Not suitable for babies under 1 month.

COMPLEMENTARY PRODUCTS

HERBAL REMEDIES

❀ Biobalm Powder

Description: A herbal remedy in powder form to relieve wind and stomach upset. Contains camomile, Irish bark, marshmallow root and slippery elm.
Dose: Half to 1 teaspoon mixed with water up to 4 times a day. Not suitable for children under 5 years.

HOMOEOPATHIC REMEDIES

❀ Chamomilla

Description: A liquid homeopathic remedy for colic.
Dose (and manufacturers): Ainsworths 30c, Weleda 3x and 30c.

CRADLE CAP

Remedies for cradle cap contain antiseptics, which should be sufficient to clear the condition. Rubbing olive oil or baby oil into the scalp is also a very effective way of treating cradle cap.

This section lists products for cradle cap and their main ingredients and instructions for use. For specific uses, cautions and warnings, read the product label or information leaflet inside the package.

WARNING NOTE

• These products should not be used on broken or inflamed skin.

• If cradle cap has spread to the baby's face, seek the advice of your GP.

• Keep all products out of the baby's eyes. If this occurs, rinse with clean water immediately.

⚞ Capasal Shampoo

Description: A shampoo containing coal tar, coconut oil and salicylic acid.
Dose: Shampoo baby's head, rinse and repeat. May be used daily, if necessary.

⚞ Dentinox Cradle Cap Treatment Shampoo

Description: A shampoo containing various detergents.
Dose: Shampoo baby's head, rinse and repeat. Do this at every bathtime until condition clears.

⚞ SCR

Description: A cream containing antiseptic.
Dose: Apply cream sparingly to baby's head. Massage in gently. Wash off after 30 minutes–2 hours, depending on severity. A second treatment can be applied, if required, after 7 days. Do not leave cream on for more than 30 minutes on babies under 12 months. Do not apply to broken or inflamed skin.

COMPLEMENTARY PRODUCTS

Not suitable.

MEASLES

See Paracetamol or Ibuprofen remedies in **General Pain Relief for Children**, page 89, to relieve pain and reduce temperature.

WARNING NOTE

• Do not give aspirin to children under 12 years.

COMPLEMENTARY PRODUCTS

Not suitable.

MUMPS

See Paracetamol or Ibuprofen remedies in **General Pain Relief for Children**, page 89, to relieve pain and reduce temperature.

WARNING NOTE

• Do not give aspirin to children under 12 years.

COMPLEMENTARY PRODUCTS

Not suitable.

NAPPY RASH

Nappy rash can often be prevented by changing dirty nappies promptly as well as by use of mild preparations such as zinc and castor oil ointment or white petroleum jelly which may be applied at each nappy change.

The main ingredients in products for the treatment of nappy rash are moisturisers, skin protectants and skin barriers. They help nappy rash by soothing and moisturising the skin, providing a barrier between the skin and the cause of the irritation and reducing the risk of infection. Some products also contain antibacterials such as cetrimide and benzalkonium chloride which also help to reduce the risk of infection.

Sometimes babies with nappy rash also develop a fungal infection. In these cases it is best to see a doctor, although there is one antifungal product available (Canesten cream). Consult a pharmacist before using this product.

This section contains a list of products for the treatment of nappy rash with their main ingredients and instructions for use. For specific uses, cautions and warnings, read the product label and leaflet inside the packaging. This also applies to all complementary products.

Canesten 1% Cream

Description: A cream containing clotrimazole (an antifungal).
Dose: Apply to baby's bottom after washing and drying 2–3 times a day. Massage into the skin gently, avoiding rubbing.

Conotrane Cream

Description: A cream containing benzalkonium chloride (an antiseptic) and dimethicone (a soothing agent).
Dose: Apply cream after each nappy change.

Curash

Description: A powder treatment containing zinc oxide (an antiseptic and astringent).
Dose: Apply powder to baby's bottom at each nappy change. Avoid inhalation by baby. Do not apply to broken skin.

Drapolene Cream

Description: A cream containing benzalkonium chloride and cetrimide (antiseptics).
Dose: Apply after washing and drying at each nappy change.

Kamillosan

Description: An ointment containing lanolin and camomile extract.
Dose: Apply cream after each nappy change.

Metanium Ointment

Description: An ointment containing titanium salts (an antiseptic and astringent).
Dose: Apply after washing and drying at each nappy change.

Morhulin Ointment

Description: An ointment containing cod liver oil (a moisturiser) and zinc oxide (an antiseptic and astringent).
Dose: Apply to baby's bottom after washing and drying.

⚞ Neo Baby Cream

Description: A cream containing cetrimide and benzalkonium (antiseptics).
Dose: Apply to baby's bottom after washing and drying.

⚞ Siopel

Description: A cream containing dimethicone (a barrier and soothing ingredient) and cetrimide (an antiseptic).
Dose: Apply 3–5 times a day after washing and drying for 3–4 days. Then apply 1–2 times a day.

⚞ Sudocrem

Description: A cream containing zinc oxide (an antiseptic and astringent) and hypoallergenic lanolin.
Dose: Apply thinly, as required.

⚞ Unguentum Merck

Description: A cream containing a variety of soothing agents.
Dose: Apply as required.

⚞ Vasogen Cream

Description: A cream containing zinc oxide (an antiseptic and astringent) and calamine (a soothing ingredient).
Dose: Apply after washing and drying at each nappy change.

⚞ Woodward's Nappy Rash Ointment

Description: An ointment containing zinc oxide (an antiseptic and astringent) and cod liver oil (a moisturiser).
Dose: Apply 3 times a day during a nappy change, after washing and drying affected area.

COMPLEMENTARY PRODUCTS

HERBAL REMEDIES

❀ Weleda Balsamicum Ointment

Description: An ointment herbal remedy for helping to heal nappy rash. Contains balsam of Peru, dog's mercury, marigold (calendula) and stibium metallicum preparatum.
Dose: Apply to clean and dry skin several times a day.

TEETHING PROBLEMS

See Paracetamol or Ibuprofen remedies in **General Pain Relief for Children**, page 89, to relieve pain and reduce temperature.

If a baby is teething, a teething ring or biscuit may be tried. However, if the baby's sleep is being disrupted, an over-the-counter remedy may be helpful. These come in the form of gels and liquids and contain a mixture of analgesics, local anaesthetics and antiseptics.

This section contains a list of products for teething with their main ingredients and instructions for use. For specific uses, cautions and warnings, read the product label and information leaflet inside the package. This also applies to complementary products.

🐴 Anbesol Teething Gel*

Description: A gel containing lidocaine (an anaesthetic) and various antiseptics.
Dose: 1 application up to 4 times a day.
* Also available as Anbesol Liquid.

🐴 Bonjela Oral Pain-Relieving Gel

Description: A gel containing choline salicylate (an analgesic) and an antiseptic.
Dose: Apply to gums no more than every 3 hours. Maximum 6 applications in 24 hours. Not suitable for babies under 4 months.

🐴 Calgel Teething Gel

Description: A gel containing lignocaine (an anaesthetic) and an antiseptic.
Dose: Apply up to 6 times a day. Ensure 20 minutes elapse between applications. Not suitable for babies under 3 months.

🐴 Dentinox Teething Gel

Description: A gel containing lignocaine (an anaesthetic) and an antiseptic.
Dose: Apply every 20 minutes when required. Suitable from birth onwards.

🐴 Dinnefords Teejel Gel

Description: A gel containing choline salicylate (an analgesic) and an antiseptic.
Dose: Apply 2cm of gel every 3–4 hours as required. Not suitable for babies under 4 months.

🐴 Rinstead Teething Gel

Description: A gel containing lignocaine (an anaesthetic) and an antiseptic.
Dose: Apply every 3 hours as required. Not suitable for babies under 3 months.

⚞ Woodward's Teething Gel

Description: A gel containing lignocaine (an anaesthetic) and an antiseptic.
Dose: Apply and then repeat application after 20 minutes. Repeat every 3 hours, as necessary.

COMPLEMENTARY PRODUCTS

❀ ⚞ Chamomilla

Description: A liquid homoeopathic remedy for teething.
Dose (and manufacturers): Ainsworth 30c, Weleda 3x and 30c.

CHAPTER 4

Vitamin, Mineral and Food Supplements

This chapter describes a wide range of vitamin, mineral and food supplements available from pharmacies, health food shops and supermarkets. The range is vast and it can be very difficult knowing which one to select.

Almost all of these supplements can be derived from natural sources and are present in a well-balanced diet. However, sometimes we do not give enough consideration to the nutritional content of what we are eating; we do not allow enough time to shop for fresh food or to cook it. Sometimes we may even skip meals. Although there is no substitute for eating wisely and eating well, it is at times like these that supplements may be of use.

Also, at different times in our lives we require more help with our nutritional needs. Athletes, slimmers, vegetarians and vegans, the elderly, teenagers, pregnant women and those who smoke or drink alcohol may find that their nutritional needs are not being met through diet alone. This is when supplements can play a role. Health food shops and pharmacies have trained staff to advise you on their products, but only a qualified nutritionist or your GP can prescribe for your individual needs.

As with all remedies, you should always stick to the recommended doses and should avoid taking multiple remedies. It can be harmful to take too many of the wrong supplements. For example, too much vitamin A or vitamin D can have a toxic effect.

How to Choose Your Supplements

Although vitamin and mineral deficiency is now extremely rare in the UK, there are certain categories of people who may benefit from taking supplements. These include those with dietary constraints, for example slimmers, vegetarians and vegans and those with eating disorders. Also there are those who may require additional supplements because of the stage of life they are at. These include the elderly, pregnant women, menopausal women and those with heavy menstrual flow. Teenagers may require additional vitamins and minerals because of the pace in which they are growing – as well as the junk food diets they tend to favour.

Lifestyle also determines whether we require supplements. For most people, taking a daily multivitamin and minerals supplement is a precautionary measure against catching a cold, missing the odd meal or having a late night. However, smokers and people with heavy alcohol consumption are at risk of having an impaired or reduced vitamin and mineral intake, either because they eat poorly or because cigarettes and alcohol prevent the adequate absorption of the nutrients. At the opposite end of the lifestyle spectrum the 'superfit' may also need to take supplements. Athletes, for example, may require more energy-inducing supplements. There are also times when additional supplements can help the body to recover from the effects of illness. Those who suffer persistent colds and flu, for example, may benefit from additional supplements to help top up depleted reserves that have been exhausted through trying to fight off germ invaders.

Identifying individual vitamin or mineral deficiencies is almost impossible for the lay-person. Knowing how to adjust the delicate balance of vitamins and minerals within the body is even more complex and can only be achieved by an expert nutritionist. Many vitamins and minerals need to work in tandem with each other. For example, taking too much of the mineral zinc can interfere with the action of other minerals and too much vitamin C could encourage kidney stones.

Some complementary nutritional therapists recommend mega-dosing – taking large amounts of supplements to combat medical conditions. Orthodox medicine frowns upon this and, indeed, in some instances it can be harmful. Vitamin A, for example, can be fatal if taken in excess.

Additional supplements can be taken if you are recovering from a cold or are in any of the above listed lifestyle groups, but you should ask your GP, pharmacist or an expert nutritionist for advice before supplementing with additional individual vitamins or minerals. For the rest, concentrating on a healthy diet and lifestyle is preferable to relying on supplements. The wisest course of action for the 'worried well' is to take just one combined multivitamin and mineral preparation a day.

As with other over-the-counter remedies, it is essential to take supplements as directed on the packaging. You will see listed the amount of the vitamin, mineral or food supplement contained in the product, together with the recommended daily allowance (RDA). The actual amount of the supplements may be higher or lower than the RDA, depending on the product. These formulations are designed to take into account how the supplements interact with each other so it is unwise to take additional individual supplements unless you have been recommended to do so by your GP or a qualified expert nutritionist.

The following brief guide explains the function of vitamins and minerals within the body and indicates when supplements may be helpful. It also introduces key ingredients from the wide range of food supplements now available and explores their role in enhancing wellbeing.

Vitamins

Vitamins are found in minute amounts in the food we eat and they are essential to health. Vitamin deficiency is rare but much of the vitamin content of food can be harmed during the cooking process. For maximum benefit from natural sources, eat vegetable and fruit sources raw or lightly cooked, rather than boiled, stewed or roasted.

Vitamin A
This vitamin helps promote good eyesight and bone, teeth, skin and hair growth. It is essential for children's proper growth. Smokers may require supplements, but only if advised by their GP or nutritionist. Vitamin A is stored in the liver and should not be taken in excess. For example, pregnant women are advised against eating liver or liver pâté as the amount stored there, together with the vitamin A in their own bodies, may mean there is an excess in the mother's body, which could harm the baby. Pregnant women should therefore watch their food intake sources and avoid supplements containing vitamin A unless advised otherwise by their GP.

• GOOD FOOD SOURCES: Liver, cod liver oil, butter, cheese and eggs.

B complex vitamins
All the vitamins within the B group, with the exception of vitamin B12, can only be stored in the body in small quantities. In addition, as they are all water-soluble their nutritional value   is easily lost during cooking. B vitamins are advised for stress, depression and premenstrual tension. Thiamine deficiency, which is especially common in alcoholics, may cause damage to the peripheral nerves and heart.

Vitamin B12 is essential for the formation of red blood cells and bone marrow. It promotes a healthy nervous system and is the only treatment for pernicious anaemia, when it has to be given by injection (this anaemia is not the same as that due to iron deficiency).

• GOOD FOOD SOURCES: red meat, fish, eggs, milk and foods with the vitamins added, such as Marmite and various tofu-containing foods.

Vitamin C

Vitamin C is an antioxidant vitamin which plays a role in fighting infection, wound-healing and absorption of iron. This vitamin cannot be stored by the body in large amounts or for long periods of time. It is also water soluble and so is easily lost in cooking.

Supplements are used to help fight illness and to promote tissue repair. Smoking damages vitamin C and so smokers could benefit from taking supplements, as can those recovering from illness or surgery.

• GOOD FOOD SOURCES: citrus fruits, blackcurrants, kiwi fruit, peas, potatoes, broccoli and brussels sprouts.

Vitamin D

This vitamin is essential for the growth of strong and healthy bones and teeth. Signs of deficiency include joint deformity, painful bones and muscle weakness. Children require relatively large amounts of vitamin D, as bone growth and turnover are so much greater than in adults. Most vitamin D is derived from sunlight so the housebound may benefit from supplements, as may those with a family tendency to osteoporosis. Too much vitamin D can be harmful by raising the level of calcium in the blood too high.

• GOOD FOOD SOURCES: dairy products, kippers and mackerel, and cod liver oil.

Vitamin E

This is a fat-soluble vitamin and a member of the antioxidant family and so helps to protect against blood and tissue damage and degeneration of nerves and muscles. It also helps protect against the damaging effects of pollution. Women taking hormone treatments such as HRT or the contraceptive pill may benefit from supplements.

• GOOD FOOD SOURCES: wheatgerm, various seed and nut oils (e.g. sunflower oil), wholemeal bread, green vegetables.

Folic acid

Folic acid is part of the B-complex vitamin group and is required for cell production. Those planning pregnancy will benefit from supplements as there is strong evidence that it helps prevent neural tube defects, such as spina bifida, in children. Supplements should be taken from when you abandon contraception and try for a baby up to the end of the first trimester of pregnancy.

Minerals

Many minerals are essential in trace amounts (e.g. iron, copper, zinc) for normal bodily processes while others are needed in larger amounts (e.g. calcium, magnesium). A balanced diet usually contains all the minerals the body requires. Mineral deficiency diseases are uncommon, except for iron deficiency. Iron supplements should only be taken under the guidance of your GP so that any, more serious causes for the deficiency can be identified and treated.

Calcium
Description: Essential for healthy bones and teeth and to promote blood clotting and muscle development. Extra calcium may be required by growing children, pregnant or breast-feeding women, menopausal women, the elderly and slimmers or vegans.

• GOOD FOOD SOURCES: Milk, cheese yoghurt, eggs, canned fish and leafy green vegetables.

Iodine
Description: Iodine helps with the formation of the thyroid hormones and regulates the body's energy production. Supplements are usually unnecessary, except on medical advice, but use iodised table salt for cooking.

• GOOD FOOD SOURCES: Kelp, sea salt and fish oils.

Iron
Description: Iron is essential for red blood cell development and helps carry oxygen within the cells. It also promotes the body's energy-producing functions. Deficiency is quite common but easily treated. Those who suspect they are anaemic should be investigated by their GP.

• GOOD FOOD SOURCES: leafy green vegetables, fortified cereals, red meat, offal, eggs, brown rice.

Phosphorus
Description: Important for cell and tissue repair and to promote energy production. Plays an important role in the structure of bones and teeth. Needs to be properly balanced with calcium to ensure calcium absorption. Phosphorous supplements need to be balanced with calcium supplements in the right pro-

portions. If they are unbalanced, it could lead to impaired calcium performance and possibly osteoporosis. Take only in balanced preparations.

• GOOD FOOD SOURCES: Dairy foods, brown rice, lentils, whole grains, fish, poultry and eggs.

Magnesium

Description: Essential for the formation of healthy bones and teeth and assisting in the absorption of calcium and the use of protein. Plays an important role in the development of nerve cells, muscle tone and the regulation of body temperature. Those with poor dietary habits or who drink excess amounts of alcohol can benefit from supplements.

• GOOD FOOD SOURCES: Wholegrains, seafood, pulses, cereals and dark, leafy vegetables such as spinach and broccoli.

Selenium

An important antioxidant, selenium helps protect the body's cells from damage and boosts the immune system. Those with constricted diets such as slimmers, vegetarians and the elderly may benefit from supplements, as might breastfeeding women.

• GOOD FOOD SOURCES: Offal, fish, shellfish and wholegrains.

Zinc

Zinc is necessary for healthy growth and helps accelerate the body's healing process. Supplements can be of benefit to those with teenage acne and there is some evidence that it can help combat male impotence. Too much zinc can impede the absorption of other vital minerals so take supplements with care or avoid supplements and boost intake from dietary sources.

• GOOD FOOD SOURCES: Lean meat, dairy products, wholemeal bread, wholegrain cereals, dried beans and seafood.

Food supplements

Food supplements contain substances derived from natural food or plant sources. The range is wide – and becoming wider still with the increasing introduction of various Native American, Australian and Chinese products. Below are listed some of the most commonly found supplements.

Cod liver oil

This fish oil is a valuable source of the vitamins A and D. Cod liver oil also contains eicosapentaenoic acid (EPA) and docosahexaenoic acid (DHA). These are essential fatty acids which help maintain healthy cell membranes, a healthy heart, circulation and joints. Supplements may help those suffering from arthritic joint disorders or poor circulation.

• GOOD FOOD SOURCES: Fresh herring, mackerel, tuna, salmon, sardines and pilchards.

Evening primrose oil

This plant-derived oil contains GLA (Gama Linolenic Acid), an essential fatty acid that helps the body form prostaglandins, which play a part in the regulation of the blood, skin and reproductive organs. Women with painful periods or painful breasts, and some patients with eczema, may find that supplements help.

• GOOD FOOD SOURCES: Cannot be derived from original source and has to be taken as a supplement.

Garlic

Garlic is beneficial in maintaining a healthy heart by its blood-thinning action and it is also thought to help increase the body's ability to fight infection. Supplements are taken as a preventive against colds and to overcome risk of heart damage.

• GOOD FOOD SOURCES: Natural garlic can be added to most food dishes. Cooked garlic loses some of its potency. Those who dislike the taste or smell of garlic may prefer taking supplements.

Ginseng

This is an ancient Eastern herbal remedy that is said to act as a tonic and stress reliever.

• GOOD FOOD SOURCES: Ginseng is not available as a food source in the UK but it is available as supplements and as a tea.

Lecithin

Lecithin plays an important role in helping to maintain healthy cells, heart and circulation. It is also thought to help reduce cholesterol levels. Those with high blood pressure may benefit from taking supplements.

• GOOD FOOD SOURCES: Liver, eggs, butter, soya beans, peanuts, trout, corn and oats.

Starflower oil

Starflower oil is similar to evening primrose oil in that it helps regulate blood, skin and reproductive organs. It, too, contains GLA but in higher concentrations than evening primrose oil. Women with painful periods or painful breasts, and some patients with eczema, may find that supplements help.

- GOOD FOOD SOURCES: Starflower is derived from the oil of the borage plant and so has to be taken as a supplement.

Royal jelly

Used as a tonic, royal jelly is the natural food of the queen bee. It is claimed to act as a 'pick you up' and provide energy to those with depleted reserves. It may be of value to those who are stressed and fatigued.

- GOOD FOOD SOURCES: Royal jelly has to be taken as a supplement.

MULTIVITAMIN PRODUCTS FOR ADULTS

The vitamin products described in this section are primarily aimed at adults and older or teenage children. Clear indications are given where the product is considered unsuitable for young children and infants, or in some cases for children of any age. Always consult your pharmacist or GP before giving vitamin supplements to younger family members.

Centrum

Description: A multivitamin and mineral preparation. Each tablet contains: vitamin A 800mcg; vitamin B1 1.4mg; vitamin B2 1.6mg; niacin 18mg; vitamin B6 2mg; vitamin B12 1mcg; vitamin C 60mg; vitamin D 5mcg; vitamin E 10mg; vitamin K 30mcg; pantothenic acid 6mg; folic acid 200mcg; biotin 0.15mg; phosphorus 125mg; molybdenum 25mcg; iodine 150mcg; calcium 162mg; iron 14mg; chromium 25mcg; copper 2mg; potassium 40mg; manganese 2.5mg; zinc 15mg; magnesium 100mg; nickel 5mcg; tin 10mcg; vanadium 10mcg; selenium 25mcg; chloride 36mg.
Dose: 1 tablet daily with water. Not suitable for children.

Centrum Select 50+

Description: A multivitamin and mineral preparation for those over 50 years. Each tablet contains: vitamin A 900mcg; niacin 40mg; vitamin B6 3mg; vitamin B12 25mcg; vitamin C 90mg; vitamin D 10mcg; vitamin E 30mg; vitamin K 30mcg; beta carotene 1800mcg; thiamine 1.8mg; riboflavin 3.2mg; folacin 400mcg; biotin 0.045mg; pantothenic acid 10mg; calcium 200mg; phosphorus 125mg; iron 4mg; magnesium 100mg; zinc 15mg; iodine 150mcg; copper 2mg; manganese 5mg; potassium 80mg; chloride 72mg; boron 100mcg; silicon 10mcg; chromium 100mcg; molybdenum 25mcg; selenium 75mcg; nickel 5mcg; tin 5mcg; vanadium 10mcg.
Dose: 1 tablet daily. Not suitable for children.

Haliborange A, C & D*

Description: A tablet multivitamin supplement. Each tablet contains vitamin A 800mcg; vitamin C 30mg; vitamin D 5mcg.
Dose: 1 tablet daily. Not suitable for children under 3 years.
* Available in four fruit flavours: orange, lemon, tropical and blackcurrant.

Haliborange High Strength Vitamin C Plus Natural Bioflavonoids and Natural Vitamin E

Description: Chewable tablet multivitamin supplement. Each tablet contains: vitamin C 500mg; vitamin E 10mg; bioflavonoids (natural) 20mg.

Dose: 1 chewable tablet daily with liquid. Dosage can be increased to 2 tablets daily. Not suitable for children under 6 years.

Haliborange Multivitamins with Calcium and Iron

Description: Each tablet contains: vitamin A 750mcg; vitamin B1 1.2mg; vitamin B2 1.5mg; nicotinic acid 10mg; vitamin B6 1mg; vitamin B12 2mcg; vitamin C 60mg; vitamin D 2.5mcg; vitamin E 6mg; pantothenic acid 5mg; folic acid 400mcg; calcium 160mg; iron 6mg.

Dose: 1 tablet daily. Not suitable for children under 3 years.

Ladytone

Description: A preparation for women. Each capsule contains: vitamin A 750mcg; vitamin B1 12mg; vitamin B2 3mg; nicotinamide 20mg; vitamin B6 8mg; vitamin B12 6mcg; vitamin C 30mg; vitamin D2 5mcg; vitamin E 15mg; pantothenic acid 6mg; folic acid 200mcg; biotin 150mcg; iodine 75mcg; iron 21.5mg; rutin 10mg; lecithin 20mg; wheatgerm oil 30mg; copper 1mg; potassium 2mg; manganese 1mg; zinc 4mg; magnesium 45mg.

Dose: 1 capsule daily with breakfast. Not suitable for children.

Menopace

Description: A preparation for women during and after the menopause. Each capsule contains: vitamin A 750mcg; vitamin B1 10mg; vitamin B2 5mg; niacin 20mg; vitamin B6 10mg; vitamin B12 9mcg; vitamin C 45mg; vitamin D3 2.5mcg; ; vitamin E 30mg; pantothenic acid 30mg; folic acid 400mcg; biotin 30mcg; iodine 225mcg; iron 12mg; para-aminobenzoic acid (PABA) 30mg; chromium 50mcg; selenium 100mcg; boron 2mg; copper 1mg; manganese 2mg; zinc 15mg; magnesium 100mg.

Dose: 1 capsule daily, after main meal with cold drink or water. Not suitable for children.

Orovite 7

Description: Powder in a sachet. Each sachet contains: vitamin A 2500iu; vitamin B1 1.4mg; vitamin B2 1.7mg; nicotinamide 18mg; vitamin B6 2mg; vitamin C 60mg; vitamin D3 100iu.

Dose: 1 sachet daily, in water. Not suitable for children under 5 years.

Pharmaton Capsules

Description: A multivitamin and mineral preparation. Each capsule contains: vitamin A 4000iu; vitamin B1 2mg; vitamin B2 2mg; nicotinamide 15mg; vitamin B6 1mg; vitamin B12 1mcg; vitamin C 60mg; vitamin D2 400iu; vitamin E 10mg; magnesium 71mg; calcium pantothenate 10mg; zinc oxide 1.25mg; manganese sulphate 3.1mg; copper sulphate 2.8mg; ferrous sulphate 33mg; calcium 307.5mg; ginseng 40mg; 2-dimethylaminoethanol hydrogen tartrate 26mg; rutin 20mg; calcium fluoride 0.42mg; potassium 18mg; lecithin 66mg.
Dose: 1 capsule daily, with breakfast. Not suitable for children.

Pregnacare

Description: A preparation for pregnant women. Each capsule contains: vitamin B1 3mg; vitamin B2 2mg; niacin 20mg; vitamin B6 10mg; vitamin B12 6mcg; vitamin C 70mg; vitamin E 20mg; vitamin D3 2.5mcg; vitamin K 200mcg; folic acid 400mcg; iodine 140mcg; iron 20mg; beta carotene 4.2mg; copper 1mg; zinc 15mg; magnesium 150mg.
Dose: 1 capsule daily, with or immediately after the main meal with water or a cold drink. Not suitable for children.

Premence

Description: A preparation for menstruating women. Each capsule contains: vitamin B1 12mg; vitamin B2 1.6mg; niacin 30mg; vitamin B6 10mg; vitamin B12 5mcg; vitamin C 60mg; vitamin E 30mg; beta carotene 3mg; folic acid 400mcg; iodine 100mcg; iron 15mg; zinc 15mg; magnesium 150mg; copper 1mg; selenium 100mcg.
Dose: 1 capsule daily, after main meal with water or a cold drink. Not suitable for children.

Red Kooga Ginseng with Multivitamins and Minerals

Description: Each tablet contains: vitamin A 800mcg; vitamin B1 1.4mg; vitamin B2 1.6mg; niacin 18mg; vitamin B6 2mg; vitamin B12 1mcg; vitamin C 60mg; vitamin D 5mcg; vitamin E 10mg; pantothenic acid 6mg; folic acid 200mcg; Korean ginseng 300mg; phosphorus 110mg; iodine 150mcg; calcium 140mg; iron 14mg; selenium 50mcg; copper 0.5mg; manganese 1mg; zinc 15mg.
Dose: 1 tablet daily. Not suitable for children.

Sanatogen Classic 50+

Description: A multivitamin and mineral preparation for those 50 years and above. Each tablet contains: vitamin A 800mcg; vitamin B1 104mg; vitamin B2 1.6mg; niacin 18mg; vitamin B6 2mg; vitamin B12 1mcg; vitamin C 60mg; vitamin D 5mcg; vitamin E 10mg; beta carotene 400mcg; copper 200mcg; folic acid 200mcg; iron 4mg; pantothenic acid 6mg; potassium 5mg.
Dose: 1 tablet daily. Not suitable for children.

Sanatogen Gold A-Z

Description: A multivitamin and mineral preparation. Each tablet contains: vitamin A 800mcg; vitamin B1 1.4mg; vitamin B2 1.6mg; niacin 18mg; vitamin B6 2mg; vitamin B12 1mcg; vitamin C 60mg; vitamin D 5mcg; vitamin E 10mg; vitamin K 30mcg; beta carotene 400mcg; biotin 0.15mg; boron 150mcg; calcium 173mg; chloride 36.3mg; chromium 25mcg; copper 2mg; folic acid 200mcg; iodine 150mcg; iron 14mg; magnesium 120mg; manganese 2.5mg; molybdenum 25mcg; nickel 5mcg; pantothenic acid 6mg; phosphorus 144mg; potassium 40mg; selenium 25mcg; silicon 2mg; tin 10mcg; vanadium 10mcg; zinc 15mg.
Dose: 1 tablet daily. Not suitable for children.

Sanatogen Gold A-Z Effervescent

Description: An effervescent multivitamin and mineral tablet. Each tablet contains: vitamin A 800mcg; niacin 18mg; vitamin B6 2mg; vitamin B12 1mcg; vitamin C 60mg; vitamin D 5mcg; vitamin E 10mg; vitamin K 25mcg; beta carotene 400mcg; biotin 0.15mg; boron 150mcg; calcium 136mg; chloride 36.71mg; chromium 25mcg; copper 0.425mg; folic acid 200mcg; iodine 25mcg; iron 2.38mg; magnesium 51mg; manganese 0.595mg; molybdenum 25mcg; nickel 5mcg; pantothenic acid 6mg; phosphorus 136mg; potassium 40mg; selenium 25mcg; silicon 2mg; tin 10mcg; vanadium 10mcg; zinc 2.55mg; thiamin 1.4mg; riboflavin 1.6 mg.
Dose: 1 tablet daily, in water. Not suitable for children.

Sanatogen Multivitamins Original

Description: A multivitamin preparation. Each tablet contains: vitamin A 800mcg; vitamin B1 1.4mg; vitamin B2 1.6mg; niacin 18mg; vitamin B6 2mg; vitamin B12 1mcg; vitamin C 60mg; vitamin D 5mcg; vitamin E 10mg; folic acid 200mcg; beta carotene 400mcg.
Dose: 1 tablet daily. Not suitable for children.

Sanatogen Multivitamins Plus Calcium

Description: Each tablet contains: vitamin A 800mcg; vitamin B1 1.4mg; vitamin B2 1.6mg; niacin 18mg; vitamin B6 2mg; vitamin B12 1mcg; vitamin C 60mg; vitamin D 5mcg; vitamin E 10mg; calcium 133.3mg; folic acid 200mcg; beta carotene 400mcg.
Dose: 1 tablet daily. Not suitable for children.

Sanatogen Multivitamins Plus Iron

Description: Each tablet contains: vitamin A 800mcg; vitamin B1 1.4mg; vitamin B2 1.6mg; niacin 18mg; vitamin B6 2mg; vitamin B12 1mcg; vitamin C 60mg; vitamin D 5mcg; vitamin E 10mg; ferrous fumerate 14mg; folic acid 200mcg; beta carotene 400mcg.
Dose: 1 tablet daily. Not suitable for children.

Sanatogen Multivitamins Plus Minerals

Description: A multivitamin and mineral preparation. Each chewable tablet contains: vitamin A 800mcg; vitamin B1 1.4mg; vitamin B2 1.6mg; niacin 9mg; vitamin B6 2mg; vitamin B12 1mcg; vitamin C 60mg; vitamin D 5mcg; vitamin E 10mg; zinc oxide 2.5mg; pantothenic acid 1mg; folic acid 200mcg; biotin 0.025mg; iodine 150mcg; iron 4mg; beta carotene 400mcg; magnesium oxide 50mg; calcium phosphate 133.3mg.
Dose: 1 tablet daily. Not suitable for children.

Sanatogen Pronatal

Description: A preparation for pregnant women or those planning pregnancy. Each tablet contains: vitamin B1 1.6mg; vitamin B2 1.8mg; niacin 19mg; vitamin B6 2.6mg; vitamin B12 4mcg; vitamin C 100mg; vitamin D 12.5mcg; vitamin E 10mg; pantothenic acid 8.7mg; folic acid 800mcg; biotin 0.2mg; phosphorus 133.3mg; calcium 133.3mg; iron 60mg; copper 1mg; manganese 1mg; zinc 7.5mg; magnesium 100mg.
Dose: 1 tablet daily. Not suitable for children.

Sanatogen Teen

Description: A preparation for teenage girls. Each capsule contains: vitamin A 400mcg; vitamin B1 0.6mg; vitamin B2 0.9mg; niacin 10.1mg; vitamin B6 10mg; vitamin B12 1mcg; vitamin C 30mg; vitamin D 2.5mcg; vitamin E 5mg; calcium 134mg; ferrous sulphate 14mg; evening primrose oil 120mg; folic acid 150mcg; magnesium 50mg.
Dose: 1 tablet daily. Not suitable for children.

Sanatogen Vegetarian

Description: A preparation for vegetarians. Each tablet contains: vitamin B2 1.6mg; vitamin B6 2mg; vitamin B12 4mcg; vitamin D3 5mcg; calcium 133.3mg; zinc 7mg; ferrous fumerate 12mg; folic acid 300mcg; copper 0.6mg.
Dose: 1 tablet daily. Not suitable for children.

Seven Seas Action Plan 50+ General Health Formula

Description: A preparation for those aged 50 years and over. Each capsule contains: vitamin A 500mcg; niacin 18mg; vitamin B6 4mg; vitamin B12 2mcg; vitamin C 60mg; vitamin D 5mcg; vitamin E 10mg; vitamin K 10mcg; riboflavin 2mg; pantothenic acid 6mg; beta carotene 500mcg; thiamine 3.5mg; calcium carbonate 133mg; iron 10mg; copper 500mcg; manganese 2.5mg; zinc 10mg; magnesium 50mg; iodine 150mcg; molybdenum 50mcg; selenium 10mcg; folic acid 300mcg; boron 1mg; chromium 100mcg; choline 5mg; ginseng 50mg; ginkgo biloba 30mg; bilberry extract 1mg; kelp 5mg; cysteine 1mg; lysine 20mg; echinacea 25mg;

evening primrose oil (GLA) 3.5mg; cod liver oil (EPA and DHA) 7.4mg; bioflavonoids 5mg.
Dose: 1 capsule daily, with liquid. Not suitable for children.

Seven Seas Action Plan 50+ Energy Formula

Description: A preparation for those aged 50 years and over. Each capsule contains: vitamin B6 10mg; niacin 30mg; vitamin B12 10mcg; vitamin C 60mg; riboflavin 2.5mg; pantothenic acid 10mg; thiamine 9mg; iron 14mg; manganese 5mg; zinc 15mg; magnesium 100mg; iodine 150mcg; folic acid 300mcg; chromium 200mcg; ginseng 100mcg.
Dose: 1 capsule daily, with liquid. Not suitable for children.

Seven Seas Multivitamins Plus Minerals and Ginseng Capsules

Description: Each capsule contains: vitamin A 800mcg; vitamin B1 2.3mg; vitamin B2 2mg; nicotinic acid 20mg; vitamin B6 8mg; vitamin B12 2mcg; vitamin C 40mg; vitamin E 20mg; pantothenic acid 5mg; folic acid 12.5mg; biotin 0.5mcg; phosphorus 15mg; molybdenum 50mcg; iodine 140mcg; calcium 20mg; iron 12mg; vitamin D2 2.5mcg; inositol 1mg; ginseng 30mg; potassium 0.5mg; manganese 5mcg; zinc 4mg; magnesium 0.5mg; choline 5mg.
Dose: 1 capsule daily, with liquid. Not suitable for children.

Seven Seas Multivitamins Plus Minerals

Description: Each capsule contains: vitamin A 800mcg; vitamin B1 2.3mg; vitamin B2 2mg; nicotinic acid 20mg; vitamin B6 8mg; vitamin B12 2mcg; vitamin C 40mg; vitamin E 20mg; pantothenic acid 5mg; folic acid 300mcg; biotin 0.5mcg; phosphorus 15mg; molybdenum 50mcg; iodine 140mcg; calcium 20mg; iron 12mg; vitamin D2 2.5mcg; inositol 1mg; copper 200mcg; potassium 0.5mg; manganese 5mcg; zinc 4mg; magnesium 0.5mcg; choline 5mg.
Dose: 1 capsule daily, with liquid. Not suitable for children under 6 years.

Seven Seas Multivitamins Natural Sources Plus Iron, Olive Oil, Sunflower Seed Oil and Siberian Ginseng One-a-Day

Description: Each capsule contains: vitamin A 2500iu; vitamin C 20mg; vitamin D 100iu; vitamin E 5mg; iron 14mg; olive oil 10mg; yeast 65mg; ginseng 10mg; sunflower seed oil 117.5mg.
Dose: 1 capsule daily. Not suitable for children under 7 years.

Seven Seas Multivitamins Plus Minerals for Vegetarians and Vegans

Description: Each tablet contains: vitamin A 800mcg; vitamin B1 2.45mg; vitamin B2 2.8mg; nicotinamide 18mg; vitamin B6 6mg; vitamin B12 2.5mcg; vitamin C 90mg; vitamin E 20mg; pantothenic acid 6mg; folic acid 300mcg; calcium 200mg; iron 14mg; zinc 15mg.
Dose: 1 tablet daily. Not suitable for children under 6 years.

Seven Seas Multivitamins with Antioxidant Vitamins E, C and Beta Carotene

Description: Each capsule contains: vitamin B1 1.4mcg; vitamin B2 1.6mcg; niacin 18mg; vitamin B6 2mg; vitamin B12 1mcg; vitamin C 100mg; vitamin E 67mg; vitamin D 5mcg; pantothenic acid 6mg; folic acid 200mcg; biotin 0.15mg; selenium 25mcg; beta carotene 1mg.
Dose: 1 capsule daily. Not suitable for children under 7 years.

Wellman

Description: A preparation for men. Each capsule contains: vitamin A 750mcg; vitamin B1 12mg; vitamin B2 5mg; niacin 20mg; vitamin B6 9mg; vitamin B12 9mcg; vitamin C 60mg; vitamin D3 5mcg; vitamin E 20mg; zinc 15mg; manganese 3mg; magnesium 50mg; iodine 150mcg; pantothenic acid 10mg; copper 1.5mg; folic acid 500mcg; biotin 50mcg; iron 6mg; chromium 50mcg; selenium 150mcg; molybdenum 50mcg; silicon 10mg; arginine 20mg; methionine 20mg; beta carotene 5mg; para-aminobenzoic acid (PABA) 20mg; ginseng 20mg; garlic 20mg; bioflavonoids 10mg.
Dose: 1 capsule daily, after main meal with a cold drink or water. Not suitable for children.

MULTIVITAMIN PRODUCTS FOR CHILDREN

The following vitamin products are specifically designed for children, although many are not suitable for very young children or infants. Always consult your pharmacist or GP before giving vitamin supplements to younger family members.

⚞ Abidec Drops

Description: A liquid multivitamin supplement for infants and children. Marked dropper provided. Each 0.6 ml drop contains: vitamin A 4000iu; vitamin B1 1mg; vitamin B2 400mcg; nicotinamide 5mg; vitamin B6 500mcg; vitamin C 50mg; vitamin D2 400iu.
Dose: Children over 12 months: 0.6ml daily. Babies under 12 months: 0.3ml daily.

⚞ Haliborange Multivitamin Orange Flavour Liquid

Description: A liquid that can be mixed with milk or water. 10ml contains: vitamin A 200mcg; vitamin B1 0.3mg; vitamin B2 0.4mg; nicotinic acid 5mg; vitamin B6 0.35mg; vitamin C 25mg; vitamin D 3.5mcg; vitamin E 2mg; pantothenic acid 1.33mg.
Dose: 10ml daily. Babies aged 1–4 months: Half a 5ml teaspoon. Children aged 4 months–4 years: 1 5ml teaspoon daily. Dilute with milk or water for babies under 6 months, if preferred. Not suitable for babies under 4 months.

⚞ Minadex Children's Vitamins A, C & D Tablets

Description: Each tablet contains: vitamin A acetate 500mcg; vitamin C 30mg; vitamin D3 5mcg.
Dose: 1 tablet daily. Not suitable for children under 3 years.

⚞ Minadex Multivitamin Syrup

Description: A liquid for mixing with a drink or child's feed. Each 10ml contains: vitamin A acetate 4000iu; vitamin B1 1.4mg; vitamin B2 1.7mg; nicotinamide 18mg; vitamin B6 0.7mg; vitamin C 35mg; vitamin D3 400iu; vitamin E 3mg.
Dose: 10 ml daily mixed in feed or a drink. Not suitable for babies under 6 months.

⚰ Minadex Vitamin Drops

Description: Liquid for children. Use special dropper supplied with the pack. Each 0.28ml dose contains: vitamin A 450mcg; vitamin C 30mg; vitamin D 10mcg.
Dose: Children from weaning up to 5 years: 0.28ml daily. Older children: 0.14ml daily. Also 0.28ml daily for breast-fed babies and babies fed on non-fortified milk.

⚰ Sanatogen Chewable Vitamins with Extra Vitamin C

Description: Chewable tablets. Each tablet contains: vitamin A 400mcg; vitamin C 75mg; vitamin D 2.5mcg.
Dose: 1 tablet daily. Not suitable for children under 3 years.

⚰ Sanatogen Children's Gold A-Z

Description: A preparation for children. Each chewable tablet contains: vitamin A 800mcg; vitamin B1 1.4mg; vitamin B2 1.6mg; niacin 9mg; vitamin B6 2mg; vitamin B12 1mcg; vitamin C 60mg; vitamin D 5mcg; vitamin E 10mg; pantothenic acid 1mg; folic acid 200mcg; biotin 0.025mg; iodine 150mcg; beta carotene 400mcg; zinc 2.5mg; magnesium 50mg; calcium 133.3mg; phosphorus 70mg; iron 4mg.
Dose: 1 tablet daily. Not suitable for children under 3 years.

⚰ Sanatogen Children's Vitamin Syrup

Description: Children's sugar-free syrup. Each 10ml dose contains: vitamin A 400mcg; vitamin B1 0.6mg; vitamin B2 0.8mg; niacin 4mg; vitamin B6 0.7mg; vitamin C 50mg; vitamin D 7mcg; vitamin E 4mg; d-pantothenol 2.67mg.
Dose: Children aged 12 months-5 years: 10ml daily. Babies aged 6–12 months: 5ml daily. Babies aged 1-6 months: 2.5ml daily.

⚰ Sanatogen Children's Vitamins Plus Minerals

Description: A preparation for children. Each chewable tablet contains: vitamin A 400mcg; vitamin B1 0.7mg; vitamin B2 0.6mg; niacin 4.5mg; vitamin B6 1mg; vitamin B12 0.5mcg; vitamin C 30mg; vitamin D 2.5mcg; vitamin E 5mg; calcium 67mg; pantothenic acid 0.5mg; ferrous fumerate 2mg; folic acid 100mcg; biotin 0.013mg; iodine 75mcg; beta carotene 200mcg; zinc 1.25mg; magnesium 25mg.
Dose: 1 tablet daily. Not suitable for children under 3 years.

MULTI-MINERAL SUPPLEMENTS

These products are primarily used for their mineral content, although they also contain vitamins.

Calcia*

Description: Each tablet contains: calcium 800mg; iron 14mg; vitamin B1 1.4mg; vitamin B2 1.6mg; vitamin B6 2mg; vitamin B12 1mcg; vitamin C 30mg; vitamin D 7.5mg.
Dose: 3 tablets daily. Not suitable for children.
* Also available as Calcia Chewable in raspberry flavour.

Calcia Plus Cod Liver Oil

Description: Each capsule contains: calcium 800mg; iron 14mg; vitamin B1 1.4mg; vitamin B2 1.6mg; vitamin B6 2mg; vitamin C 30mg; vitamin B12 1mcg; vitamin D 7.5mcg; cod liver oil 550mg.
Dose: 4 capsules daily. Not suitable for children.

Iron Jelloids

Description: Each tablet contains: ferrous fumerate 60.12mg; vitamin B1 0.17mg; vitamin B2 0.29mg; nicotinamide 1.67mg; vitamin C 4.17mg.
Dose: 2 tablets daily after meals or with a drink. Not suitable for children.

Osteocare Tablets

Description: A tablet for those at risk of developing osteoporosis. Each tablet contains: calcium 400mg; zinc 5mg; magnesium 150mg: vitamin D3 2.5mcg.
Dose: 2 tablets daily (or 1 tablet twice daily) before meals). Not suitable for children.

Osteocare Liquid

Description: A liquid to help promote strong bone formation. Each 10ml contains: calcium 300mg; zinc 6mg; magnesium 150mg; vitamin D3 3.8mcg.
Dose: Adults: 10ml twice daily. Children aged 3–12 years: 10ml 2–3 times daily. Children aged 12 months–2 years: 5ml twice daily. Babies aged 6–12 months: 2.5ml twice daily. Not suitable for babies under 6 months.

Seven Seas Calcium Plus Vitamin D

Description: Each tablet contains: calcium 400mg; vitamin D 2.5mcg.
Dose: Chew 1–2 tablets daily. Not suitable for children under 7 years.

Seven Seas Chewable One-a-Day Calcium with Vitamin D

Description: Each capsule contains: calcium 400mg; vitamin D 5mcg.
Dose: 1 or 2 capsules daily. Not suitable for children under 7 years.

Seven Seas Chewable One-a-Day Iron with Vitamin C

Description: Each capsule contains: vitamin C 30mg; ferrous fumerate 7mg.
Dose: Chew 1–2 capsules daily. Not suitable for children under 7 years.

Seven Seas Chewable One-a-Day Zinc Plus with Vitamin C

Description: Each capsule contains: zinc 3.75mg; vitamin C 60mg.
Dose: Chew or swallow whole 1–4 capsules daily. Not suitable for children under 7 years.

Seven Seas One-a-Day Minerals for Bones

Description: Each tablet contains: vitamin D 5mcg; calcium 400mg; magnesium 150mg; zinc 7.5mg; copper 0.5mg; boron 2mg.
Dose: 1–2 tablets daily, with liquid. Not suitable for children.

Seven Seas One-a-Day Minerals for Energy

Description: Each tablet contains: vitamin C 60mg; iron 14mg; magnesium 75mg; copper 1mg.
Dose: 1 tablet daily, with liquid. Not suitable for children.

Seven Seas One-a-Day Minerals for a Healthy Immune System

Description: Each tablet contains: vitamin C 60mg; zinc 15mg; copper 1mg.
Dose: 1 tablet daily, with liquid. Not suitable for children.

Seven Seas One-a-Day Minerals for Hormonal Balance

Description: Each tablet contains: vitamin B6 2mg; magnesium 300mg; zinc 15mg.
Dose: 1 tablet daily, with liquid. Not suitable for children.

SINGLE VITAMIN SUPPLEMENTS

The following products contain vitamins in a variety of strengths.

SUPPLEMENTS CONTAINING VITAMIN B

Cytacon Liquid

Description: 5ml contain: vitamin B12 35mcg.
Dose: Adults: 5–10ml 2–3 times daily. Children: 5ml 2–3 times daily.

Cytacon Tablets

Description: Each tablet contains: vitamin B12 50mcg.
Dose: Adults: 1–3 tablets or more daily. Children: 1 tablet twice daily.

Sanatogen Vitamin B Complex

Description: Each tablet contains: vitamin B1 1.4mg; vitamin B2 1.6mg; niacin 18mg; vitamin B6 2mg; vitamin B12 1mcg; folic acid 200mcg.
Dose: 1 tablet daily. Not suitable for children.

Seven Seas One-a-Day Super Vitamin B6 Capsules*

Description: Each capsule contains: vitamin B6 40mg.
Dose: 1 capsule daily, with liquid. Not suitable for children.
* Also available as 10mg capsules.

Seven Seas One-a-Day Vitamin B Complex Capsules with Folic Acid

Description: Each capsule contains: vitamin B1 1.4mg; vitamin B2 1.6mg; nicotinic acid 18mg; vitamin B6 2mg; vitamin B12 1mcg; pantothenic acid 6mg; folic acid 400mcg; biotin 0.15mg; inositol 5mg; brewers yeast 100mg.
Dose: 1 capsule daily. Not suitable for children.

SUPPLEMENTS CONTAINING FOLIC ACID

Folic Plus

Description: Each tablet contains: vitamin D 2.5mcg; folic acid 133mcg; calcium 266mg.
Dose: 3 tablets daily. Not suitable for children.

Preconceive Tablets

Description: Each tablet contains: folic acid 400mcg.
Dose: 1 tablet daily with food and water before conception and until the end of the third month of pregnancy.

SUPPLEMENTS CONTAINING VITAMIN C

Haliborange Effervescent High Strength Vitamin C 1000mg Orange*

Description: Each tablet contains: vitamin C 1000mg.
Dose: 1 tablet 1–3 times daily, dissolved in water. Not suitable for children.
* Also available in lemon flavour.

Redoxon C Tablets 500mg*

Description: Each tablet contains: vitamin C 500mg.
Dose: 1–3 tablets daily. Not suitable for children.
* Also available in 200g strength.

Redoxon Double Action Chewable Tablets

Description: Each tablet contains: vitamin C 500mg; zinc 5mg.
Dose: Adults: 1–3 tablets daily. Children: Half of 1 tablet.

Redoxon Double Action Effervescent Tablet

Description: Each tablet contains: vitamin C 1000mg; zinc 10mg.
Dose: Adults: 1–2 tablets daily. Children aged 6–12 years: Half of 1 table daily, or as directed by GP. Not suitable for children under 6 years.

Redoxon Slow Release Vitamin C

Description: Capsules. Each capsule contains: vitamin C 500mg.
Dose: 1–2 capsules daily, taken with liquid. Not suitable for children.

Redoxon Vitamin C Effervescent Tablets*

Description: Each tablet contains: vitamin C 1000mg.
Dose: Adults: 1–3 tablets daily, dissolved in a glass of water. Children aged 6–12 years: Half of 1 tablet daily, or as directed by a doctor. Not suitable for children under 6 years.
* Available in blackcurrant, orange, lemon or plain flavours.

Redoxon Vitamin C Tablet Chewable 500mg*

Description: Each tablet contains: vitamin C 500mg.
Dose: Adults: 1 tablet daily. Children: Half of 1 tablet daily.
* Also available in 250mg size.

Sanatogen Chewable High Strength Vitamin C Tablets 500mg

Description: Each tablet contains: vitamin C 500mg.
Dose: 1 tablet daily. Not suitable for children.

Sanatogen Vitamin C Tablets 60mg

Description: Each tablet contains: vitamin C 60mg.
Dose: Adults and children: 1 tablet daily.

Seven Seas Chewable One-a-Day Vitamin C

Description: Each capsule contains: vitamin C 250mg.
Dose: 1-2 capsules daily. Not suitable for children under 7 years.

Seven Seas One-a-Day Vitamin C Plus Capsules

Description: Each capsule contains: vitamin C 200mg; citrus bioflavonoids 10mg; blackcurrant concentrate 10mg.
Dose: 1 capsule daily. Not suitable for children.

SUPPLEMENTS CONTAINING VITAMIN E

Sanatogen Vitamin E Capsules

Description: Each capsule contains: vitamin E 250mg.
Dose: 1 capsule daily, taken with food. Not suitable for children.

Seven Seas Antioxidant Vitamin E 200iu Capsules

Description: Each capsule contains: vitamin E 200iu.
Dose: 1 capsule daily, with liquid. Not suitable for children.
* Also available in 400iu strength.

COMBINED MULTIVITAMINS, MINERALS AND FOOD SUPPLEMENTS

The following products include combined multivitamin and mineral supplements, as well as a range of easily available food supplements.

Calcia Plus Evening Primrose Oil

Description: Each capsule contains: calcium 800mg; iron 14mg; vitamin B1 1.4mg; vitamin B2 1.6mg; vitamin B6 2mg; vitamin B12 1mcg; vitamin C 30mg; vitamin D 7.5mcg; evening primrose oil 250mg.
Dose: 4 capsules daily. Not suitable for children.

Floresse Body Boost 500mg Starflower Oil 115mg GLA

Description: Each capsule contains: starflower oil 500mg; folic acid 200mcg; pantothenic acid 6mg; vitamin B1 1.4mg; vitamin B2 1.6mg; niacin 3mg; vitamin B6 2mg; vitamin B12 1mcg; vitamin C 10mg.
Dose: 1–2 capsules daily prior to or during monthly period. Not suitable for children.

Floresse Skin Vitality Starflower Oil 115mg GLA

Description: Each capsule contains: starflower oil 500mg; vitamin C 10mg; vitamin E 2mg.
Dose: 1–2 capsules daily prior to or during monthly period. Not suitable for children.

Floresse Starflower Oil*

Description: Each capsule contains: starflower oil 1000mg; vitamin E 2mg.
Dose: 1 capsule daily prior to or during monthly period. Not suitable for children.
* Also available in 250mg and 500mg strengths.

Hofels Cardiomax Garlic Pearles

Description: Each capsule contains: garlic oil 4mg.
Dose: 1 capsule daily, with food and a cold drink, if preferred. Not suitable for children.

Hofels High Strength Concentrated Ginger Pearles One-a-Day

Description: Each capsule contains: ginger 100mg.
Dose: 1 capsule daily, with a cold drink or a meal. Not suitable for children.

Hofels Odourless Neo Garlic Pearles One-a-Day

Description: Each capsule contains: garlic paste 2mg.
Dose: 1 capsule daily, with a cold drink or a meal. Not suitable for children.

Immunace

Description: Each capsule contains: vitamin B1 7.5mg; vitamin B2 5mg; vitamin B6 15mg; vitamin B12 4.5mcg; vitamin C 150mg; vitamin D3 2.5mcg; vitamin E 60mg; vitamin K 100mcg; folic acid 250mcg; iodine 100mcg; iron 3mg; chromium 50mcg; selenium 100mcg; cystine 20mg; methionine 20mg; beta carotene 3mg; copper 1mg; manganese 2mg; zinc 7.5mg; magnesium 50mg; bioflavonoids (citrus) 15mg; pantothenic acid 10mg.
Dose: 1–2 capsules daily, taken with or immediately after main meals with water or a cold drink. Not suitable for children.

Red Kooga Betalife

Description: Each capsule contains: vitamin C 30mg; vitamin E 33mg; Korean ginseng 300mg; fish oil 150mg; selenium 50mcg; beta carotene 5mg.
Dose: 1 capsule daily. Not suitable for children.

Red Kooga CO-Q-10 and Ginseng

Description: Each tablet contains: Korean ginseng 300mg; co–enzyme Q10 15mg.
Dose: 1 or 2 tablets daily, taken with a meal. Not suitable for children.

Red Kooga Ginkgo Biloba and Ginseng

Description: Each tablet contains: Korean ginseng 300mg; ginkgo biloba 2000mg.
Dose: 1 or 2 tablets daily, taken with a meal. Not suitable for children.

Red Kooga Ginseng Capsules 600mg

Description: Each capsule contains: Korean ginseng 600mg.
Dose: 1 capsule daily. Not suitable for children.

Red Kooga Ginseng Elixir

Description: 10ml contains: Korean ginseng 600mg.
Dose: 10ml daily. Not suitable for children.

Red Kooga Ginseng Tablets 600mg

Description: Each tablet contains: Korean ginseng 600mg.
Dose: 1 tablet daily. Not suitable for children.

Redoxon Protector

Description: Each capsule contains: vitamin A (as beta carotene) 3mg; vitamin B2 1.6mg; vitamin B6 2mg; vitamin C 60mg; vitamin E 6.5mg; selenium 50mcg; zinc 15mg; copper 1.5mg; manganese 2.5mg.
Dose: 1 capsule daily, with liquid. Not suitable for children.

Sanatogen Multivitamins Plus Evening Primrose Oil Capsules

Description: Each capsule contains: vitamin A 800mcg; vitamin B1 1.4mg; vitamin B2 1.6mg; niacin 18mg; vitamin B6 2mg; vitamin B12 1mcg; vitamin C 60mg; vitamin D 5mcg; vitamin E 10mg; pantothenic acid 6mg; evening primrose oil 100mg; folic acid 200mcg; biotin 0.15mg; beta carotene 400mcg.
Dose: 1 capsule daily, with liquid. Not suitable for children.

Seven Seas Antioxidant Vitamins A, C, E with Selenium Capsules

Description: Each capsule contains: vitamin C 100mg; vitamin E 50mg; selenium 25mcg; beta carotene 12mg.
Dose: 1 capsule daily. Not suitable for children.

Seven Seas Antioxidant Beta Carotene Capsules

Description: Each capsule contains: beta carotene 15mg.
Dose: 1 capsule daily, with liquid. Not suitable for children.

Seven Seas Chewable Evening Primrose Oil Plus Starflower Oil

Description: Each capsule contains: gamma-linolenic acid (GLA) 34mg; vitamin E 10mg.
Dose: 1 capsule daily, chew or swallow whole. Not suitable for children.

Seven Seas Evening Primrose Oil Plus Starflower Oil 1000mg*

Description: Each capsule contains: gamma linolenic acid (GLA) 130mg; vitamin E 10mg.
Dose: 1–2 capsules daily, with liquid. Not suitable for children.
* Also available as 500mg capsules containing 67mg GLA.

Seven Seas Garlic Oil Pearles

Description: Each capsule contains: garlic oil 2mg.
Dose: 1 capsule daily. Not suitable for children.

Seven Seas One-a-Day Korean Ginseng Capsules

Description: Each capsule contains: Korean ginseng 600mg.
Dose: 1 capsule daily, with liquid. Not suitable for children.

Seven Seas One-a-Day Lecithin Capsules

Description: Each capsule contains: lecithin 600mg.
Dose: 1 capsule daily, with liquid. Not suitable for children.

Seven Seas Pure Starflower Oil

Description: Each capsule contains: gamma-linolenic acid 102mg; vitamin E 10mg.
Dose: 1–2 capsules daily, with liquid. Not suitable for children.

Seven Seas Royal Jelly with Honey

Description: Each capsule contains: honey 50mg; royal jelly 100mg.
Dose: 1 capsule daily, with liquid. Not suitable for children.

FISH OIL SUPPLEMENTS

Sanatogen Cod Liver Oil with Garlic

Description: Each capsule contains: vitamin A 800mcg; vitamin D 5mcg; vitamin E 10mg; eicosapentaenoic acid 69mg; docosahexaenoic acid 55mg; garlic powder 75mg.
Dose: 1 capsule daily. Not suitable for children.

Sanatogen High Strength Cod Liver Oil

Description: Each capsule contains: vitamin A 800mcg; vitamin E 10mg; eicosapentaenoic acid (EPA) 84mg and docosahexaenoic acid (DHA) 73.5mg; cod liver oil 700mg.
Dose: 1 capsule daily, with liquid.

Sanatogen Super Cod Liver Oil Liquid

Description: Each 10ml dose contains: vitamin A 800mcg; vitamin D 5mcg; vitamin E 7.67mg; eicosapentaenoic acid (EPA) 1200mg and docosahexaenoic acid (DHA) 600mg.
Dose: 10ml daily.

Sanatogen Super Cod Liver Oil Plus Multivitamins Capsules

Description: Each capsule contains: vitamin A 800mcg; vitamin B2 1.6mg; niacin 18mg; vitamin B6 2mg; vitamin B12 1mcg; vitamin C 60mg; vitamin E 10mg; vitamin D 5mcg; pantothenic acid 6mg; folic acid 200mcg; eicosapentaenoic acid 61mg; docosahexaenoic acid 42mg.
Dose: 1 capsule daily.

Sanatogen Super Cod Liver Oil One-a-Day Capsules

Description: Each capsule contains: cod liver oil 500mg; eicosapentaenoic acid 61mg; docosahexaenoic acid 42mg; vitamin A 800mcg; vitamin D 5mcg; vitamin E 5mg.
Dose: 1 capsule daily.

Seven Seas High Strength Pure Cod Liver Oil

Description: Each capsule contains: cod liver oil, enriched with fish oil omega 3 1050mg; omega 3 400mg (EPA and DHA 360mg); vitamin A 800mcg; vitamin D 5mcg; vitamin E 10mg.
Dose: 1 capsule daily. Not suitable for children.

Seven Seas High Strength One-a-Day Pure Cod Liver Oil

Description: Each capsule contains: cod liver oil, enriched with fish oil omega 3 525mg; omega 3 200mg (EPA and DHA 180mg); vitamin A 800mcg; vitamin D 5mcg; vitamin E 10mg.
Dose: 1 capsule daily with liquid. Not suitable for children.

Seven Seas High Strength Pure Cod Liver Oil (Liquid)

Description: Each 10ml dose contains: cod liver oil, enriched with fish oil omega 3 9.2g; EPA 1200mg; DHA 600mg; vitamin A 800mcg; vitamin D 5mcg; vitamin E 10mg.
Dose: 10 ml daily. Not recommended for babies under 12 months.

Seven Seas Lemon Flavour Pure Cod Liver Oil with Evening Primrose Oil

Description: Each 10ml dose contains: cod liver oil, enriched with fish oil omega 3 9.2g; EPA 744mg; DHA 661mg; evening primrose oil 460mg; vitamin A 800mcg; vitamin D3 2.5mcg; vitamin E 6.7mg.
Dose: 10ml daily. Not suitable for babies under 12 months.

Seven Seas One-a-Day Pure Cod Liver Oil Capsules

Description: Each capsule contains: cod liver oil 500mg; EPA 43.9mg; DHA 39.3mg; vitamin A 800mcg; vitamin D 2.5mcg; vitamin E 0.33mg.
Dose: 1 capsule daily.

Seven Seas Orange Syrup and Cod Liver Oil

Description: 10ml contains: vitamin A 4000iu; vitamin B6 0.7mg; vitamin C 35mg; orange juice 700mg; vitamin D 400iu; vitamin E 3iu; cod liver oil 3ml; EPA 252mg; DHA 224mg.
Dose: Adults and children over 12 months: 10ml daily. Pregnant or lactating women: 5ml daily. Babies aged 1–6 months: 2.5ml daily, diluted with previously boiled and cooled water. Babies aged 7–12 months: 5ml daily.

Seven Seas Pulse High Strength Triomega Pure Fish Oils Capsules

Description: Each capsule contains: triomega fish oils 600mg (EPA 200mg, DHA 60mg); vitamin E 1.5mg.
Dose: 1 or 2 capsules daily. Not suitable for children.

Seven Seas Pulse Pure Fish Oils Capsules

Description: Each capsule contains: fish oils 500mg (EPA 65mg, DHA 42mg); vitamin E 0.3mg.
Dose: 1 capsule twice daily.

Seven Seas Pure Cod Liver Oil and Vitamin E

Description: Each capsule contains: cod liver oil 695mg (EPA 58.5mg, DHA 52mg); vitamin A 800mcg; vitamin D3 5mcg; vitamin E 67.1mg.
Dose: 1 capsule daily.

Seven Seas Pure Cod Liver Oil and Calcium

Description: Each capsule contains: cod liver oil 500mg (EPA 42.1mg, DHA 37.4mg); calcium 267mg; vitamin A 800mcg; vitamin D3 5mcg; vitamin E 10mg.
Dose: 1 capsule daily. Not suitable for children.

Seven Seas Pure Cod Liver Oil and CO-Q-10

Description: Each capsule contains: cod liver oil 785mg (EPA 66.1mg, DHA 58.8mg); co-enzyme Q 10 10mg; vitamin A 800mcg; vitamin D3 5mcg; vitamin E 1.34mg.
Dose: 1 capsule daily.

Seven Seas Pure Cod Liver Oil and Evening Primrose Oil

Description: Each capsule contains: cod liver oil 615mg (EPA 52.5mg, DHA

46.7mg); evening primrose oil 200mg; vitamin A 800mcg; vitamin D3 2.5mcg; vitamin E 0.33mg.
Dose: 1 capsule daily.

Seven Seas Pure Cod Liver Oil and Ginkgo Biloba

Description: Each capsule contains: cod liver oil 790mg (EPA 66.5mg, DHA 59.1mg); ginkgo biloba 80mg; vitamin A 800mcg; vitamin D3 5mcg; vitamin E 1.34mg.
Dose: 1 capsule daily.

Seven Seas Pure Cod Liver Oil and Multivitamins

Description: Each capsule contains: cod liver oil 500mg (EPA 42.1mg, DHA 37.4mg); vitamin A 800mcg; vitamin B1 1.4mg; vitamin B2 1.6mg; nicotinamide 18mg; vitamin B6 2mg; vitamin B12 1mcg; vitamin C 60mg; vitamin D3 5mcg; vitamin E 10mg; pantothenic acid 6mg; folic acid 200mcg; biotin 0.01mg.
Dose: 1 capsule daily.

Seven Seas Pure Cod Liver Oil and Odourless Garlic

Description: Each capsule contains: cod liver oil 800mg (EPA 67mg, DHA 60mg); vitamin A 800mcg; vitamin D3 5mcg; vitamin E 1.34mg; garlic powder 6mg.
Dose: 1 capsule daily. Not suitable for children.

Seven Seas Pure Cod Liver Oil and Starflower Oil

Description: Each capsule contains: cod liver oil 584mg (EPA 49.2mg, DHA 43.7mg); starflower oil 250mg; vitamin A 800mcg; vitamin D3 5mcg; vitamin E 10mg.
Dose: 1 capsule daily. Not suitable for children.

Seven Seas Pure Cod Liver Oil and Vitamin C

Description: Each capsule contains: cod liver oil 500mg (EPA 42.1mg, DHA 37.4mg); vitamin A 800mcg; vitamin C 250mg; vitamin D3 5mcg; vitamin E 1.34mg.
Dose: 1 capsule daily.

Seven Seas Pure Cod Liver Oil Capsules

Description: Each capsule contains: cod liver oil 0.32ml (EPA 26mg, DHA 24mg); vitamin A 670iu; vitamin D3 67iu; vitamin E 0.3iu.
Dose: Adults and children over 6 years: 2 capsules with liquid, 3 times daily. Pregnant or lactating women: 1 capsule 3 times daily, with liquid. Not suitable for children under 6 years.

Seven Seas Pure Cod Liver Oil Lemon Flavour

Description: 10ml contain: cod liver oil 9.2mg (EPA 788mg, DHA 700mg); vitamin A 800mcg; vitamin D3 2.5mcg; vitamin E 6.7mg.
Dose: 10ml daily. Not suitable for babies under 12 months.

Seven Seas Pure Cod Liver Oil Liquid

Description: 10ml contain: cod liver oil 9.2mg (EPA 828mg, DHA 736mg); vitamin A 4000iu; vitamin D 400iu; vitamin E 10iu.
Dose: Adults and children over 1 year: 10ml daily. Pregnant women: 5ml daily. Babies aged 7–12 months: 5 ml daily. Babies aged 0–6 months: 2.5ml daily.

INDEX